I0471621

THE COUNTERFEIT
CONSTITUTION

VOLUME II

How Voluntary Confessions
Became Inadmissible Evidence

THE COUNTERFEIT CONSTITUTION

VOLUME II

How Voluntary Confessions
Became Inadmissible Evidence

———————

LEON F. SCULLY, JR.

Copyright © 2017. All rights reserved.

ISBN-13: 978-1547077410
ISBN-10: 1547077417

Cover and interior design by Kristina Phillips

Typeset in Caslon 540,
an edition of a typeface by William Caslon,
adapted by American Type Founders in 1902

For Eileen

Contents

Preface

Brewer, Warden v. Williams
CERTIORARI TO THE UNITED STATES COURT OF APPEALS
FOR THE EIGHTH CIRCUIT
430 U.S. 387
NO. 74-1263 ARGUED OCTOBER 4, 1976 – DECIDED MARCH 23, 1977

Mr. JUSTICE STEWART delivered the opinion of the Court.

An Iowa trial jury found the respondent, Robert Williams, guilty of murder. The judgment of conviction was affirmed in the Iowa Supreme Court by a closely divided vote. In a subsequent habeas corpus proceeding a Federal District Court ruled that under the United States Constitution Williams is entitled to a new trial, and a divided Court of Appeals for the Eighth Circuit agreed. The question before us is whether the District Court and the Court of Appeals were wrong.

On the afternoon of December 24, 1968, a 10-year-old girl named Pamela Powers went with her family to the YMCA in Des Moines, Iowa, to watch a wrestling tournament in which her brother was participating. When she failed to return from a trip to the washroom, a search for her began. The search was unsuccessful.

Robert Williams, who had recently escaped from a mental hospital, was a resident of the YMCA. Soon after the girl's disappearance Williams was seen in the YMCA lobby carrying some clothing and a large bundle wrapped in a blanket.

He obtained help from a 14-year-old boy in opening the street door of the YMCA and the door to his automobile parked outside. When Williams placed the bundle in the front seat of his car the boy "saw two legs in it and they were skinny and white." Before anyone could see what was in the bundle Williams drove away. His abandoned car was found the following day in Davenport, Iowa, roughly 160 miles east of Des Moines. A warrant was then issued in Des Moines for his arrest on a charge of abduction.

On the morning of December 26, a Des Moines lawyer named Henry McKnight went to the Des Moines police station and informed the officers present that he had just received a long-distance call from Williams, and that he had advised Williams to turn himself in to the Davenport police. Williams did surrender that morning to the police in Davenport, and they booked him on the charge specified in the arrest warrant and gave him the warnings required by *Miranda v. Arizona*, 384 U.S. 436. The Davenport police then telephoned their counterparts in Des Moines to inform them that Williams had surrendered.

McKnight, the lawyer, was still at the Des Moines police headquarters, and Williams conversed with McKnight on the telephone. In the presence of the Des Moines chief of police and a police detective named Leaming, McKnight advised Williams that Des Moines police officers would be driving to Davenport to pick him up, that the officers would not interrogate him or mistreat him, and that Williams was not to talk to the officers about Pamela Powers until after consulting with McKnight upon his return to Des Moines. As a result of these conversations, it was agreed between McKnight and the Des Moines police officials that Detective Leaming and a fellow officer would drive to Davenport to pick up Williams, that they would bring him directly back to Des Moines, and that they would not question him during the trip.

In the meantime Williams was arraigned before a judge in Davenport on the outstanding arrest warrant. The judge advised him of his *Miranda* rights and committed him to jail. Before leaving the courtroom, Williams conferred with a lawyer named Kelly, who advised him not to make any statements until consulting with McKnight back in Des Moines.

Detective Leaming and his fellow officer arrived in Davenport about noon to pick up Williams and return him to Des Moines. Soon after their arrival they met with Williams and Kelly, who, they understood, was acting as Williams' lawyer. Detective Leaming repeated the *Miranda* warnings, and told Williams:

> [W]e both know that you're being represented here by Mr. Kelly and you're being represented by Mr. McKnight in Des Moines, and . . . I want you to remember this because we'll be visiting between here and Des Moines.

Williams then conferred again with Kelly alone, and after this conference Kelly reiterated to Detective Leaming that Williams was not to be questioned about the disappearance of Pamela Powers until after he had consulted with McKnight back in Des Moines. When Leaming expressed some reservations, Kelly firmly stated that the agreement with McKnight was to be carried out—that there was to be no interrogation of Williams during the automobile journey to Des Moines. Kelly was denied permission to ride in the police car back to Des Moines with Williams and the two officers.

The two detectives, with Williams in their charge, then set out on the 160-mile drive. At no time during the trip did Williams express a willingness to be interrogated in the absence of an attorney. Instead, he stated several times that "[w]hen I get to Des Moines and see Mr. McKnight, I am going to tell you the whole story." Detective Leaming knew that Williams was a former mental patient, and knew also that he was deeply religious.

The detective and his prisoner soon embarked on a wide-ranging conversation covering a variety of topics, including the subject of religion. Then, not long after leaving Davenport and reaching the interstate highway, Detective Leaming delivered what has been referred to in the briefs and oral arguments as the "Christian burial speech." Addressing Williams as "Reverend," the detective said:

> I want to give you something to think about while we're traveling down the road . . . . Number one, I want you to observe the weather conditions, it's raining, it's sleeting, it's freezing, driving is very treacherous, visibility is poor, it's going to be dark early this evening. They are predicting several inches of snow for tonight, and I feel that you yourself are the only person that knows where that little girl's body is, that you yourself have only been there once, and if you get a snow on top of it you yourself may be unable to find it. And since we will be going right past the area on the way into Des Moines, I feel that we could stop and locate the body, that the parents of this little girl should be entitled to a Christian burial for the little girl who was snatched away from them on Christmas [E]ve and murdered. And I feel we should stop and locate it on the way in rather than waiting until morning and trying to come back out after a snow storm and possibly not being able to find it at all.

Williams asked Detective Leaming why he thought their route to Des Moines would be taking them past the girl's body, and Leaming responded that he knew the body was in the area of Mitchellville—a town they would be passing on the way to Des Moines.* Leaming then stated: "I do not want you to answer me. I don't want to discuss it any further. Just think about it as we're riding down the road."

As the car approached Grinnell, a town approximately 100 miles west of Davenport, Williams asked whether the police had found the victim's shoes. When Detective Leaming replied that he was unsure, Williams directed the officers to a service station where he said he had left the shoes; a search for them proved unsuccessful. As they continued towards Des Moines, Williams asked whether the police had found the blanket, and directed the officers to a rest area where he said he had disposed of the blanket. Nothing was found. The car continued towards Des Moines, and as it approached Mitchellville, Williams said that he would show the officers where the body was. He then directed the police to the body of Pamela Powers.

*The fact of the matter, of course, was that Detective Leaming possessed no such knowledge. [Footnote in original].

By a vote of five-to-four the Supreme Court of the United States set aside the murder conviction of Robert Williams. In the event of a retrial, neither Williams' incriminating statements themselves nor any testimony describing his having led the police to the victim's body could constitutionally be admitted into evidence. No member of the Court had the slightest doubt of the defendant's guilt. All accepted tacitly, and Justice Marshall expressly, the fact that Williams committed the unspeakable murder of the little girl. It was not fear of convicting an innocent man in this or any future case that caused the majority to rule as they did; guilt or innocence was simply irrelevant.

This is the jurisprudence that prevails in the United States today. Williams was deprived of his "liberty" by Iowa, said the majority, without the "due process of law" required by the Fourteenth Amendment. This is so because he was "compelled" in a "criminal case to be a witness against himself" in violation of that provision of the Fifth Amendment.

Before 1961, a defendant in a state criminal prosecution was constitutionally guaranteed a "fair trial." Nothing more was required by, and nothing less would satisfy, the due process of law demanded by the Fourteenth Amendment, the *only* amendment applicable to state criminal cases. This jurisprudence was called "fundamental fairness" and what it required was equity; that justice be done in the case at hand. Its underlying purpose was to prevent the conviction of an innocent defendant. Once a defendant's guilt was established, however, fundamental fairness never required that he be let go. This dissent in *Williams* exemplifies its philosophy:

MR. CHIEF JUSTICE BURGER, dissenting.

The result in this case ought to be intolerable in any society that purports to call itself an organized society. It continues the Court—by the narrowest margin—on the much-criticized course of punishing the public for the mistakes and misdeeds of law enforcement officers, instead of punishing the officer directly, if in fact he is guilty of wrongdoing. It mechanically and blindly keeps reliable evidence from juries whether the claimed constitutional violation involves gross police misconduct or honest human error.

Williams is guilty of the savage murder of a small child; no member of the Court contends he is not. While in custody, and after no fewer than five warnings of his rights to silence and to counsel, he led police to the concealed body of his victim. The Court concedes Williams was not threatened or coerced and that he spoke and acted voluntarily and with full awareness of his constitutional rights. In the face of all this, the Court now holds that because Williams was prompted by the detective's statement—not interrogation but a statement—the jury must not be told how the police found the body.

On the shelves of every law library in the country lie the numbered volumes of the United States Reports. In them you will find the opinions of the Justices of the Supreme Court from the beginning of the republic. The majority opinion in the *Williams* case is something few of them would have recognized as constitutional law. It is, in fact, a sophistry responsible for the crime-ridden society we have today. Crime has not changed, it is just more prevalent because it goes unpunished. But it was not always thus.

Introduction

IN 1982 I WAS AN INDEPENDENT oil operator with an office and a home in both Houston, Texas and Denver, Colorado. I had been in the oil business since 1956, and, in the middle 1970's, after their graduation from college, my two oldest sons had joined me to make it a family endeavor. Times had been good and business prospered. I had not the slightest inclination to write a book. Then, in July of 1982, I had a heart attack.

This, as it turned out, was not the first I had suffered, nor was it to be the last. My doctors' advice was that I must at all costs avoid stress and they strongly recommended that I retire. My partners, of whom one was my wife, were adamant I heed this advice. And so, in early 1983, at the age of 53 and at the beginning of what I had thought would be my most productive years, I was "forced" into retirement. Reading became a full time occupation.

One subject in which I had an abiding interest was criminal law and my sense of justice was being offended with great regularity by accounts of dangerous criminals being released by federal judges, not because there was any doubt of their guilt, but because the evidence used to prove it was said to have been obtained in violation of the Bill of Rights. This ran counter to everything I had ever learned about constitutional law.

In what now seemed to have happened to someone else in another time in another world, I had started off my career not in the oil business, but as a lawyer in private practice. It was mostly civil practice but I had done some work in criminal law as well. In the 25 years that had passed since I had tried a criminal case, however, I had not kept abreast of events. Now that time was something I had plenty of, I decided to catch up.

Over the next five years, I read everything I could find on the Fourth and Fifth Amendments and the exclusionary rules of evidence the Court has read into them. If an expert may be defined as someone who knows more and more about less and less, I became an expert. The most puzzling aspect of this study, it turned out, was the curious fact that the rules now being used to free robbers, rapists and murderers were formulated entirely in cases involving petty gamblers.

For example, the offense of Fremont Weeks, the defendant in *Weeks v. United States*, the case which originally established the search and seizure exclusionary rule, was to send lottery tickets through the mail. *Mapp v. Ohio*, the case which applied the *Weeks* rule to the states, involved a search for lottery tickets, although you would not know this by reading the official report. In *Malloy v. Hogan*, the case in which the so-called "Privilege against Self-Incrimination" was created, the underlying crime was "pool selling," a "pool" in this context being a bet on a sporting event. *Malloy v. Hogan* is the foundation upon which *Miranda v. Arizona* rests; overrule *Malloy* and the *Miranda* rule falls with it.

But how, I wondered, did rules which have had such a devastating effect on criminal justice arise from cases which, if they were to be prosecuted at all, should have been decided at the lowest echelon of our court system? The answer was simple. These cases were faked—every single one of them was bogus. The prosecutors and the defense attorneys, far from being the adversaries they pretended to be, were colluding behind the scenes to achieve the same end. The idea was to obtain in a non-controversial case involving a petty gambler a precedent which then could be used in cases of serious crime. This, it seemed to me, was a scandal of immense proportion and I thought about writing what eventually became this book.

From the beginning I could foresee a problem of "credentials." A lawyer who had spent most of his working life in oil exploration—a "wildcatter," to use an outmoded expression—is a most unlikely commentator on our criminal justice system. There was also the question of credibility. It seems highly implausible that such critical cases could be set up and colluded without the Court and the bar becoming aware of it. Yet you can scour the shelves of the nation's law libraries without coming across a reference that even alludes to such a possibility.

But upon reflection, the factors that seemed to work against me might actually be my strong points. While my experience in the practice of criminal law was indeed limited, it did take place before the 1960's. So, unlike those lawyers who came of age later on, I had not been conditioned to accept these exclusionary rules as emblematic of a free society.

This is of critical importance because the prevailing opinion among lawyers, especially young lawyers, seems to be quite the opposite. In 1989, Joseph Grano, one of the few law professors to question the *Miranda* doctrine, wondered how "what started out as revolutionary and extremely controversial has become in many circles unassailable dogma."

> While slanted and deficient training may explain the inability and unwillingness of many students and young lawyers to challenge critically the assumptions of the existing orthodoxy, the similarly broad reluctance of the practicing and academic lawyers who well recall the period of change is more baffling.[1]

One of these academic lawyers is Yale Law School Professor Steven B. Duke, a protégé of the late Justice William O. Douglas. In 1976, Professor Duke, on the occasion of the retirement of Justice Douglas, stated that before Douglas took his seat on the

---

1 "Remembering the Past of Criminal Procedure," 22 University of Michigan Journal of Law Reform (1989), 399-400.

Supreme Court: "Police and prosecutors could suppress and fabricate evidence, self-incrimination could be compelled and the accused denied access to the defense witnesses . . . Trial could be without a jury or an unbiased judge; double jeopardy and cruel and unusual punishments could be imposed; a speedy trial could be denied."[2] Now I know this to be a litany of absolute falsehoods. But how many of his students do? And future generations of lawyers, will they challenge it, or accept it as a fair and accurate restatement of the past? Professor Grano does not offer much encouragement.

> My students, however, cannot make the comparison: to them the old world has no flesh, and the new world is all they know. For those to whom a world without *Miranda* is as antiquarian as a world without satellites or video cassette records, the question of whether we made wrong choices, or of whether we should re-embrace some of what we so precipitously and often casually discarded, does not call for serious analysis.

Well perhaps we can put flesh on some old bones so that they *can* make a comparison between the world they know and the constitutional law which was our patrimony. We will take the Fifth Amendment, the fourteenth amendment, the writ of habeas corpus, each in turn, and see how they fitted into our constitutional scheme of things under a jurisprudence in which the sole object in a criminal trial in a state court was to determine the truth of the accusation against the defendant. You will learn how, and by what chicanery, this jurisprudence, known as "fundamental fairness," was overthrown by a cabal of rogue justices acting in concert with the American Civil Liberties Union and perverted into a system in which travesties of justice such as *Brewer v. Williams* are commonplace.

---

[2] 11 Harvard Civil Rights-Civil Liberties Law Review, 241 (1976).

CHAPTER 1

THE WAY IT WAS

WHEN FIRST OUT OF LAW SCHOOL and newly admitted to the bar, I took up the general practice of law. The year was 1954 and the place was the Borough and County of Bronx in the City and State of New York. This was made easier by the fact that my father was a successful lawyer with his own practice, and I had only to move in with him. He gave me an office and a desk and assigned me tasks within my competence so that I could gain experience and make a living at the same time.

For some reason now beyond recall, I became afflicted with the notion that I should become versed in the criminal as well as the civil law. My father didn't think much of this idea, but he had decided, he told me, that I was old enough to make my own mistakes. Free at last to act upon my misapprehensions, I set out to learn.

At that time it was the obligation of lawyers to represent indigent criminal defendants *pro bono publico*—that is, for the public good, without pay. While all members of the bar were supposed to bear their share of the burden, it did not work out that way, particularly in the large cities where lawyers tend to specialize. In this scenario volunteers were welcome. I wrote letters to some criminal court judges announcing my availability, and in due course was interviewed and found fit. Each of the judges gave me a short lecture on criminal justice, and a promise to assign some cases.

In the beginning they were misdemeanor cases, all of which were disposed of by a plea bargain of one sort or another I negotiated with the assistant district attorney (A.D.A.) in charge of the case. In some cases, where the defendant had no prior record, the charge might simply be dropped and the defendant let off with a warning. For youthful offenders there was a procedure whereby a defendant might enter a tentative plea of guilty and receive a suspended sentence. If he stayed out of trouble for a specified period of time, the plea was vacated, the charge dropped and the record expunged.

Only one of my misdemeanor clients, in fact he was my very first client, received an actual jail sentence. He had been serving a sentence for a misdemeanor at Riker's Island Prison in greater New York harbor when he made a spectacular escape. Riker's is in that turbulent stretch of the East River aptly named "Hellgate," considered to be New York's equivalent of Alcatraz and equally escape-proof. One day in December of 1954, just before Christmas, he made his way up an air shaft three stories to the roof and then, on a rope made of bed sheets, let himself down to the yard. Somehow he managed to get over the wall and to the river where he launched himself into the icy waters clutching some wood he had lashed together as a raft. Rescued by a police boat and taken to the hospital, he told them that he was a painter who had been working on one of the East River bridges when the scaffolding collapsed and he fell into the river.

The bridge painter must have been pretty convincing because the front page of the tabloids the following morning showed him in a hospital bed flanked by the officer who had pulled him out of the water and some of the brass who wanted to get their picture in the newspaper. The patient was discharged from the hospital and released into the general population before the police realized that he was an escaped convict. A manhunt ensued, the zeal of which had not been seen since the days of Bonnie and Clyde. Gleeful reporters kept the public duly informed on its progress. Escaping from prison in and of itself was a crime; if you were serving a felony sentence, it was a felony; if a misdemeanor, escape was a misdemeanor. My client understood that there was no defense to the charge and accepted his fate equably.

Of some 20 felony cases I tried only two. The first was a rape case which ended in a plea bargain. After the trial was over, but before the jury returned a verdict, the prosecution offered the defendant a plea to simple assault, a misdemeanor. We accepted it. The second trial was a mundane case of felonious assault. One bad guy cut another bad guy on the arm. It would have been a band-aid rather than a felony case but for my client's record.

The defendant had three prior felony convictions of which the last was a murder committed during the course of a bank robbery in Pennsylvania. Sentenced to life imprisonment, he'd been released on parole after serving some 20 years. By moving to New York without permission he was in violation of the terms of his parole. If my client were to be convicted of felonious assault, he would receive from New York, as a fourth felony offender, a mandatory sentence of 25 years to life. If he lived long enough he would then be returned to Pennsylvania as a parole violator to finish his sentence there.

There was no plea bargaining. The defendant could not accept a felony plea and the prosecution would not settle for a misdemeanor. There had to be a trial, and at stake was whether the defendant, who was about forty, would spend the rest of his life in the penitentiary. The complainant and all the other witnesses testified it was an unprovoked assault which took place during a card game. My client told me it was a "frame-up" engineered by the complainant as a result of a dispute over a woman. There was no choice but to put him on the witness stand to give his version of events. To impeach his credibility the prosecution was permitted to show his prior convictions, and when he admitted to the murder the jury was visibly shocked.

But they acquitted him on the felony charges and convicted him of simple assault. He was sentenced to what amounted to the time he had already served while awaiting trial. As far as New York was concerned, he was free and would be held only so long as it took Pennsylvania to pick him up as a parole violator. When I saw him after his sentence, he was effusive in his thanks and sanguine about his future. Six months would see him a free man and after that it was the straight and narrow path for him.

These two aside, I never had a case in which my client had a chance of winning an acquittal. A short interview would reveal not only that they had committed the crimes of which they were charged, but had also admitted everything to the police. If there was any tangible evidence, such as a weapon, or the fruits of the crime, the police had it neatly tagged and filed away. If my client had an accomplice he had already implicated him, and had been implicated in return.

If in the 1950's you accused a New York City detective of extorting a confession he would have been insulted. As a matter of professional pride detectives were convinced that given sufficient time and absent "outside interference," they could get any suspect to tell the truth of his own free will. The time most critical was the first few hours following arrest and by outside interference they meant lawyers.

A case would start off with my getting a copy of an indictment in the mail together with a notice from the court of my appointment to represent the defendant. The notice would give the date for pleading. Let's assume the defendant has been indicted for burglary in the first, second and third degrees. The first degree of a crime is the most serious and the third the least. The penal statutes are so drawn that a crime in the first degree would also be a crime in the lesser degrees, but not the other way around. A conviction of an "attempt" to commit a crime was punishable by one-half of the time provided for a conviction of the crime itself.

The first step would be a trip to the county jail to talk to my new client and get an idea of what the case against him was like. The interviews were not always informative. Many defendants, after telling the police everything they knew, would later, upon reflection, tell their lawyer the story they wished they had told the police. When still new at the game I got batted back and forth like a shuttlecock between client and A.D.A. learning a new unpleasant fact with each stroke. After a while I learned to question them more closely which saved a lot of wear and tear, not to mention loss of face.

Let's say I had already achieved this degree of proficiency and in a 30-minute conversation have elicited from my client that he committed the burglary charged in the indictment and has told the police all about it. With his consent, and probably with him in tow, they went to his home and found some of the loot which can be traced to the crime. I also ascertain from the defendant that the police did not threaten or abuse him; that neither food nor drink was withheld from him, and that he was not questioned for a length of time or under circumstances which could be regarded as coercive.

My client has no complaint about his treatment and agrees that his admissions were voluntary. "In that case," I would ask, "why did you talk?" The refrain was always: "Well, the cops knew most of the story so I just told them the rest," or words to that effect. What this meant was that the police had psyched him into thinking his situation was hopeless so he would tell them all. If his case wasn't hopeless to begin with, it was now, and the only thing I do at this point was to make the best plea bargain for him that I could.

The next step would be to talk to the A.D.A. about a "disposition." A disposition is the final result of a plea bargain whereby the defendant pleads guilty to one of the charges against him, in return for which the prosecution dismisses the rest. In this and every other case of mine, except the two cases tried, the ADA knew that he had the defendant dead to rights. He knew that if he tried the case he would obtain a conviction, and it was just a question of what it was worth to him to avoid a trial. Once a disposition had been arranged, the judge would set a date for sentencing and order a report from the probation department.

The probation report would show not just the defendant's prior convictions but his complete police record. Where he had been arrested and let off with a warning, or otherwise been given a break, the report would so indicate. Also included were interviews with people in a position to know the defendant and his prospects for reformation and rehabilitation. These were given in the strictest of confidence, and for that reason the probation report was absolutely confidential and unavailable to the defense attorney.

On the appointed day for sentence to be imposed the defendant and his counsel stood side by side in front of the bench. The lawyer would then make a short speech on why the court should show mercy to his client. Some attorney, some time, must have said something on behalf of a client which resulted in mitigating his sentence. It had to have happened, but I wasn't there when it did. Between pleas, sentences and postponements thereof I daresay I made at least a hundred appearances in court, and hardly ever without hearing a defense attorney deliver a peroration on compassion. I never heard one that was effective. That having been said let me quickly add that I could do no better.

There are a finite number of categories in which mitigating factors may be found. If you wanted to touch every base, for example, you could start by making a brief allusion to the fact that no one was hurt or that restitution had been made. If this is not the case, by all means leave it alone. It is a mistake to say that the victim is doing nicely or that the money will be paid back when your client gets a job.

Next would be the defendant's working record and perhaps military service. Was he a useful citizen and one who had served his country; if so, and most important, he could then, if the court sees fit not to imprison him, support his wife and children who otherwise will become a "public charge." These are the magic words. Convince the sternest of judges that this is the case and he will bend over backward to be lenient. The problem is that such defendants occur with the frequency of hen's teeth.

It is important to bear in mind that the judge, while this little speech is going on, has in front of him the confidential probation report in which all of the pertinent facts about the defendant have been synthesized. You, the defense counsel, can only go on what your client has told you. The judge, as he pleases, will interrupt and interject as you are speaking. You, of course, must respectfully pause and let him finish and respond to his questions.

Judges particularly liked to do this to young lawyers. They would tolerate a pompous old gas bag but would pounce upon a neophyte. These encounters were sort of a game whose ostensible purpose was to teach a fledgling lawyer a lesson. Properly played they were a spectacle enjoyed by all, in particular the court attendants and those members of the bar not at risk. The judge always won and the defendant always lost, and hopefully the young lawyer learned a lesson. I learned mine early on, the hard way, of course.

My client, so he told me, was a married man with three children. He had served in the Navy until he was injured and received a medical discharge. Thereafter he held a number of jobs but because of his injury was unable to work and support his family. He had pleaded guilty to an attempted robbery. He and an accomplice held up a small Hispanic grocery store, a "bodega," using knives as weapons.

The proprietors of the bodega had bigger and better knives, as well as a meat-cleaver, and with help from some willing customers went after the two banditos. The other man got away, but my client was overcome and severely beaten. But for the timely arrival of the police he most likely would have been kicked to death. He had been hit across the forehead with the cleaver which left his vision impaired and his features distorted. I started by pointing out that no one was hurt in the robbery but was immediately interrupted by the judge. Etched in my memory is what followed:

JUDGE: How about your client. He was hurt, wasn't he?

DEFENSE COUNSEL: Yes, Your Honor, he was severely hurt. He was in the hospital for months.

JUDGE: (Gravely) I hope they took good care of him. He doesn't look very good. This is a most unusual case. Let me see if I have the facts straight. (Restates the account of the robbery loudly enough for all to hear.) Does that sound right to you? Have I got it straight?

D.C.: I think everyone does, Your Honor. (Laughter)

JUDGE: Good, please proceed.

D.C.: My client...

JUDGE: Is not a very successful robber, is he? Did you have a lot of trouble with the DA getting the robbery charge reduced to an attempt? (Laugher)

D.C.: No, Your Honor, he was most cooperative.

JUDGE: Good, I'm glad to hear it. Please proceed.

D.C.: He was severely injured as a result of the robbery.

JUDGE: As a result of the apprehension, you mean.

D.C.: Yes, Sir.

JUDGE: Good thing it wasn't the police.

D.C.: What I'm getting at is that the defendant has probably suffered more than if he went to jail; that he has learned more of a lesson.

JUDGE: You're probably right.

D.C.: (Seeing things have taken a turn for the better.) Your Honor, my client is a veteran having served in the Navy until, as the result of an injury, he was given a medical discharge. After...

JUDGE: It says here he got a dishonorable discharge.

D.C.: I beg your pardon?

JUDGE: Dishonorable—he was discharged because he was a thief.

D.C.: (After a hurried, whispered conversation with defendant) Your Honor, it is my understanding it was a medical discharge. He was hospitalized right up to the point of discharge.

JUDGE: He got beaten up for stealing. (Laughter) It happens, you know. It was dishonorable. I have the certificate here. Would you like to see it?

D.C.: Yes, Your Honor, I would. (Judge hands paper to bailiff, who brings it to D.C., who scrutinizes document and after whispered conversation with defendant, returns it to bailiff who brings it back to Judge. During this time a stillness has fallen over the courtroom befitting the solemnity of the occasion.)

JUDGE: Well?

D.C.: Well, it appears to be genuine, Your Honor, but...

JUDGE: I'm glad of that. (Laughter) I'd hate to think the probation department would give me a fake. (More laughter)

D.C.: (With great dignity) What I started to say, Your Honor, is that the defendant has a common Hispanic name, and the possibility exists that it could be a mistake, someone with a similar name.

JUDGE: True. Perhaps it is the person using that name who keeps getting arrested here in this city. (Reads the defendant's extensive police record item by item.) (Sustained laughter) But the FBI says it's the same man. Same fingerprints, the arrests, the Navy discharge—same man. *Your man.* Did he tell you about the larceny?

D.C.: I'm aware of the petit larceny, Your Honor, but I thought it was a Y.O. (Youthful Offense) and was wiped out.

JUDGE: Oh no, he was too old for that. It was a second-degree burglary. He got a break. They let him off on a misdemeanor. He's gotten a lot of other breaks too. It's not wiped out. It counts all right. It surely does. (Laugher) Anything else?

D.C.: Your Honor, the defendant is a married man with three children to...

JUDGE: How many?

D.C.: (Warily) Three, Your Honor.

JUDGE: The number is five (pause).

D.C.: Your Honor, I...

JUDGE: Three by his wife and two by his paramour (pause).

D.C.: Your Honor, I...

JUDGE: (Spacing his words) Not – to – one – of – whom – has – he – ever – shown – the – least – semblance – of – parental – responsibility. He never supported any of them. The women, the children, any of them, ever, not even for a day. (Pause) Is there anything else?

D.C.: No, your Honor.

The center stage was mine, all right; the audience hung on my every word. It must have been like watching a prizefight where one of the contestants, hopelessly outclassed, doggedly refuses to quit. Met by stiffening jabs to the head, he shakes the cobwebs from his eyes and keeps coming in, awaiting the right hand which will mercifully end the unequal contest. But in the end it was the defendant who took the count.

From there on out, I questioned my clients a lot more closely. It was not just a matter of self-preservation; if I was to help them I had to know the truth. After a while I had no illusions. My clients were never soldiers or sailors or workers or providers. Any assertion to the contrary was received with the greatest of caution. None ever checked out. There was precious little to be said in mitigation of sentence. Most of the time the result could not be influenced by anything the defendant's lawyer said anyway, so it didn't really matter.

Much more effective would it have been had a defendant exercised his right of allocution and said something on his own behalf. An expression of contrition and resolve to change, if genuine, could mean a great deal no matter how poorly articulated. My efforts in this regard met with no success; they just didn't seem to care that much. One defendant, when brought out to be sentenced, swaggered to his place before the bar in an exaggerated manner, winked and waved to his friends in the courtroom and, hand on hip, turned contemptuously toward the bench in a taunting posture. He had picked the wrong time and the wrong judge for that. His little grandstand play must have cost him at least a year of his life. I have no doubt that he thought it was worth every day.

In this situation defense counsel had only one factor working in his favor. If every defendant exercised his right to a jury trial the criminal justice system would break down in short order. The system was predicated on the assumption that no more than one in ten cases would have a factual situation which would admit of a possible defense and that the vast majority would plea bargain once they learned the police had built an airtight case against them. This was the way the criminal justice system functioned in New York City at the time, and I suspect that this was true throughout the country. A prosecutor would bargain because he had to, up to a point.

It had always been the law in the United States that the due process required of the states by the Fourteenth Amendment did not bar the use of a confession that was made voluntarily. Any confession procured by force, fear or favor was deemed involuntary. In this discussion, therefore, we are not talking about incriminating statements obtained from defendants by torture, physical brutality, deprivation of sleep, food, drink, toilet facilities, exhaustion or menace. For the sake of brevity we will use the word *duress* as a compendium of the foregoing circumstances. Any incriminating statement obtained under duress is barred. This has always been our law and anyone who says otherwise speaks out of ignorance or with intent to deceive.

The validity of confessions obtained under pressures not amounting to duress were judged by the facts and circumstances of the case. They always included the defendant's inculpatory statements to the police, who then corroborated them. Such statements most often were made at the scene of the crime, in a police car, or at the station house. But wherever they were made, the defendant did not have a lawyer by his side. The only time a confession was made once he was represented by counsel was after a bargain had been struck. In exchange for leniency the defendant talked and implicated himself along with his accomplices.

One day I took stock. I had taken up criminal work to get trial experience and because I thought it would be interesting. My interest had waned and the trials were far and few between. At the rate things were going, I would never live long enough to try 100 cases. Over a period of 15 months I had spent about 30 working days on felony cases. The two trials took about seven days between them and with the interviews, plea-bargaining and speaking for my clients in mitigation of punishment, maybe each of my "dispositions" came to a day apiece. The misdemeanors I'll throw in for good measure. And I served *pro bono publico* true to the end. The experience was neither enriching nor useful. It's been almost half a century and I haven't been in a criminal courtroom since.

To some readers, particularly those whose memories do not reach back to the 1950s, some questions might occur. "What about the Fifth Amendment?" you might ask. Was Joey read his "*Miranda*" rights? Did you move to have Joey's statements suppressed? The answer to all three questions is "no." You would not speak of *Miranda* because the only *Miranda* anyone had ever heard of was rhumba-dancer Carmen. If you suggested to a judge that the police should have advised your client that he had a right to remain silent, he would have told you that the duty of a police officer is to elicit the truth from a suspect, not to give him legal advice.

If you alluded to the Fifth Amendment the judge would have told you that it is basic, fundamental, constitutional law that the Fifth Amendment, like the rest of the Bill of Rights, applies solely to the federal government. The Fourteenth, he would have reminded you, is the only constitutional amendment which applies in a state criminal trial, and what it guarantees a defendant is a *fair* trial. There is nothing *unfair* about admitting his incriminating statements to the police provided those statements were voluntary, and if there was a question as to their voluntariness, the jury, after hearing all the evidence, would decide it.

The trial would involve one issue and one issue only, and that was whether or not the defendant was guilty of the crime of which he stood indicted. The prosecution had to produce evidence which if true was sufficient to prove him guilty beyond a reasonable doubt. If they failed to do this the judge would dismiss the case without letting it go to the jury. If the prosecution made such a case it was for the jury to decide the truth.

The fact of the matter is that the cases against most of my clients were ironclad; they didn't have a chance of an acquittal. The wise defendant accepted the realities of his predicament and made the best deal he could. Those who did not went to trial and were convicted. When sentence was passed, they paid the price of folly.

CHAPTER 2

THE EXEMPTION
FROM COMPULSORY
SELF-INCRIMINATION

IN MEDIEVAL ENGLAND THERE EXISTED two rival and distinctly different systems of law. One was the Common Law. It had its own courts, judges, processes and procedures, and answered ultimately to the highest temporal authority in the realm—the King. The other was the Inquisition whose jurisdiction covered sin, most particularly heresy. Its functionaries were men under holy orders who answered to the highest ecclesiastical authority in Christendom, the Pope. All that it did was done in the name of the Church of Rome, the only church in England, and the overriding purpose of the Inquisition was to see that it so remained.

A serious crime against the King's law was called a *felonie*. Where a felony had been committed, and there was cause to believe a certain individual was the perpetrator, that person was arrested and brought before a judge for arraignment. This was a proceeding most often conducted by a magistrate, a minor judicial officer similar to a present-day justice of the peace. He began by informing the prisoner of the charge made against him.

The prisoner was entitled, but not obliged, to make a statement. He had the right to a preliminary hearing that looked to the substance of the charge against him. If the magistrate found substance lacking, he dismissed the charge and released the prisoner. On the other hand, if the evidence proved substantial, the suspect was held or "bound over."

The prosecution's evidence was then presented to a panel of jurors called a *grand* jury, because of their large number. Sworn to secrecy, they met in closed session. The suspect did not have the right to hear the evidence or confront the witnesses against him. If the grand jury concluded the evidence was insufficient, they voted "no bill." In this event the charge was dropped and the suspect released.

The grand jury consisted of not fewer than 12, nor more than 23 men. If 12 of them found probable cause to believe the accused had committed the crime charged, they voted a "true bill." This meant the accused stood indicted on a charge of felony. The truth or falsity of the indictment was tried before a *petit* jury, so called because it numbered only twelve. In this trial the accused, now the defendant, could not be required to testify against himself.

In the ecclesiastical courts the inquisitor would conduct his own investigation and examine the witnesses at a time and place of his choosing. The suspect, called the *examinate*, had no right to confront or question the witnesses against him. He was required to take an oath called the *oath ex officio*, and to answer any and all queries put to him by the inquisitor. In a case of heresy the inquisitor might question the examinate on his understanding of Christian dogma in an attempt to ensnare him. Should he decline to take the oath, or after taking it refuse to answer a question, he might be imprisoned until he did.

These are the origins of the two systems of criminal justice that exist in western Europe today. In Great Britain and the English-speaking world, the "accusatorial" system of the common law obtains. In France, Italy and Spain, among others, where the Inquisition lasted into the eighteenth century, variations on the inquisitorial process prevail. What are in the United States some of the functions of the police, grand jury and prosecutor are combined into the office of magistrate. A magistrate investigates, takes testimony, including that of the accused, and decides whether to prosecute. If he does, he may call the defendant as a witness.

Most of these legal principles took shape during the Plantagenet Dynasty which came to an end on Bosworth Field in 1485. The first of the Tudors, Henry VII, succeeded to the throne, and the following year married Elizabeth of York. Their son, Henry VIII, of the six wives, became King in 1509 shortly after marrying Catherine of Aragon, the daughter of the King and Queen of Spain.

Henry and Catherine had one child, a daughter named Mary. Henry desperately wanted a male heir which Catherine was unable to produce. His other great desire was to rid England of the spiritual sovereignty of the Church of Rome and its ecclesiastical courts. When the Pope refused to sanction the dissolution of his marriage to Catherine, Henry broke with Rome, and with the consent of Parliament assumed the title of Supreme Head of the Church, henceforward to be called the Anglican Church or the Church of England. At this point in the history of England religion and politics fused; heresy became treason and treason heresy.

The Protestant Reformation, which began in Germany in 1517, had spread to England, keeping the ecclesiastical courts and its inquisitors busy indeed. They now became the hunted. Henry seized the monasteries and the property of the Roman Church, and expelled or executed those clergymen who would not plight their allegiance to him and the Church of England. For refusing to take the oath recognizing Henry's supremacy, Thomas More, the Lord Chancellor and author of *Utopia*, was beheaded in 1535 for treason. Adultery by the queen was another form of treason, and for this Anne Boleyn, Henry's second wife, and the mother of his daughter Elizabeth, was beheaded. The persecution of those who continued to recognize the Pope as the leader of the Church, Roman Catholics, continued throughout Henry's reign, and after his death in 1547 through the six-year regency of his son, the child-King Edward VI who died at the age of 16.

Mary, Henry's daughter by Catherine of Aragon, became Queen in 1553. She was a Catholic and had married her Catholic cousin,

Philip, the future King of Spain. Mary attempted to reverse the Reformation and return England to Catholicism by force. During the five year reign of "Bloody Mary," large numbers of Protestants were convicted of heresy or treason and condemned to death. Two Anglican bishops were burned at the stake. Mary Tudor died childless in 1558, and her half-sister Elizabeth, the daughter of Henry VIII and Anne Boleyn, became Queen.

Henry VIII had four children of whom Elizabeth was now the lone survivor. All had died without issue, and Elizabeth was judged medically incapable of bearing children. She never married. The next in the line of succession was Mary Stuart, Queen of Scotland, and a Catholic. Elizabeth was a Protestant. Roman Catholics did not accept the divorce of Henry VIII from Catherine of Aragon nor the validity of his subsequent marriage to the mother of Elizabeth, Anne Boleyn.

The corollary of this was that if you were a Catholic you accepted Mary, Queen of Scots, as being the rightful Queen of England and considered Elizabeth a bastard and a usurper. It was unwise to banter this about. Even to speculate on the order of succession should something untoward happen to "Good Queen Bess," could get you in a lot of trouble. The Elizabethan period was not an age of tolerance in merry old England; plots abounded. In 1587 the Queen of Scots was beheaded.

The reigning monarchs of England had a council to advise them and see to the functions of government. Of this council there was an inner circle, something akin to a president's cabinet, called the Privy Council. Since at least the time of Henry VII they performed judicial as well as executive functions. This they did in a room off the Great Hall at Westminster the sky-blue ceiling of which was adorned with gold stars.

Sometime during the middle of the sixteenth century it acquired the name, as did the court which sat there, of the *Camera Stellata*, or the Star Chamber. "Generally speaking, it may be said that the Council both at its private Table and publicly in the

Star Chamber took cognisance . . . of [offenses such as] sedition, or insubordination to constituted authority; slander; political or religious dissidence, and disobedience to Proclamations.[1]

"Lewd words" reflecting on the character or policy of the monarch were very severely punished, and so were insults to peers, members of Council and officials. Offenders against the statutes concerning religion, both Roman Catholic recusants and Puritan nonconformists, frequently felt the weight of the Privy Council's displeasure.[2]

The Star Chamber was an excellent place for dealing with mischievous fellows given to vexatious oral exchanges bothersome to someone who had the ear of the Council or one of its members. "A great many cases of all kinds were initiated in the Star Chamber by bills or petitions of private persons."[3] Where a forfeiture or a fat fine was in the offing, jurisdiction was never an impediment nor, so it seems, was double jeopardy a defense.

In the reign of Elizabeth there were some very large fines. The Earl of Hertford, in 5 Elizabeth, was fined £15,000, £5000 for deflouring Lady Catherine Grey, £5000 for breaking out of his prison and coming to her, and £5000 "for iterating the said vicious act." Sir Robert Stapleton, in 1583, was fined £3000 for plotting scandal against the Archbishop of York, while one of his confederates was fined £500 and another £300 . . . Elizabeth . . . got a goodly income from the Star Chamber . . .[4]

---

[1] Charles Ogilvie, *The King's Government and the Common Law, 1421-1641*, Oxford: Basil Blackwood (1958). Republished in 1978 by Greenwood Press, Westport, Connecticut, 102.

[2] Id., 100.

[3] Id., 102

[4] Cora L. Scofield, *A Study of the Court of Star Chamber*. New York: Burt Franklin, originally published 1900, reprinted 1969, 78.

While the Star Chamber took jurisdiction over other offenses, it is remembered today for its treatment of religious or political deviants. Catholic monarchs used it to persecute Protestants, and Protestant monarchs to persecute Catholics. Both persecuted Anabaptists and, later, Puritans. The Puritans were an abstemious and priggish lot opposed to both the Catholic and Anglican Churches, as well as everything that was fun in Elizabethan England. They were forever printing seditious pamphlets on unlicensed printing presses, and being haled before the Star Chamber. The Star Chamber was essentially a political–ecclesiastical tribunal, and its procedure was inquisitorial. The accused was compelled to take the *oath ex officio* and answer the questions put to him.

Elizabeth died in 1603 and was succeeded by the first of the Stuarts, James VI of Scotland, who as King of England became James I. He was the son of Mary, Queen of Scots, but had been separated from her as an infant and raised as a Protestant in the Court of Elizabeth. His wife, however, was a Catholic. An absolutist and a believer in the divine right of kings, James reigned 22 years and died a natural death. His son, Charles I, would not be so lucky.

It was the seventeenth-century conflicts between the Stuarts and their enemies that brought about the legal reforms that are part of our heritage. The Stuarts were a cruel and vindictive clan, but not markedly more so than the Tudors before them. The Stuarts were absolute monarchs, but so also were their predecessors. It was not so much the ruling family of England, but the world around them which was changing, and the Stuarts were on the throne when it did.

Absolute monarchy could exist only in an agricultural society of pedigreed landlords and tenants, where one's status was determined by his rank in the feudal pecking order. It was a closed society in which advancement was possible only through inheritance, marriage or service to the King or one's liege. But all of this was changing. A commercial revolution was underway, and trade had been expanded to the new world. An entreprenurial class of merchants, bankers and manufacturers was accumulating wealth, its members demanding political power commensurate with their new status. They wanted a more mobile society based on freer trade and ideas, and a judicial system free from arbitrary power. Their allies were the common lawyers.

In the coming revolution it would be the Stuart King Charles I on one side and Parliament on the other. The King would have the support of the nobles and the lower classes and Parliament the classes in between. The religious alignment defies simple description; but venturing one anyhow, it seems fair to say that the Royalists, or Cavaliers as they were called, had the allegiance of Catholics and many Anglicans. Parliament had the support of the Puritans, known also as the "Roundheads," Presbyterians, and all others.

Far more important for us and for history is that the Royalists stood for a past of absolute and arbitrary power in which political and religious deviance was judged by the Star Chamber and punished with the utmost ferocity. The forces arrayed against them portended a future of parliamentary democracy and ever increasing religious and political tolerance. The Star Chamber was abolished by Parliament in 1641.

Viewed in its historical context, this tribunal was but an instrument used by ruthless and powerful men to deal with those who challenged their ascendancy. An ordinary criminal plying his trade, who did not fall afoul of one of them personally, had nothing to fear from *Camera Stellata*. Common criminals who committed common crimes against common people continued to be tried, as they had always been, in the common law courts.

A person charged with robbery or burglary was tried to a jury at the Old Bailey in London or its local equivalent elsewhere. He need have no fear of being compelled to testify against himself, since he could not testify at all. Only disinterested persons were competent to testify at common law as it existed at the end of the eighteenth century. The maxim, *nemo debet esse testis in propria causa*—"no man should be a witness in his own case"—was the rule of law that prevailed.[5]

♀ ♀ ♀

It was the common law of England, and it remained so until 1898, that a defendant was not competent to be a witness in his own case. In other words, a person on trial for a felony, even at his own request, would not be permitted to take the witness stand and testify as to his version of events. He was disqualified because he was deemed to be an untrustworthy witness. This was the law, and the only law on the subject in the United States, when in 1791 these words were added to the Constitution as the Fifth Amendment:

> "*No person* shall be held to answer for a capital, or otherwise infamous crime, unless on a presentment or indictment of a grand jury, except in cases arising in the land or naval forces, or in the militia, when in actual service in time of war or public danger; nor shall any person be subject for the same offense to be twice put in jeopardy of life or limb; nor *shall be compelled in any criminal case to be a witness against himself*, nor be deprived of life, liberty, or property, without due process of law; nor shall private property be taken for public use without just compensation."

There are five prohibitions in the Fifth Amendment, the last of which concerns a civil matter not within the purview of this book. The first three are specific provisions relating to criminal procedure. The fourth is the antithesis of a specific provision. Deliberately vague, it provides that "No person shall . . . be deprived of life, liberty, or property, without due process of law." This will be iterated in the Fourteenth Amendment and applied to the indi-

---

[5] Leonard W. Levy, *Origins of the Fifth Amendment: The Right Against Self-Incrimination*. New York: Macmillan Publishing Company (1986), 423.

vidual states. Due process of law is omnipresent in constitutional discussion and its reach knows no categorical bounds.

A private civil suit is the occasion in which our "process of law" is most often invoked. The very purpose of such a suit is to "deprive" the defendant of "property" of one kind or another for the benefit of the plaintiff. A civil action is initiated by the service upon the defendant of a written complaint by the plaintiff, alleging a wrong done him by the defendant. To set things right, the plaintiff asks the court to grant him damages and such other relief as may be just and proper. The complaint is accompanied by a summons issued under the authority of the court in which the suit is brought, giving the defendant a certain time in which to appear and file an answer. His failure to answer will be deemed an admission of the facts alleged, and would result in a default judgment.

There are procedures in civil suits whereby each party may make "definite and certain" their adversary's contention as to the facts. Through motions and interrogatories one side may compel the other to confirm or deny the relevant facts under oath. Where a fact is true, a party is put in the position in which he must either admit it or perjure himself. A fact admitted is thereafter taken as true. If the case comes to trial it is only the controverted facts, now isolated and placed in issue, which must be proven. At trial both plaintiff and defendant must submit to cross-examination. The entire civil process is nothing but a search for the truth of the matter. This is not so in our criminal law.

The chain of events which established the United States as an independent nation culminated with the ratification of the Constitution in 1789 and the Bill of Rights in 1791. This did not lead us to cast aside the experience of centuries. The law which governed us in most matters, including criminal procedure, continued to be that of the erstwhile mother country. The English common law survived the American Revolution relatively unscathed.

The basic legal codes adopted by each state of the Union included in them a proviso to the effect that the common law of

England, to the extent it was not inconsistent with the constitution or statutes of that state, remained in force. When they decided a rule of the common law no longer suited their needs, state legislatures would abrogate it by statute. The judicial branch did the same by evolution. Case by case, state courts accepted, rejected or modified English precedents according to their own notions of justice and public policy. But if a case arose, and there was nothing in that state's constitution, statute books, or case law to the contrary, the common law of England was the law in that jurisdiction.

The law we inherited upon our independence was that a defendant in a criminal case was incompetent to testify at his own trial whether he wished to or not. Whether by statute or by case law, this remained the law in the United States, and in each state, up until the Civil War. In the mother country, meanwhile, reformers—the philosopher Jeremy Bentham chief among them—had been pressing for change.

> Bentham led the movement for reform in England, contending always for rules that would not exclude but would let in the truth . . . The basic ground of the attack was, as Macaulay said, that "[A]ll evidence should be taken at what it may be worth, that no consideration which has a tendency to produce conviction in a rational mind should be excluded from the consideration of the tribunals."[6]

In the United States "reform was largely the work of Judge John Appleton of the Supreme Court of Maine, an American disciple of Bentham" whose efforts were successful in getting Maine in 1864 to enact "a general competency statute for criminal defendants, the first such statute in the English-speaking world."[7] Judge Appleton wrote a book in which he made the case for permitting the defendant to testify.

---

[6] *Ferguson v. Georgia*, 365 U.S. 570, 575 (1961).

[7] *Ferguson*, 577.

Of these rules the effect is to screen the guilty, by exempting them from what they most dread—interrogation. Were the criminals to frame a code for their own special protection, their first provision would be to protect themselves from all inquiry into their conduct. The present law benefits the criminal, by exempting him from the dangers of detection, and injures the innocent by depriving him of the benefits arising from an inquiry into his conduct.[8]

Appleton was quite persuasive. "Within 20 years most of the States now comprising the Union had followed Maine's lead . . . Before the end of the century every State except Georgia had abolished the disqualification."[9] The federal government had done so in 1878 so that in all federal criminal trials: "the person so charged shall, at his own request but not otherwise, be a competent witness. And his failure to make such a request shall not create any presumption against him."[10]

By the beginning of the twentieth century it was the law in the United States, and in each of them, Georgia aside, that a defendant in a criminal case could if he wished, but not otherwise, take the witness stand and testify on his own behalf. His right *not* to do so became known as the exemption from compulsory self-incrimination. If the defendant chose to testify, he was deemed to have waived the exemption and could then be cross-examined by the prosecution. But, one must keep in mind, that when the words were written into the Fifth Amendment that "no person . . . shall be compelled in any criminal case to be a witness against himself," he could not be a witness for himself either. He was not permitted to testify at all.

---

8 John Appleton, *The Rules of Evidence*. Philadelphia: T. & J.W. Johnson & Co., 1860, 134.

9 Georgia's incompetency statute was held unconstitutional in *Ferguson v. Georgia, supra*, from which this quotation is taken at 577. On the same page are the "dates on which the general competency statutes of the States were enacted."

10 March 16, 1878, c.37, 20 Stat. 30.

When the first post-Civil War Congress met in 1865, except for Maine and John Appleton, nothing new with respect to compulsory self-incrimination had taken place since the ratification of the Fifth Amendment in 1791. In the time in between the passage of the Fourteenth Amendment by that Congress in 1866, and its ratification in 1868, eight more states removed the defendant's disqualification.[11] This was due largely to the influence of Appleton and his writings. These are his views on why a criminal defendant should be permitted to testify:

> The accused innocent, he would rejoice at such a rule. To dissipate the clouds which encircle and surround him; to expose, detect and refute the false and calumnious charges, which have been made against him, would be to him a source of pride. Innocent, he would rejoice at an opportunity of stating, under the most solemn sanctions, the several exculpatory facts by which such innocence would be proved. To him interrogation brings no terrors. To the guilty alone is it a source of dread.[12]

If an innocent defendant would rejoice at the opportunity to confront his accusers and refute the false and calumnious charges against him, what does that bespeak of the defendant who chooses *not* to exercise his right to testify on his own behalf? May the trial judge or the prosecution comment on his failure to take the witness stand? May a jury infer guilt from his silence? Here again is Judge Appleton:

> If, in answer to interrogation from either the judge or public prosecutor, he be silent,—for he may be so,—it is at the risk of that inference which is ordinarily drawn from silence. He would obviously answer, were such answer to be favorable to his own interest. If, then, with an opportunity for excul-

---

[11] *Ferguson*, 577: 1866 California, Massachusetts, South Carolina and Vermont; 1867 Connecticut, Nevada, Ohio; 1868 Minnesota.

[12] *Appleton*, 127.

pation,—if exculpation be possible,—if, with the opportunity of asserting, and, so far as his solemn asservations can be of any avail, of establishing his innocence, he will not avail himself of that opportunity, what is it, but an admission that an answer would be dangerous; that he even prefers the natural inference of guilt from silence to answering. If, then, knowing this inference will be drawn, he prefers it should be, what is it but an admission of its correctness. *Silence is tantamount to confession.*[13]

There was but one area of contention. A criminal defendant may, but is not obliged to, testify on his own behalf. His election to do so opens him up to cross-examination which may incriminate him. Suppose in a criminal case evidence is presented against a defendant, both damaging to him and within his knowledge to explain or deny. He chooses not to testify, leaving the evidence against him unexplained and unrefuted. May the prosecution allude to his silence, and may the court instruct the jury that they may, if they see fit, draw from it inferences unfavorable to the defendant? Under some circumstances may the jury infer that, as Appleton put it, "silence is tantamount to confession"?

With respect to federal cases the answer is no. The 1878 statute has always been construed to prohibit such comment. We therefore need not concern ourselves as to whether the Fifth Amendment forbids it as well. It is only in state criminal cases, to which neither the federal statute nor the Fifth Amendment apply, where controversy arises. The question of whether the Fourteenth Amendment prohibits such a practice in state criminal trials was answered in 1904.

❦   ❦   ❦

Albert Twining and David Cornell were convicted of fraud by the state of New Jersey. The two had been officers and directors

---

[13] *Appleton*, 129 (emphasis added).

of a bank that had failed. Shortly before the bank had closed its doors to its depositors, it paid out a large sum of money for certain shares of stock, a transaction which impaired the bank's solvency. In the audit that followed, the validity of this transaction was questioned by a bank examiner. In response to the questions, Twining and Cornell produced a paper purporting to be a certified copy of the minutes of a special meeting at which the bank's directors had passed a resolution authorizing the acquisition of the stock.

The copy of the minutes certified that all five members of the board of directors, including Twining and Cornell, were present at the special meeting. One of the three other directors testified that to his knowledge no such meeting had taken place, and that if it had, he was not present. He testified further that he had never assented to the purchase of the stock. The defendants called no witnesses and did not testify themselves, although the law of New Jersey gave them the right to do so if they chose. In charging the jury the trial judge made this allusion to the defendants' silence:

> Now, it is not necessary for these men to prove their innocence. It is not necessary for them to prove that this meeting was held. But the fact that they stay off the stand, having heard testimony which might be prejudicial to them, without availing themselves of the right to go upon the stand and contradict it, is sometimes a matter of significance.[14]

The jury convicted Twining and Cornell of making false entries in the books of a banking corporation and they were sentenced to prison. They appealed this conviction to the Supreme Court of the United States on the grounds that the trial court's comment "upon the failure of the accused to testify was a violation of the fundamental rights of the plaintiff in error and was a denial of due process of law as guaranteed by the Fourteenth Amendment."[15]

---

14 *Twining v. New Jersey*, 211 U.S. 78, 80-81 (1908).

15 *Twining*, 83.

The Court traced the history of the "exemption from compulsory self-incrimination."

> None of the great instruments in which we are accustomed to look for the declaration of the fundamental rights made reference to it. The privilege was not dreamed of for hundreds of years after Magna Carta (1215), and could not have been implied in the "law of the land" there secured. The Petition of Right (1629), though it insists upon the right secured by Magna Carta to be condemned only by the law of the land, and sets forth by way of grievance divers violations of it, is silent upon the practice of compulsory self-incrimination, though it was then a matter of common occurrence in all the courts of the realm.[16]

In America only four of the thirteen original states insisted upon incorporating the exemption in the Constitution, and only two of the four had such a provision in their own state constitutions.[17] The Court did not rate the exemption "as an immutable principle of justice which is the inalienable possession of every citizen of a free government . . . It has no place in the jurisprudence of civilized and free countries outside the domain of the common law, and it is nowhere observed among our own people in the search for truth outside the administration of the law."[18] By a vote of eight to one, the Court concluded "that the exemption from self-incrimination in the courts of the States is not secured by any part of the Federal Constitution."[19]

> Due process of law, guaranteed by the Fourteenth Amendment, does not require the State to adopt a particular form of procedure, so long as it appears that the accused has had sufficient notice of the accusation and an adequate opportunity

---

16 *Twining*, 107-108.

17 *Twining*, 109.

18 *Twining*, 113.

19 *Twining*, 114.

to defend himself in the prosecution. It is impossible to reconcile the reasoning of these cases and the rule which governed their decision with the theory that an exemption from compulsory self-incrimination is included in the conception of due process of law.[20]

In 1931 the American Bar Association Convention debated the following resolution: "That by law it should be permitted to the prosecution to comment to the jury on the fact that a defendant did not take the stand as a witness; and to the jury to draw the reasonable inferences." The resolution was adopted by a vote of more than two-to-one, 242 "for" to 115 "against."[21] As a result of this resolution, and a study by the American Law Institute, California amended its constitution to permit comments to be made and inferences to be drawn upon a defendant's silence. In 1947, almost 40 years after the *Twining* decision, in a murder case arising in California, the exemption from compulsory self-incrimination was again before the Supreme Court of the United States.

The body of Stella Blauvelt, a widow 64 years of age, was found on the floor of her Los Angeles apartment on July 25, 1944. The evidence indicated that she died on the afternoon of the preceding day. The body was found with the face upward covered with two bloodstained pillows. A lamp cord was wrapped tightly around the neck three times and tied in a knot. The medical testimony was that death was caused by strangulation. Bruises on the face and hands indicated that the deceased had been severely beaten before her death.[22]

Entry into the apartment had been gained by means of a small aperture in the back door used for milk deliveries and trash collections. It had an unlocked outside door through which the trashman or milkman could either place or remove cans or bottles, and

---

20 *Twining*, 112.

21 56 *American Bar Association Reports* 159.

22 People v. Adamson, *27 Cal. 2d 478, 165 P.2d 3, 5-6 (1946)*.

on the inside of this miniature vestibule was a similar but locked door leading into the kitchen. This inside door had been forced. The defendant, Admiral Dewey Adamson, was small enough to have made his way in through the vestibule. Six of his fingerprints were found on the inner door.

Some diamond rings were missing and there was testimony that not long after the murder the defendant had offered to sell a diamond ring. In addition, the top of one of the victim's silk stockings had been shorn off and taken away. A search of the defendant's home revealed a collection of the tops of women's stockings. Adamson, who had two prior felony convictions, did not testify. Had he done so, the jury would have become aware of his criminal record.

California law permitted the court and prosecution to comment upon, and the jury to consider, the defendant's failure to explain facts within his knowledge, whether he took the witness stand or not. Thus the jury could infer that there was no innocent explanation for the fingerprints, the offer to sell a diamond ring or the defendant's keen interest in ladies lingerie. This they did and Adamson was convicted of murder in the first degree and sentenced to death. He appealed to the Supreme Court of the United States. California, argued Adamson, by permitting comment to be made and inference to be drawn on his silence, was attempting to deprive him of life and liberty without the due process of law required by the Fourteenth Amendment. Not so, held the Court:

> Specifically, the due process clause does not protect, by virtue of its mere existence, the accused's freedom from giving testimony by compulsion in state trials that is secured to him against federal interference by the Fifth Amendment. *Twining v. New Jersey*, 211 U.S. 78, 99-114; *Palko v. Connecticut, supra*, p. 323. For a state to require testimony from an accused is not necessarily a breach of a state's obligation to give a fair trial. Therefore, we must examine the effect of the California law applied in this trial to see whether the

comment on failure to testify violates the protection against state action that the due process clause does grant to an accused. The due process clause forbids compulsion to testify by fear of hurt, torture or exhaustion.[23]

California has prescribed a method for advising the jury in the search for truth. However sound may be the legislative conclusion that an accused should not be compelled in any criminal case to be a witness against himself, we see no reason why comment should not be made upon his silence. It seems quite natural that when a defendant has opportunity to deny or explain facts and determines not to do so, the prosecution should bring out the strength of the evidence by commenting upon defendant's failure to explain or deny it.[24]

The measure of the due process of law the Fourteenth Amendment required of state criminal trials was known as "fundamental fairness." If a trial was fair, it was constitutional, these two words being interchangeable. While this may place prior felony offenders like Adamson on the horns of dilemma, there is nothing unfair about that.

It is true that if comment were forbidden, an accused in this situation could remain silent and avoid evidence of former crimes and comment upon his failure to testify. We are of the view, however, that a state may control such a situation in accordance with its own ideas of the most efficient administration of criminal justice. *The purpose of due process is not to protect an accused against a proper conviction but against an unfair conviction.* When evidence is before a jury that threatens conviction, it does not seem *unfair* to require him to choose between leaving the adverse evidence unexplained

---

[23] *Adamson v. California*, 332 U.S. 46, 54 (1947).

[24] *Adamson*, 56.

and subjecting himself to impeachment through disclosure of former crimes.[25]

Let us observe that there was no self-incrimination, compulsory or otherwise. Adamson said not a word, nor under California law could he be compelled to do so. The law did, however, permit the prosecutor and judge to comment on his silence, and the jury to draw inferences from it. The exemption from self-incrimination was not in issue, and was in fact exercised. The question was whether due process of law requires its exercise to pass unremarked, and prohibits a judge or jury from attaching any significance to it. Justice Felix Frankfurter concurred separately:

> This does not create an issue different from that settled in the *Twining* case. Only a technical rule of law would exclude from consideration that which is relevant, as a matter of fair reasoning, to the solution of a problem. Sensible and just-minded men, in important affairs of life, deem it significant that a man remains silent when confronted with serious and responsible evidence against himself which it is within his power to contradict. The notion that to allow jurors to do that which sensible and right-minded men do every day violates the "immutable principles of justice" as conceived by a civilized society is to trivialize the importance of "due process."[26]

With respect to criminal justice, due process has but one standard and that standard is "fairness." Anything interfering with a fair trial falls within its ambit. The due process of law required by the Fourteenth Amendment does not ask whether reference to, or inference from, the defendant's silence is a species of the genus of the compulsory self-incrimination prohibited by the Fifth Amendment. It asks but one question: Is it fair?

---

25 *Adamson*, 57. (Emphasis added)

26 *Adamson*, 60.

In the late 1950's there was a judicial inquiry by the Supreme Court of New York into what used to be called "ambulance chasing." For refusing to answer questions regarding his professional conduct, a Brooklyn lawyer named Albert M. Cohen was disbarred. His appeal to the Supreme Court of the United States rested essentially on two propositions: "(1) that the Fourteenth Amendment forbade the State from making his refusal to answer the Inquiry's questions put to him a *per se* ground for disbarment; (2) that in any event such a ground is not permissible when refusal to answer rests on a *bona fide* claim of a privilege against self-incrimination."[27] "The issue is not," said the Court, "*whether* lawyers are entitled to due process of law in matters of this kind, but rather *what* process is constitutionally due them in such circumstances . . . [W]hat procedures are fair, what state process is constitutionally due . . . all depend upon the particular situation presented . . . Clearly enough, factual distinctions are the determinative consideration upon the question of what process is due in each of these cases."[28] "As a lawyer [the appellant] was 'an officer of the court, and like the court itself, an instrument . . . of justice.'"[29] By a vote of five-to-four the Court affirmed the disbarment.

> In this regard all that New York has in effect held is that petitioner, by resort to a privilege against self-incrimination, can no more claim a right not to be disbarred for his refusal to answer with respect to matters within the competence of the Court's supervisory powers over members of the bar, than could a trustee claim a right not be removed from office for failure to render accounts which might incriminate him.[30]

---

27 *Cohen v. Hurley*, 366 U.S. 117, 123 (1961).
28 Ibid., 129-131 (emphasis in original).
29 Ibid., 126.
30 Ibid., 127.

Chief Justice Warren, and Associate Justices Black, Douglas and Brennan dissented. The Fifth Amendment provides "no person . . . shall be compelled in any criminal case to be a witness against himself." This provision, they say, applies to the states by virtue of the Fourteenth Amendment. Justice Brennan wrote a separate dissenting opinion. "I would reverse because I think that the petitioner was protected by the immunity from compulsory self-incrimination guaranteed by the Fifth Amendment, which in my view is *absorbed* by the Fourteenth Amendment, and therefore is secured against impairment by the States."[31]

---

31 Ibid., 154. [Emphasis added]

CHAPTER 3

CONFESSIONS

U NDER THE COMMON LAW OF ENGLAND a confession was admitted into evidence in a criminal trial provided it was voluntary. For more than a century the common law rule prevailed in the United States in all jurisdictions, state as well as federal. If an incriminating statement was made voluntarily it was admitted into evidence; if not, it was excluded as both unfair and unreliable. The leading case was *Wilson v. United States*, involving a murder that took place in Oklahoma, then a United States territory and not yet a state.

> Wilson was convicted of the murder of one Thatch . . . and sentenced to be hanged. There was evidence tending to show that Thatch's body was found in a creek near where Wilson and Thatch had camped together two weeks before, in a state of decomposition indicating that deceased had been dead for that length of time. Wilson was arrested the day the body was discovered, and had in his possession five horses and a colt, a wagon, gun, bed clothing and other property that had belonged to Thatch.[1]

Wilson was arrested and brought before a U. S. Commissioner who questioned him "without giving him the benefit of counsel, or warning him of his right of being represented by counsel, or in any way informing him as to his right to be thus represented."[2] While Wilson did not confess he did not remain silent either.

---

[1] *Wilson v. United States*, 162 U.S. 613, 614 (1896).

[2] *Wilson*, 615.

He told the commissioner that Thatch owed him money and in return for the forgiveness of this debt had given most of his possessions to Wilson. Soon after that, according to Wilson, Thatch rode away. The problem with this story was that Wilson was found in possession of the deceased's shoes, hat, coat and saddle. This meant, if his story was true, that Wilson had last seen Thatch riding away bareback clad only in the undershirt, overalls and a pair of socks in which his body was found. His explanation of how he came to be in possession of Thatch's property, meant to be exculpatory, was taken by the jury to be incriminating. The Court treated Wilson's statement as a confession; to be admissible it must be voluntary. It was involuntary, contended Wilson, because he had not been informed of his right to counsel:

> The true test of admissibility is that the confession is made freely, voluntarily and without compulsion or inducement of any sort . . . The fact that he is in custody and manacled does not necessarily render his statement involuntary . . . [I]t is not essential to the admissibility of a confession that it should appear that the person was warned that what he said would be used against him, but on the contrary, if the confession was voluntary, it is sufficient though it appear that he was not so warned.[3]

All of the above "were matters which went to the weight or credibility of what he said of an incriminating character, but . . . were not of themselves sufficient to require his answers to be excluded on the ground of being involuntary as matter of law."[4] The jury had weighed Wilson's statements and found them both voluntary and true. The murder conviction was affirmed.

In 1896, the same year the decision in *Wilson* was handed down, a triple murder was committed on board an American ship while on the high seas, thus making it a federal crime. The sailing ship, the *Herbert Fuller*, out of Boston, was under the command of Cap-

---

3 *Wilson*, 623.

4 *Wilson*, 624.

tain Charles Nash. Thomas Mead Bram was the first mate. The murders took place in the aftercabin where there were five separate compartments. Captain Nash slept in one and his wife in another. Bram and the second mate each had their own compartment and the fifth was occupied by a passenger. A crew of six seaman and the steward slept forward by the bow.[5]

On the night of July 13, when the watch was changed at midnight, First Mate Bram took the deck, two seaman went forward on the lookout, and Charles Brown, another seaman, took the wheel. Sometime near two o'clock, the passenger, whose room was between the room occupied by Mrs. Nash and that of Captain Nash, was awakened by a scream. He arose, went to the captain's quarters, and saw him lying on the floor. He then went on deck and told Bram what had happened. Bram got a lantern and he and the passenger went below to investigate.[6]

Captain Nash, his wife and Blomberg, the second mate, were all dead, each with several wounds upon the head, apparently given with a sharp instrument like an axe, penetrating the skull and into the substance of the brain, and the second mate lying on his back with his feet crossed, in his berth; Mrs. Nash in her room . . . and Captain Nash in his room, as already stated.

The whole crew was called at or about daylight and were informed of the deaths.

The bodies were removed from the cabin and placed in the jolly boat, and the boat was towed astern to Halifax. The cabin was then locked, Bram taking the keys, and it remained locked till the vessel reached Halifax . . . No blood or spots of blood were ever discovered on the person or the clothing of any person on board, nor did anything direct suspicion to anyone.[7]

---

5 *Bram v. United States*, 168 U.S. 532, 534-535 (1897).

6 Id., 535.

7 Id., 535-536.

With Bram now in command, the ship came about and set a course toward Nova Scotia. A few days later suspicion fell upon seaman Brown and he was put in irons. When the vessel made landfall, on the basis of an accusation by seaman Brown, the crew overpowered Bram and took over the ship. Bram avowed his innocence. When the *Herbert Fuller* docked at Halifax, Bram and Brown, both in irons, were taken into custody by the Halifax police.[8]

> [T]he police detective caused Bram to be brought from jail to his private office, and when there alone with the detective *he was stripped of his clothing*, and either whilst the detective was in the act of stripping him, or after he was denuded, the conversation offered as a confession took place. The detective repeats what he said to the prisoner, whom he had thus stripped, as follows:
>
> "When Mr. Bram came into my office I said to him: "Bram, we are trying to unravel this horrible mystery.' I said: 'Your position is rather an awkward one. I have had Brown in this office, and he made a statement that he saw you do the murder.' He said: 'He could not have seen me. Where was he?' I said: 'He states he was at the wheel.' 'Well,' he said, 'he could not see me from there."[9]

It is hard to believe, in view of his continuing protestations of innocence, that Bram meant by this statement to confess to murder. It is far more likely that Bram, obviously under great stress, had misspoken, and that what he was trying to say was that Brown, had Brown been at the wheel, could not see from this position the aftercabin where the murders took place. And if there was any other evidence pointing toward Bram's guilt, no reference was made to it in the Court's opinion.

Nevertheless, when Bram was tried for murder in Boston, and this statement introduced into evidence, he was convicted and

---

8 Id., 536-537.

9 Id., 560-561.

sentenced to death. By a vote of six-to-three, the Supreme Court reversed the conviction. Bram, said the Court, had been compelled to be a witness against himself in violation of that clause of the Fifth Amendment.

In criminal trials, in the courts of the United States, wherever a question arises whether a confession is incompetent because not voluntary, the issue is controlled by that portion of the Fifth Amendment to the Constitution of the United States, commanding that no person "shall be compelled in any criminal case to be a witness against himself."[10]

> The rule is not that in order to render a statement admissible the proof must be adequate to establish that the particular communications contained in a statement were voluntarily made, but that it must be sufficient to establish that the making of the statement [itself] was voluntary; that is to say, that from the causes, which the law treats as legally sufficient to engender in the mind of the accused hope or fear in respect to the crime charged, the accused was not involuntarily impelled to make a statement, when but for the improper influences he would have remained silent.[11]

If there is any difference between the amount of pressure required to render a suspect's confession involuntary, and that necessary to compel a suspect in a "criminal case to be a witness against himself," the Court did not make the distinction. Nor did they retreat from their unanimous holding in *Wilson v. United States* the year before that "it is not essential to the admissibility of a confession that it should appear that the person was warned that what he said would be used against him, but on the contrary, if the confession was voluntary, it is sufficient though it appear that he was not so warned."[12]

---

10 *Bram v. United States*, 168 U.S. 532, 542 (1897).

11 *Bram*, 549.

12 *Wilson*, 623.

In 1919, during the pandemic of influenza then raging, Ziang Sung Wan, a native of China, was taken into custody by Washington D.C. police as a suspect in a murder case. District detectives took him to a room in a hotel where he was held incommunicado for more than a week. During this entire period Wan was sick and spent most of the time in bed.[13]

> Wan was held in the hotel room without formal arrest, *incommunicado*. But he was not left alone. Every moment of the day, and of the night, at least one member of the police force was on guard inside his room. Three ordinary policemen were assigned to this duty. Each served eight hours . . . From 7 o'clock in the evening until 5 o'clock in the morning the questioning continued. Before it was concluded . . . [T]he superintendent of police had returned to his home, apparently exhausted. One of the detectives had fallen asleep. To Wan, not a moment of sleep was allowed.[14]

On the twelfth day of his detention, after relentless and unremitting questioning, Wan signed a confession. The following day he was visited and examined by the chief medical officer of the jail who found Wan lying in a bunk exhausted, emaciated and suffering from intense abdominal pain. The doctor diagnosed his condition as spastic colitis. At the trial, the doctor was questioned by the court:

> QUESTION. Would he be liable to sign a confession that would lead him to the gallows in that condition?
> ANSWER. I think he would, if he wanted to be left alone.
> QUESTION. With spastic colitis, if he was accused of crime he would simply sign a paper and say, "You hang me?" This is your opinion as a medical man?

---

[13] *Ziang Sung Wan v. United States*, 266 U.S. 1 (1924).
[14] Id., 11, 12.

ANSWER. I say, if he was as sick as that and in as great pain as that, he would do anything to have the torture stopped.[15]

A unanimous Court held the confession to be involuntary. "In the federal courts, the requisite of voluntariness is not satisfied by establishing merely that the confession was not induced by a promise or a threat. A confession is voluntary in law if, and only if, it was, in fact, voluntarily made . . . [A] confession obtained by compulsion must be excluded . . . *Bram v. United States*, 168 U.S. 532."[16] But while *Bram* was cited, it was not cited for its proposition that the accused would, but for improper influences, have remained silent. Voluntariness, under the totality of the circumstances surrounding a confession, remained the requisite of admissibility in both state and federal courts.

Then, in 1943, the Supreme Court created a rule which limited the admissibility of confessions in federal but not state cases. It was predicated not upon the Fifth Amendment or any other provision of the Constitution, but incidental to the Court's power and duty to supervise the administration of criminal justice in the federal courts. The case arose out of a raid by federal agents on a moonshine operation run by a clan of Tennessee mountaineers named McNabb. During this nocturnal foray one of the agents was shot and killed, and five of the McNabbs known to have been near the scene of the homicide were arrested. Questioning them separately, and playing one off against the other, the officers were able to elicit from the McNabbs both accusations against one another and self-incriminating statements.

After a trial in which these statements were admitted into evidence, three of the McNabbs were convicted of murdering a federal officer while he was engaged in the performance of his official duties. They appealed their convictions to the Supreme Court of

---

15 Id., 13,14.

16 Id., 14, 15.

the United States, arguing that the statements used against them were coerced. The Court, speaking through Justice Felix Frankfurter, never reached this question or crossed the constitutional threshold.

> In the view we take of the case, however, it becomes unnecessary to reach the Constitutional issue pressed upon us. For, while the power of this Court to undo convictions in state courts is limited to the enforcement of those "fundamental principles of liberty and justice," *Hebert v. Louisiana*, 272 U.S. 312, 316, which are secured by the Fourteenth Amendment, the scope of our reviewing power over convictions brought here from the federal courts is not confined to ascertainment of Constitutional validity. Judicial supervision of the administration of criminal justice in the federal courts implies the duty of establishing and maintaining civilized standards of procedure and evidence.[17]

A federal statute provided: "It shall be the duty of the marshal, his deputy or other officer, who may arrest a person charged with any crime or offense, to take the defendant before the nearest United States commissioner or the nearest judicial officer . . . for a hearing, commitment, or taking bail for trial."[18] The convictions of the McNabbs were reversed. Because the officers who arrested the McNabbs had not complied with the statute, held the Court, the confessions were inadmissible even if they were otherwise voluntary. This became known as the *McNabb* rule.

The case had been briefed and argued on the question of voluntariness. No thought was given nor significance attached as to when the defendants were arraigned before a judicial officer. As Justice Stanley Reed pointed out in his dissent, the record was silent in this regard. The McNabbs were tried a second time and once again convicted. This time their convictions were upheld on

---

17 *McNabb v. United States*, 318 U.S. 332, 340 (1943).

18 *McNabb*, 342.

appeal[19] when it was proven that the officers *had* complied with the statute; the defendants in fact *had* been promptly arraigned before the nearest U.S. magistrate. So, the McNabbs went to prison while their famous rule survived.

The *McNabb* rule excluded from evidence incriminating statements, regardless of their volition and probity, if they were obtained from a defendant prior to arraignment, when the arresting officer had not taken him to a magistrate forthwith. In practice, few confessions are made after arraignment. The *McNabb* decision provoked an uproar in Congress, and legislation was introduced in the House of Representatives which would have had the effect of reversing it. A bill introduced by Representative Samuel F. Hobbs of Alabama provided "that a failure to observe the requirements of law as to the time within which a person under arrest must be brought before a committing officer shall not render inadmissible any evidence otherwise admissible."[20] The Hobbs Bill was passed thrice by the House but failed in the Senate.

In 1957 the *McNabb* rule became the *McNabb-Mallory* rule. Andrew Mallory was convicted of rape in the District of Columbia. He had confessed after his arrest but before his arraignment, during a lie detector test administered in between. Such interrogations were standard operating procedure. The idea was to confront the suspect with the evidence against him and encourage him to talk until he either cleared or ensnared himself. A law enforcement officer interrogating a suspect considered himself under no obligation to caution him that he had a right to remain silent.

The best policy for one wrongfully suspected of crime was to tell the police the truth. For a suspect who was guilty, however, unless he was interested in clearing his conscience and unburdening his soul, silence was the safest course. If he lied, the police inevitably would catch him in inconsistencies and it would only

---

19 *McNabb v. United States*, 142 F. 2nd 904 (1944).

20 38 *Journal of Criminal Law and Criminology*, 137.

be a matter of time until he confessed. The result was that dumb criminals, such as Andrew Mallory, made confessions which, while voluntary and true, were ill-advised from the standpoint of pure self-interest. His smarter and better counseled brethren, on the other hand, stood mute and often "walked." Apparently the underlying purpose of the *McNabb-Mallory* Rule was to level the playing field.

> When this inquiry of a nineteen-year-old lad of limited intelligence produced no confession, the police asked him to submit to a "lie-detector" test. He was not told of his rights to counsel or to a preliminary examination before a magistrate, nor was he warned that he might keep silent and "that any statement made by him may be used against him." After four hours of further detention at headquarters, during which arraignment could easily have been made in the same building in which the police headquarters were housed, petitioner was examined by the lie-detector operator for another hour and a half before his story began to waver. Not until he had confessed, when any judicial caution had lost its purpose, did the police arraign him.[21]

It must be kept in mind that the *McNabb* rule, like its Fourth Amendment cousin, the *Weeks* rule, applied only in federal cases. In the case of *Weeks v. United States*, the Court specified that it was only the letters seized by a United States marshal which must be excluded. Evidence which had been obtained by state police officers would have been admissible had Weeks been tried again.[22] Justice Frankfurter, the author of the *McNabb* opinion, had made clear that the rule of exclusion being created was *not* of constitutional dimension. That being the case, the resolution of the controversy lay with Congress, which had only to change the statute upon which the *McNabb-Mallory* rule rested. On July 2, 1958, the

---

[21] *Mallory v. United States*, 354 U.S. 449, 455 (1957).

[22] *Weeks v. United States*, 232 U.S. 383, 398 (1914).

Willis-Keating Bill, drafted for this purpose, passed in the House of Representatives by a vote of 294 to 79. On August 19 it passed in the Senate by a vote of 65 to 12. In the early morning of August 23, 1958, however, in the closing minutes of the 85th Congress, the Bill was blocked by a parliamentary maneuver by Senator John Carroll of Colorado.[23]

In the state courts, voluntariness remained the test of admissibility. Any amount of force, fear or favor, however slight, was sufficient to vitiate a confession. In the next case the means used was anything but slight: "It is sufficient to say that in pertinent respects the transcript reads more like pages torn from some medieval account, than a record made within the confines of a modern civilization which aspires to an enlightened constitutional government."[24]

⚡ ⚡ ⚡

On the afternoon of Friday, March 30, 1934, in Kemper County, Mississippi, a white farmer was found murdered. That night a mob, led by a deputy sheriff, seized three black men including Ed Brown. The mob took them to the farm of the victim, where they were tortured. One was chained to a tree and whipped. They were then taken to the county jail where they were beaten some more and told that this treatment would continue until they confessed. On Sunday, they confessed.

On Monday, the confessions were repeated in open court after the three men had been warned that if they recanted more beatings awaited them. The trial was a sham. It was over in two days. On Friday, April 5, seven days after the body was found, the three defendants were convicted and sentenced to death. That their confessions were extorted was a fact known to everyone connected with the trial.

---

[23] Otis H. Stephens, *The Supreme Court and Confessions of Guilt.* Knoxville, Tennessee, University of Tennessee Press, 1984, 82-87.

[24] *Brown v. Mississippi*, 297 U.S. 278, 282 (1936).

The facts are not only undisputed, they are admitted, and admitted to have been done by officers of the state, in conjunction with other participants, and all this was definitely well known to everybody connected with the trial, and during the trial, including the state's prosecuting attorney and the trial judge presiding.[25]

Mississippi's argument was that the Court's holding in *Twining v. New Jersey*, that the "exemption from compulsory self-incrimination in the courts of the States is not secured by any part of the Federal constitution," meant that a state was free, if it so chose, to coerce confessions and use them in evidence against those from whom they had been extorted.[26] Not only was this proposition monstrous, said the Court, it was also a non-sequitur.

But the question of the right of the State to withdraw the privilege against self-incrimination is not here involved. The compulsion to which the quoted statements refer is that of the processes of justice by which the accused may be called as a witness and required to testify. Compulsion by torture to extort a confession is a different matter.

The State is free to regulate the procedure of its courts in accordance with its own conceptions of policy, unless in so doing it "offends some principle of justice so rooted in the traditions and conscience of our people as to be ranked as fundamental." *Snyder v. Massachusetts, supra, Rogers v. Peck, 199 U.S. 425, 434* . . . But the freedom of the State in establishing its policy . . . is limited by the requirement of due process of law . . . Because a State may dispense with a jury trial, it does not follow that it may substitute trial by ordeal. The rack and the torture chamber may not be substituted for the witness stand.[27]

---

25 *Brown*, 286.

26 *Id.*

27 *Brown*, 285.

The convictions were reversed by a unanimous Supreme Court as a violation of the Fourteenth Amendment. It was fundamental fairness that prevailed; the Fifth Amendment and its exemption from compulsory self-incrimination did not enter into the decision. "It would be difficult," said the Court, "to conceive of methods more revolting to the sense of justice than those taken to procure confessions of these petitioners, and the use of the confessions thus obtained as the basis for conviction and sentence was a clear denial of due process."[28]

In 1940, in a case out of Florida, a murder conviction was reversed because of a confession obtained by intimidation and exhaustion. The defendant, Isaiah Chambers, had been picked up in a dragnet search in which a number of young black men were arrested and interrogated about the murder of a white man. Extended, all-night questioning while the police held a lynch-mob at bay produced a "sunrise confession" ruled by a unanimous court to be coerced.[29]

The unanimous rulings in *Brown v. Mississippi* and *Chambers v. Florida* established once and for all, if there were any doubts about it before, that violence and intimidation are outlaws, and that no statement obtained under such influences will be considered voluntary.[30] The test for custodial self-incriminating statements in state as opposed to federal courts remained the English common law rule going back for centuries. If the statements were voluntary they were both constitutional and admissible; if not, they were neither.

In 1949 the Supreme Court decided three state cases involving incriminating statements made to the police and later recanted by the defendant. The pattern was the same. In each case, the prosecution put policemen and stenographers on the witness stand who testified to the defendant's statements and the events and

[28] *Brown*, 286.

[29] *Chambers v. Florida*, 309 U.S. 227 (1940).

[30] See also *Ward v. Texas*, 316 U.S. 547 (1942).

circumstances surrounding them. Evidence, both physical and testimonial, was introduced to corroborate the truthfulness and voluntary character of the confession.

The defense in each case then tried to prove that the statements were coerced. The jury, after seeing and hearing the witnesses, accepted the account of the prosecution and rejected that of the defendant. Jurors found the incriminating statements both voluntary and true, and the defendants guilty. Each defendant then appealed his conviction to the highest court of the state, which after a painstaking, point-by-point examination upheld both convictions. The cases were then appealed to the Supreme Court of the United States, where a majority, or substantial minority, voted for reversal by accepting the testimony of the defendant's witnesses and rejecting those of the prosecution on every controverted issue. By inflection and innuendo, the resulting opinions put a sinister import on the interrogations, pronouncing them "inquisitorial."

These three cases have other things in common. In each, the defendant was neither physically abused nor threatened, but was subjected to intense and prolonged questioning. This, at the time, was called the "third degree," and exemplified in cartoons by a suspect sitting in a police station under an overhead light closely ringed by detectives watching his every twitch. The charge in each case was a murder unwitnessed except by victim and perpetrator. The police had no suspects but the defendants, and the alternative to interrogating them was to close the books on the case and forget it.

Two competing definitions of "voluntary" emerged. One focused on the standard of reliability. Manifestly a coerced confession is unreliable evidence. Were the pressures on the defendant such as would test his will to stand by the truth? This, of course, depends on the character of the defendant and the pressures brought to bear. Those charged with this judgment in the first instance are the jury and trial judge who decided the statements were voluntary. Their findings, one would think, should stand in the absence of a clear showing of error. So said the Supreme Court in 1942:

> In such a case, we accept the determination of the triers of fact, unless it is so lacking in support in the evidence that to give it effect would work that fundamental unfairness which is at war with due process. Here, judge and jury passed on the question whether the petitioner's confessions were freely and voluntarily made . . . Furthermore, in passing on the petitioner's claim, the Supreme Court of the State found no violation of the Fourteenth Amendment. Our duty, then, is to determine whether the evidence requires that we set aside the finding of two courts and a jury, and adjudge the admission of the confessions so fundamentally unfair, so contrary to the common concept of ordered liberty, as to amount to a taking of life without due process of law.[31]

Some judges simply do not like a defendant, particularly one without legal counsel, to incriminate himself in any event. By taking the defendant's version of things, opposite of what the jury did, they simply characterize the prolonged interrogation as an "inquisition" and "inherently coercive" without regard to its effect on the defendant, or the other circumstances of the case. While any amount of force or violence is sufficient to vitiate a confession, the same is not true of questioning.

> Actual or threatened violence have no place in eliciting truth and it is fair to assume that no officer of the law will resort to cruelty if truth is what he is seeking . . . When, however, we consider a confession obtained by questioning, even if persistent and prolonged, we are in a different field. Interrogation *per se* is not, while violence *per se*

---

[31] *Lisenba v. California*, 314 U.S. 219, 238 (1941).

is, an outlaw. Questioning is an indispensable instrumentality of justice.[32]

In *Harris v. South Carolina*, the owner of a country store and his wife were shot dead, in cold blood, by a robber determined to leave no witnesses.[33] Time and space prevent its discussion. In the second case two robbers entered a small factory in Philadelphia after closing time and robbed and murdered two men, while a third acted as a lookout.

The lookout was arrested on other charges six months later, and confessed to a series of crimes including this one, in which he implicated his two accomplices. Each of them confessed, including the actual murderer, one "Tree-top" Turner. Turner was interrogated 15 to 30 hours, depending on whom you believe, over a six-day period before he confessed. No force, threats or physical abuse were involved. The Supreme Court of Pennsylvania unanimously affirmed the conviction with the absolute certitude that justice had been done. They also left us with some words to remember.

Anyone with experience in the administration of criminal law who reads the answers Turner made to the questions put to him will readily conclude that the statements he made to the officers were not those of a coerced or scared witness but that they were the statements of a man who had committed a murder and whose recital of its details was clear and explicit. The teller of the gruesome story of this double murder was obviously drawing on his memory and not on a fear-fired imagination. His narrative dovetailed so accurately with the physical facts surrounding the crime and with the story told by his accomplices that there can be no reasonable doubt of the story's truthfulness.[34]

---

32 *Ashcraft v. Tennessee*, 322 U.S. 143, 160 (1944), Jackson J., dissenting.

33 *Harris v. South Carolina*, 338 U.S. 68 (1949).

34 *Commonwealth v. Turner*, 358 Pa. 350, 58 A. 2nd 61, 63-64 (1948).

In cases of this kind the duty of the judiciary is to hold the balance true between the safety of society and fair play for an accused. Solicitude for the feelings of an accused must not be permitted to blind either judicial or police officers to the rights of the multitude to have criminals apprehended and their further depredations prevented. Any method of extracting confessions by means which would cause a prisoner to falsely confess guilt in order to be relieved of unendurable immediate suffering will not be tolerated in any civilized state. On the other hand, for a court to hold that a confession made by a well fed and decently cared for prisoner after he has been held in custody a few days without counsel or contact with friends and after he has been questioned a few hours every day by police officers in reference to a crime of which he is suspected, is inadmissible as being a coerced confession would be unrealistic and impractical. Such a judicial holding would result in a vast increase in the already too large number of felons who go unpunished and are free to prey upon law abiding citizens. These enemies of society naturally endeavor to commit their crimes where there are no witnesses except themselves and their victims. When the victim is killed the murderer feels himself safe.[35]

By a vote of five to four, the Supreme Court of the United States found the confessions involuntary, reversed the South Carolina and Pennsylvania Supreme Courts, and set aside the convictions of Harris and Turner. With respect to the *Turner* case, the Court let pass the pointed remarks of the Pennsylvania Supreme Court as to criminal psychology and the desire to confess, which they said was known to every criminal trial judge and the police for generations: "The only ones who apparently do not know it are some of the [U.S.] Supreme Court judges."[36] Furthermore:

---

[35] Id., 67, 68.
[36] Id., 69.

Anyone believing Turner's later assertions that he had been coerced into making his incriminating statements about the commission of these murders would be too credulous to be safely entrusted with any part in the realistic work of administering the criminal law with justice both to the accused and to society.[37]

In the third case, arising out of Indiana, a man had driven a municipal dump truck to the Indianapolis home of one Harriet Stout. He knocked on her door and asked if she had ordered a load of gravel. When told she had not he asked to use the phone. Once inside he threatened her with a knife and forced her to disrobe. On the pretext of locking the back door Mrs. Stout ran out of the house naked and escaped. The man fled and the police were called.

Robert Austin Watts, a city truck driver Mrs. Stout identified as her assailant, was arrested. In the meanwhile, two other women in the neighborhood identified Watts as the man who had knocked on their door that morning with the same story. That evening, Mary Lois Burney, who lived in the same neighborhood, was found murdered in her bedroom, shot in the face at close range with a shotgun. Two empty shell casings were found at the scene of the crime and her husband's shotgun was missing. From bruises on her body and the disarray of the house, it was apparent a struggle had taken place. Watt's fingerprints were found on her door.

Watts professed his innocence of the murder. He admitted, however, attacking Mrs. Stout and going to the homes of the other two women before the murder was discovered. He was interrogated three to four hours a day, for six days, until he confessed. Indicted for the murder of Mrs. Burney, Watts "entered a plea of not guilty and a special plea of insanity."[38] When he came to trial Watts repudiated the confession on the grounds it was coerced.

---

[37] Id., 67.

[38] *Watts v. State*, 226 Ind. 655, 82 N.E.2d 846, 848 (1948).

He was starved and beaten, so he said, and forced to sleep in a cell without a bed. This cell was called "the hole." Every other witness, including fellow prisoners, said Watts never missed a meal, and the commissary officer testified Watts had used the money he had at the time of his arrest to purchase cigarettes and candy in substantial amounts.

There was testimony that Watts was visited every day by his wife or mother; that Watts had said he didn't want a lawyer; that the cell without a bed, No. 7, was kept for fractious prisoners. Watts had gotten into a fight with another prisoner soon after his arrival. He was in "the hole" for two nights as a punishment for fighting, before being transferred to cell No. 2, with four beds, together with other prisoners.

He was in solitary confinement when he was in cell No. 7 only in the sense that he was the only one in the cell. The other prisoners could and did talk to him through the bars and hand him cigarettes, candy and the like. There was a toilet in cell No. 7, just as there was in the other cells. The only difference was that there was no bed. In a six-to-three decision, the U.S. Supreme Court reversed the conviction.

> On review here of State convictions, all those matters which are usually termed issues of fact are for conclusive determination by the State courts and are not open for reconsideration by this court. Observance of this restriction in our review of State courts calls for the utmost scruple. But "issue of fact" is a coat of many colors. It does not cover a conclusion drawn from uncontroverted happenings.[39]

That being said, the Court's majority went on to accept Watts's version of events very much controverted by the witnesses whose testimony the jury had accepted. Most telling is Watts's reference to cell No. 7, which became a place as wicked as the infamous "Black Hole of Calcutta." The specter of the Star Chamber was

---

[39] *Watts v. Indiana*, 338 U.S. 49, 50-51 (1949).

raised. We are reminded that ours is an accusatorial as opposed to an inquisitorial system.

Ignored was the fact that under the accusatorial system of the common law, and under American jurisprudence since, it had always been permissible for police to question a defendant unrepresented by legal counsel, and to use as evidence, in a state criminal trial, incriminating statements thereby obtained, provided, and provided only, they were voluntary. The reason cannot be over emphasized: The use of an involuntary statement is a violation of due process of law is because it is unreliable and untrustworthy evidence. The reliability of Watts's confession was never discussed by the majority. Nor did they mention that Watts had led the police to the murder weapon, a fact noted by the state court:

> [S]hortly after making this confession, he [Watts] led the officers in whose custody he was, to a lonely place in the City of Indianapolis, where he had tossed the shotgun. This spot was far from the scene of the crime. The gun was still there. The gun was the property of the husband of the deceased and he had kept it in the home where he and the deceased resided; that the empty shotgun shells found at the place of the crime had been fired from this gun.[40]

⚡ ⚡ ⚡

The three confession cases—*Harris v. South Carolina, Turner v. Pennsylvania,* and *Watts v. Indiana*—were decided in June of 1949 at the every end of the 1948/49 term. In each case Justices Murphy and Rutledge had found the confessions to be coerced. When the Court met again in October Frank Murphy and Wiley Rutledge were dead and with them, so it appeared, had died the notion that true confessions voluntarily made and later regretted were inadmissible in state criminal trials.

---

[40] *Watts v. State,* 82 N.E. 2d 846, 850 (1948).

In the spring of 1950, a *Reader's Digest* truck in Pleasantville, New York, carrying bank deposits, was held up. In the course of the holdup a guard was murdered. Some time afterward, four men were arrested and charged. Three of them, Harry Stein, Calman Cooper and Nathan Wissner, were hoodlums of long standing. The fourth, his case severed from the other three, turned state's evidence.

Two of the three defendants had signed confessions which they recanted before their trial as involuntary. All were tried and convicted of first degree murder and sentenced to death. They appealed to the Supreme Court on the grounds that the admission of the confessions at their trial deprived them of life and liberty without the due process of law required by the Fourteenth Amendment. Justice Robert H. Jackson, speaking for a majority of six, wrote the Court's opinion. He first addressed the respect which should be accorded the findings of fact in the state court below.

> Petitioners' argument here essentially is that the conclusions of the New York judges and jurors are mistaken and that by reweighing the same evidence we, as a super-jury, should find that the confessions were coerced. This misapprehends our function and scope of review . . .
>
> It is common courtroom knowledge that extortion of confessions by "third-degree" methods is charged falsely as well as denied falsely. The practical problem is to separate the true from the false. Primary, and in most cases final, responsibility for determining contested facts rests, and must rest, upon state trial and appellate courts.
>
> A jury and the trial judge—knowing local conditions, close to the scene of events, hearing and observing the witnesses and parties—have the same undeniable advantages over any appellate tribunal in determining the charge of coercion of a confession as in determining the main charge of guilt of the crime. When the issue has been fairly tried and

reviewed, and there is no indication that constitutional standards of judgment have been disregarded, we will accord to the state's own decision great and, in the absence of impeachment by conceded facts, decisive respect.[41]

In New York a confession was admissible if it was voluntary. It was considered voluntary if not induced by fear or favor. If the prosecution offered a confession into evidence, the trial judge made a preliminary determination. If he found that under no circumstance could it have been voluntary, he excluded the confession; otherwise the judge admitted the confession, leaving the ultimate determination of voluntariness to the jury.

The jury then would hear the confession and the evidence going to its volition, as well as the other evidence in the case. If they found the confession voluntary they gave it whatever credence they chose. If they found it involuntary they were instructed to disregard it. If the remaining evidence was sufficient to prove the defendant's guilt beyond a reasonable doubt, they could convict him solely on that.

Defense lawyers did not like the New York law, or any law, in which the determination of the voluntariness of a confession is left with the jury. Such a rule, of course, puts the defendant on the horns of a dilemma. If he stays off the stand, the testimony of the police that the confession was voluntary in most cases will stand unrebutted. If he does testify, and he has a criminal record, his convictions may be shown to impeach his credibility. The three defendants, for good reason, did not testify.

We now know that each had an impressive felony record, one including murder and another perjury [12 felony convictions for the three defendants are here footnoted]. Doubtless, to have testified would have resulted in disclosing this to the jury, while silence would keep it from being brought to light until after the verdict. We think, on any realistic

---

[41] *Stein v. New York*, 346 U.S. 156, 180-182 (1953).

view of this case, they stayed off the stand not because the State would subject them to any improper cross-examination but because their records made them vulnerable to any proper one . . .

In trial of a coercion issue, as of every other issue, when the prosecution has made a case to go to the jury, an accused must choose between the disadvantage from silence and that from testifying. The Constitution safeguards the right of a defendant to remain silent; it does not assure him that he may remain silent and still enjoy the advantages that might have resulted from testifying. We cannot say that petitioners have been denied a fair hearing of the coercion charge.[42]

Jackson distinguished between confessions obtained by force and those obtained by interrogation. "Interrogation is not inherently coercive, as is physical violence. Interrogation does have social value in solving crime, as physical force does not. By their own answers many suspects clear themselves, and the information they give frequently points out another who is guilty. Indeed, interrogation of those who know something about the facts is the chief means to solution of crime. The duty to disclose knowledge of crime rests upon all citizens."[43]

The fact that the defendants were held incommunicado was relevant circumstantial evidence of coercion which the jury considered. The jury found, and there was ample evidence for them to find, that the defendants were not coerced into confession. "Of course, these confessions were not voluntary in the sense that petitioners wanted to make them or that they were completely spontaneous, like a confession to a priest, a lawyer, or a psychiatrist. But in this sense no criminal confession is voluntary."[44] Note was taken of the fact that the *Reader's Digest* killers were hardened criminals who would not easily break. "Stein held out until after

---

[42] *Stein*, 176-177.

[43] *Stein*, 184.

[44] *Stein*, 186.

Cooper had confessed and implicated him." His motive for confessing was not fear but revenge. "I was the best friend he ever had; well, if I must go, I will take him with me."[45]

Corroboration was critical. A 10 page summary under two headings: "I. Facts About The Crime" and "II. Facts About The Confessions," noted the physical evidence connecting the defendants with the crime and the incriminating statements made after the alleged coercive pressure was removed.[46] Once the possibility of convicting, and in this case condemning, an innocent man had been eliminated, the Court was not about to free those who had murdered the guard. "We are not willing to discredit constitutional doctrines for protection of the innocent," said the Court, "by making of them mere technical loopholes for the escape of the guilty. The petitioners have had fair trial and fair review. The people of the State are also entitled to due process of law. Affirmed."[47]

In 1958 the Court heard two companion cases, one arising in California and the other in New Jersey, which brought to the forefront how deeply the Court was divided on the issue of confessions. Both were murder cases and in each case the vote was five-to-four. In the California case the defendant, under sentence of death, appealed on the grounds that his confession was involuntary because state authorities denied his request to consult with a lawyer.

> Petitioner, however, contends that . . . every state denial of a request to contact counsel be an infringement of the constitutional right *without regard to the circumstances of the case* . . . [T]he doctrine suggested by petitioner would have a lesser but still devastating effect on enforcement of criminal law, for it would effectively preclude police questioning—*fair as well as unfair*—until the accused was afforded opportunity to call his attorney. Due process, a concept "less rigid and

---

45 *Stein*, 186.

46 *Stein*, 160-170.

47 *Stein*, 196-197.

more fluid than those envisaged in the specific and particular provisions of the Bill of Rights . . . demands no such rule."[48]

In the New Jersey case a suspect's lawyer went to the police station where his client was being interrogated about the murder of a storekeeper. The police did not permit the lawyer to confer with his client for some seven hours by which time the suspect had signed a written confession and implicated two confederates who in turn confessed to the murder and implicated him. Before trial all three of the co-defendants moved to suppress their confessions on the ground they had been illegally obtained. When their motion was denied they pleaded guilty and were sentenced to life imprisonment.

After serving some 10 years one of them commenced a habeas corpus proceeding that ended up in the Supreme Court. Due process of law, held the Court, cannot be determined by rule. While "the right to counsel in a criminal case has a high place in our scheme in procedural safeguards," it must be reconciled with the people's right to have murderers brought to justice. "A satisfactory formula for reconciling these competing concerns is not to be found in any broad pronouncement that one must yield to the other in all instances . . . This Court, in judging whether state prosecutions meet the requirements of due process, has sought to achieve a proper accommodation by considering a defendant's lack of counsel one pertinent element in determining from all the circumstances whether a conviction was attended by *fundamental unfairness*."[49] The convictions were upheld.

---

[48] *Crooker v. California*, 357 U.S. 433, 440, 441 (1958).

[49] *Cicenia v. Lagay* 357 U.S. 504, 508-509 (1958). (Emphasis added)

CHAPTER 4

THE GREAT WRIT

O N THE 15TH OF JUNE, 1215, "John, by the grace of God, King of England, Lord of Ireland, Duke of Normandy and Acqui-taine, and Count of Anjou," accepted and swore to uphold the Magna Charta pressed upon him by the barons. Article 39 guar-anteed: "No free man shall be taken; imprisoned . . . except *per legale judicium parium suorum vel per legum terrae*—"by the lawful judgment of his peers and by the law of the land."

Noble words indeed, but words are only words, and paper is but paper. What happens if this guarantee is not met? More to the point, what does a free man do if he finds himself cooling his heels in the gaol of the Sheriff of Nottingham, being incarcerated not *per legale judicium parium suorum*, but because the Sheriff, quite contrary to the *legem terra*, has imprisoned him? He gets a writ of habeas corpus, that's what he does.

In the four centuries after Magna Charta, there were constant jurisdictional disputes between the common law courts and eccle-siastical tribunals, particularly in cases where a monetary fine or an escheat of property was involved. If, for example, a person was detained unlawfully under ecclesiastical authority, the King's Jus-ticiary could set matters right by serving the presiding inquisitor with a writ of habeus corpus commanding him in the King's name to deliver the prisoner before the King's Bench forthwith. That way the offender would pay to the proper temporal authorities for his crime in this world, and for his sins in the next.

And so it is today that when a person is detained, the detainee, or someone acting on his behalf, may obtain a writ of habeus corpus, which, when served upon the person holding him in custody, commands him to bring the prisoner forthwith, or at a specified time, before the court which issued the writ, so that court has (*habe*) his body (*corpus*) before it. At that point the custodian must show cause to the court for the detention. If sufficient legal cause is shown the prisoner is remanded to custody. If not, he is released or bailed.

Habeus corpus may be used in civil matters such as the custody of a child or someone held as a mental patient. Here, however, we are concerned exclusively with its use on behalf of persons in the custody of the law, almost invariably being held by a sheriff or a warden. Each of the 50 states has procedures under which a person so detained, or someone on his behalf, may apply to a state judge or court for a writ of habeas corpus. But in this book, unless otherwise stated, the term habeas corpus refers to a writ issued under federal authority.

The Great Writ worked in medieval England because it was done in the name of the king. If you were a jailer and you flouted his writ, all of the forces at the command of the king would be brought to bear. But what if you were in jail not by a judgment of your peers, as Magna Charta requires, but by an order of the king himself?

In 1626 the second Stuart king, Charles I, found himself short of the funds he needed to prosecute his war with Spain. Unable to get Parliament to levy the necessary taxes, he decided to "borrow" the money. These were somewhat unusual loans, bearing a suspicious resemblance to taxes. The king sent a commissioner around to inventory your property, and, based upon their value, decided how much you should lend. These loans matured at "such time as *We*"—the royal W—"shall think fit."

To create a financial climate more conducive to money lending, he gave his subjects an incentive. You really had to give Charles credit, because if you didn't, he clapped you in jail. And he kept you there "for such a time as *We* shall see fit," or until you loosened

your purse-strings, whichever came first. Since most property owners preferred being the king's creditor to being his prisoner, they
complied. Some bold and stout fellows resisted, however, among
them five knights of the realm. Imprisoned, they obtained a writ
of habeas corpus, being held, so they say, without *legale judicium
parium suorum vel per legem terra*. This became the case of the Five
Knights, sometimes called Darnell's Case after Sir Thomas Darnell, one of the knights.

At the appointed time, the jailer returned the writ and the
corpi of the knights to the court. He then showed cause for their
detention. The prisoners were being held *per speciale mandatum
domini regis*—by special command of the king—and, as everyone
in the realm knew—*quod placuit principe legis habet vigorem*—"what
is pleasing to the King is the law." No mention was made of loans
or anything of that sort.

Being able to imprison his subjects is a royal prerogative, said
the court, for which good and sufficient reason must be presumed.
Besides that, the whole idea of a *speciale mandatum* is so that the
king can exercise his powers without going into a lot of detail.
This is a right inherent in kings, vested in them by God. And if
God didn't want things to be this way, he would not have used
His grace to make Charles the King of England—or Lord of Ire-
land, either, for that matter.

The case of the *Five Knights* created the *per speciale mandatum
domini regis* exception to the *legale judicium parium suorum vel per
legem terrae* rule of Magna Charta. In practical terms, this means
habeus corpus won't work if all the king's horses and all the king's
men are arrayed against you. Unless, of course, you have enough
horses and men on your side. This lesson was not lost on the
knights or their allies in Parliament.

Parliament convened in 1628. Included among its members
were some of the recalcitrant creditors newly released from prison.
Under the leadership of Sir Edward Coke, they presented the king
with a "Petition of Right." This petition condemned the forced

loans and arbitrary imprisonment, and prayed their rights under Magna Charta henceforth be observed by the king. The following year Charles sent Parliament packing and ruled by fiat from 1629 to 1640. During these "Eleven Years of Tyranny" he continued to levy illegal taxes and imprison those who refused to pay them. With his appointees on the Star Chamber, the writ of habeus corpus was to those who opposed him but a scrap of paper.

In 1641 Parliament met and abolished the Star Chamber. At the same time it directed that the writ of habeus corpus be available to all who might be imprisoned. Every sheriff, gaoler, minister, officer or other person served with the writ was constrained to deliver the prisoner before the King's Bench or the Court of Common Pleas. However valid the detention, the custodian must nevertheless return the writ along with the prisoner, and certify the true cause of his detainer in open court. The court would have three days to determine whether the detention was just and legal and, accordingly, to free, bail or remand the prisoner. Any person, judge or gaoler, who violated these provisions, forfeited treble damages to the aggrieved person.

Civil war began in 1642 after the king attempted to arrest five members of the House of Commons on a charge of treason. In the end, the forces of the "Long Parliament" led by Oliver Cromwell prevailed, and in 1649 Charles was beheaded at Westminster. There followed the "Interregnum," with Cromwell ruling as Lord Protector until his death in 1658. The anti-royalist forces were able to coalesce only so long as it took to defeat the king. In victory they were divided and intolerant, and those who had fought the absolutism of the Stuarts became tyrants themselves once they had the upper hand. In 1660 the monarchy was restored, and Charles II succeeded to the throne of his father.

One day in 1676 an obstreperous fellow named Francis Jencks attended a meeting at London Guildhall. Jencks had definite opinions about the current state of affairs in the realm and was not bashful about voicing them. He had the effrontery to move the meeting to petition the king to call a new Parliament. The following day, he was summoned before the king and his privy counsel, and by their warrant arrested and imprisoned on a charge that he did "'in a most seditious and mutinous manner . . . stir the persons then present' in Guildhall, and that, when later before the Council, he 'did in a presumptuous and arrogant manner endeavor to justify his offence.'"[1] His friends applied everywhere for a writ of habeus corpus but got the runaround. No judge or magistrate wished to take sides against the king. Jencks was in jail for months until the king, tiring of the game, let him go. Habeus corpus once again had been tried and found wanting.

> Because of such defects in the common-law writ of habeas corpus, the King and his ministers were able to imprison anybody they objected to, for considerable periods. Low judges were afraid to block high officials, high judges would not stoop to bother with obscure prisoners, all judges were reluctant to lift a finger while their courts were not in session, which meant a good part of the year. There were other tricks. A gaoler would be served with the writ, rush his prisoner to the Tower, and then make a return that he did not have him in his custody. The head of the Tower could do likewise, and so on, always keeping one jump ahead of the courts.[2]

A new Parliament met and passed legislation to put an end to these evasions. The Habeas Corpus Act of 1679 stipulated that any gaoler, or other custodian, who refused to obey the writ forfeited his right to hold office, as well as the then considerable sum of 100£, to the aggrieved party. Any judge who refused to issue the writ forfeited 500£. There was a list of out-of-the-way places to which a prisoner might not be sent.

We shall take the Act of 1679 as a legacy from the mother-country, and leave its enforcement over the next 110 years to

---

1 Chafee, *The Most Important Human Right in the Constitution*. 32 Boston University Law Review 143, 149, (1952).

2 Id., 150.

history with but a brief note. As a matter of practice, habeas corpus worked where religion and politics, then inextricable, were not involved, and poorly where they were. The legacy was accepted by our Founding Fathers by its insertion in Article I, Section 9 of the Constitution: "2. The privilege of the writ of *habeus corpus* shall not be suspended, unless when in cases of rebellion or invasion the public safety may require it." In *Federalist Paper No. 84* Alexander Hamilton cited Blackstone for the historical necessity of the writ of habeas corpus.

> But confinement of the person, by secretly hurrying him to jail where his sufferings are unknown or forgotten, is a less public, a less striking and therefore a more dangerous engine of arbitrary government. And as a remedy for this fatal evil he is everywhere peculiarly emphatical in his encomiums on the habeas corpus act, which in one place he calls "the Bulwark of the British Constitution."

In 1804, Hamilton was killed in a duel with Vice President Aaron Burr, who, as it turned out, would figure in one of the earliest tests of habeas corpus. In 1806, the year after his term had expired, Burr embarked on a seditious undertaking to establish a new republic in what is now Louisiana and Texas. Erick Bollman and Samuel Swartwout were Burr's advance men, whose mission was to recruit army officers in the plot. They approached James Wilkinson, the U.S. Army General commanding at New Orleans, and made the mistake of showing him correspondence between themselves and Burr outlining the plan. Instead of enlisting, General Wilkinson arrested the conspirators and sent them to Washington in irons.

Held on a charge of treason in levying war against the United States, Bollman and Swartwout sought habeas corpus directly from the Supreme Court of the United States. The Court looked to the English common law for the meaning of the term habeas corpus. As to whether the imprisonment was illegal, the Court noted the affidavits supporting the detainment did not state facts which, if true, would constitute treason. In any event, the crime, if such it was, was committed in New Orleans and, under the Sixth Amendment, must be tried in that judicial district. The prisoners were discharged.[3]

Article I, Section 9 of the Constitution specifically provides that the privilege of the writ of habeas corpus may be suspended when in cases of rebellion or invasion the public safety may require it. Rebellion came in 1861 with our Civil War. When Abraham Lincoln was inaugurated on the 4th of March, most of the southern states had already seceded. Others were in the process, and the border states were in ferment with partisans of both sides attempting to seize armories and to take over state courts and legislatures.

The first shot was fired on Fort Sumter, in Charleston Harbor, on April 12, 1861. On Sunday, April 14th, the fort was surrendered, and on the following day Lincoln issued his call to arms. On the 19th of April the 6th Massachusetts Volunteers, a regiment en route to Washington, was beset by armed mobs in Baltimore, Maryland, and while making a portage between railway stations had to fight its way through the city in what was called the battle of Pratt Street.[4] The unit's casualties included four killed. Shortly thereafter the railroad bridges to Philadelphia and New York were destroyed. Other troops arriving from the north were landed at Annapolis, where they found the railroad sabotaged, and had to march the 50 miles to Washington. Federal troops occupied key points in the Baltimore area and began arresting southern sympathizers.

One of these was John Merryman, who was said to be raising a company of rebel infantry. Merryman was rousted from his bed at two o'clock one morning in May by federal troops, and imprisoned in Fort McHenry in Baltimore harbor. A lawyer

---

3 *Ex Parte Bollman And Ex Parte Swartwout*, 8 U.S. (4 Cranch) 75 (1807).

4 Currier and Ives made a print of this engagement called "The Lexington Of 1861." It shows "The Massachusetts Volunteers fighting their way through the streets of Baltimore on their march to the defense of the National Capital, April 19, 1861. Hurrah for the Glorious 6th!"

acting on Merryman's behalf sought a writ of habeus corpus. It was granted the following day by none other than Roger B. Taney, Chief Justice of the United States, sitting as a circuit court justice in Baltimore. Served on Major General George Cadwalader, the commandant of the fort, the writ ordered him to bring the body of John Merryman before the court the following morning.

The only appearance was a messenger from Cadwalader stating that Merryman was being held in custody, charged with various acts of treason, and that Cadwalader had been authorized by the President in such cases, and hereby did in this case, to suspend the writ of habeus corpus for the public safety. Taney promptly held General Cadwalader in contempt, and ordered the U.S. marshal to arrest him. The marshal was not permitted to enter the gate of Fort McHenry. The Chief Justice summed up the situation in one long sentence:

> The case then is simply this: a military officer, residing in Pennsylvania, issues an order to arrest a citizen of Maryland, upon vague and indefinite charges, without any proof, so far as appears; under this order, his house is entered in the night, he is seized as a prisoner, and conveyed to Fort McHenry, and there kept in close confinement; and when a habeas corpus is served on the commanding officer, requiring him to produce the prisoner before a justice of the supreme court, in order that he may examine into the legality of the imprisonment, the answer of the officer, is that he is authorized by the president to suspend the writ of habeas corpus at his discretion, and in the exercise of that discretion, suspends it in this case, and on that ground refuses obedience to the writ.[5]

Only Congress, held Taney, can suspend the writ of habeus corpus, and even in that event a civilian arrested by the military must be immediately turned over to the civil authorities to be dealt with

---

[5] *Ex Parte Merryman*, 17 Fed. Cas. 144, 147-148, (1861).

according to law. Otherwise: "[T]he people of the United States are no longer living under a government of laws, but every citizen holds life, liberty and property at the will and pleasure of the army officer in whose military district he may happen to be found."[6]

But the chief justice could not make his writ good. Though he had, in his view, "exercised all the power which the Constitution and laws confer . . . that power had been resisted by a force too strong for me to overcome." He sent the record to President Lincoln, who, under the Constitution, had the duty to "'take care that the laws be faithfully executed,' to determine what measures he will take to cause the civil process of the United States to be respected and enforced."[7] The President gave his answer in a message to Congress when both houses convened on July 4th in special session.

> Soon after the first call for militia, it was considered a duty to authorize the Commanding General, in proper cases, according to his discretion, to suspend the privilege of the writ of habeas corpus; or, in other words, to arrest, and detain, without resort to the ordinary processes and forms of law, such individuals as he might deem dangerous to the public safety. . . . Of course some consideration was given to the questions of power, and propriety, before this matter was acted upon. . . . Are all the laws, but one, to go unexecuted, and the government itself go to pieces, lest that one be violated? Even in such a case, would not the official oath be broken, if the government should be overthrown. . . . It was decided that we have a case of rebellion. . . . Now it is insisted that Congress, and not the Executive, is vested with this power. But the Constitution itself, is silent as to which, or who, is to exercise the power . . .[8]

---

6 Id, 152.

7 Id., 153.

8 4 Collected Works of *Abraham Lincoln*, 421, 430 (Roy P. Basler, ed. 1953).

In 1863 Congress authorized the President to suspend the
writ of habeus corpus when in his judgment such action was
required to preserve the public safety. Lincoln did so by procla-
mation, with the result that any civilian arrested by the military
was denied the use of the writ to obtain his release. In practice
this means the prisoner stays in jail until his captors decide to let
him go. One such civilian was Clement L. Vallandigham, a former congressman from Ohio, and well known rebel sympathizer,
who was arrested and convicted by court-martial of making dis-
loyal statements. As a punishment he was passed through the
southern lines and banished to the Confederacy. The Supreme
Court declined to intervene.[9]

A private citizen of Indiana by the name of Lambdin P. Milligan was arrested there in October of 1864 by the army—the Union
Army. He was charged with being a member of a secret society
of secessionist persuasion known as the Knights of the Golden
Circle, the "Copperheads," as they were called, and with having
conspired to give aid to the enemy through sabotage and guerrilla
warfare. Though a civilian, he was tried before a military tribunal
and sentenced to be hanged. Luckily for Milligan the war ended
before he could be executed and his case was considered in a climate more congenial to the judicial process.

> During the late wicked Rebellion, the temper of the times
> did not allow that calmness in deliberation and discussion
> so necessary to a correct conclusion of a purely judicial
> question. *Then*, considerations of safety were mingled with
> the exercise of power; and feelings and interests prevailed
> which are happily terminated. *Now* that the public safety is
> assured, this question, as well as all others, can be discussed
> and decided without passion or the admixture of any ele-

---

[9] *Ex Parte Vallandigham*, 68 U.S. 243 (1863). Vallandigham returned from exile
by way of Canada. At the Democratic National Convention of 1864 he was a "Peace
Candidate" for the Presidential nomination which went to General George B.
McClellan.

ment not required to form a legal judgment. We approach the investigation of this case, fully sensible of the magnitude of the inquiry and the necessity of full and cautious deliberation.[10]

On the return of a writ of habeus corpus from the U.S. Circuit Court in Indiana, Milligan argued that his detention by the military was illegal. He was a civilian not subject to military discipline, and if he had committed any crime in Indiana as alleged, he was entitled, the courts there being open, to be tried by an impartial jury, and to the other benefits of the Fifth and Sixth Amendments. The Supreme Court agreed, and in its opinion spoke to the exigencies required by the Constitution to justify the suspension of civil processes and the imposition of martial law in the event of rebellion or invasion.

> It follows, from what has been said on this subject, that there are occasions when martial rule can be properly applied. If, in foreign invasion or civil war, the courts are actually closed, and it is impossible to administer criminal justice according to law, *then*, on the theatre of active military operations, where war really prevails, there is a necessity to furnish a substitute for the civil authority, thus overthrown, to preserve the safety of the army and society; and as no power is left but the military, it is allowed to govern by martial rule until the laws can have their free course. As necessity creates the rule, so it limits its duration; for, if this government is continued *after* the courts are reinstated, it is a gross usurpation of power. Martial rule can never exist where the courts are open, and in the proper and unobstructed exercise of their jurisdiction. It is also confined to the locality of actual war. Because, during the late Rebellion it could have been enforced in Virginia, where the national authority was overturned and the courts driven out, it does not follow that

---

10 *Ex Parte Milligan*, 71 U.S. (4 Wall) 2, 109 (1866).

it should obtain in Indiana, where that authority was never disputed, and justice was always administered. And so in the case of a foreign invasion, martial rule may become a necessity in one state, when, in another, it would be "mere lawless violence."[11]

History records, however, that while Milligan was arguing his cause before the federal court in Indiana, another case was being tried before a military tribunal in Washington, D.C. virtually in the shadow of the Supreme Court. There were eight defendants, all civilians, including one woman. All were convicted. On July 7, 1865, four of the eight defendants—including the woman—were hanged; the other four were imprisoned.

The late wicked rebellion and the Civil War were over. The courthouses, including the Supreme Court, were open, and the public safety assured. What was missing was the calmness in deliberation and discussion so necessary to a correct conclusion of a purely judicial question. The temper of the times was anything but calm, and the question was not purely judicial. The defendants were in fact convicted of complicity in the assassination of President Abraham Lincoln.

⚜ ⚜ ⚜

In the first Judiciary Act of 1789 Congress had extended to the federal courts jurisdiction to grant writs of habeas corpus only to persons detained under color of federal authority. They could not entertain, therefore, petitions from those in state custody.[12] With the Civil War over and Reconstruction under way, Congress enlarged the jurisdiction of the federal courts to grant the writ of habeas corpus to include prisoners held under state as well as federal authority.

In 1913, in the Superior Court of Fulton County, Georgia, Leo Frank was convicted of the murder of Mary Phagan and

---

[11] Id., 127.

[12] *Ex Parte Dorr* 4 U.S. 103 (1845).

sentenced to death. Frank was the superintendent of an Atlanta pencil factory and the victim a 13-year-old factory worker. Frank appealed on 103 separate grounds, claiming, among other things, that because of public disorder in and near the courthouse he was denied the fair and impartial trial to which he was constitutionally entitled. These grounds were reviewed at length by the Supreme Court of Georgia.[13] With respect to the allegations of disorder, it was held that the events of which he complained either did not in fact occur, or amounted to no more than irregularities of little substance which were adequately addressed and dealt with by the trial court. The Supreme Court of the United States declined to hear his appeal.[14]

Then, more than six months after his conviction, Frank raised a new objection. At the trial he had waived his right to be present when the jury rendered its verdict. This waiver, he claimed, hence his absence, was involuntary, being made only to avoid possible danger if the verdict was for acquittal. His argument was rejected by the trial court, and Frank appealed once again to the Georgia Supreme Court. He could not, held that court, argue this point in the second appeal when he could have and did not include it in the first appeal.[15] Under sentence of death Frank applied to the federal district court for a writ of habeas corpus. When his petition was denied he appealed to the Supreme Court of the United States. This is the opening paragraph in *Frank v. Mangum, Sheriff of Fulton County, Georgia*:

> Leo M. Frank, the present appellant, being a prisoner in the custody of the Sheriff in the jail of Fulton County, Georgia, presented to the District Court of the United States for the Northern District of Georgia his petition for a writ of *habeas corpus* under Rev. Stat., '753, upon the ground that he was in custody in violation of the Constitution of the United States,

---

13 *Frank v. State*, 141 Georgia 243 (1913).

14 235 U.S. 694 (1914).

15 *Frank v. State*, 142 Ga. 617 (1914).

especially that clause of the Fourteenth Amendment which declares that no State shall deprive any person of life, liberty, or property without due process of law. The District Court, upon consideration of the petition and accompanying exhibits, deeming that upon his own showing petitioner was not entitled to the relief sought, refused to award the writ. Whether this refusal was erroneous is the matter to be determined upon the present appeal.[16]

The Supreme Court began by stating that Frank's allegations, if true, constituted adequate grounds to set aside the conviction. "We of course agree that if a trial is in fact dominated by a mob, so that the jury is intimidated and the trial judge yields . . . [that there is] a departure from due process of law. . . . And if the State, supplying no corrective process, carries into execution . . . a verdict thus produced by mob domination, the State deprives the accused of his life or liberty without due process of law."[17] But to what extent would the petitioner be permitted to litigate anew the questions of fact found against him in the state courts?

[W]e hold that such a determination of the facts as was thus made by the court of last resort of Georgia respecting the alleged interference with the trial through disorder and manifestations of hostile sentiment cannot in this collateral inquiry be treated as a nullity, but must be taken as setting forth the truth of the matter, certainly until some reasonable ground is shown for an inference that the court which rendered it either was wanting in jurisdiction, or at least erred in the exercise of its jurisdiction; and that the mere assertion by the prisoner that the facts of the matter are other than the state court upon full investigation determined them to be will not be deemed sufficient to raise an issue respecting

16 *Frank v. Mangum*, 237 U.S. 309, 311 (1915).

17 Id., 335.

the correctness of that determination; especially not, where the very evidence upon which the determination was rested is withheld by him who attacks the finding.[18]

"The Georgia courts," said the Supreme Court of the United States, "proceeded upon the theory that Frank would have been entitled to this relief had his charges been true, and they refused a new trial only because they found his charges untrue save in a few minor particulars not amounting to more than irregularities, and not prejudicial to the accused. There was here no denial of due process of law." With respect to the argument raised for the first time in Frank's second state appeal which the Georgia Supreme Court refused to consider:

> [T]hat because Frank, shortly after the verdict, was made fully aware of the facts, and he then made a motion for a new trial upon over 100 grounds, without including this as one, and had the motion heard by both the trial court and the Supreme Court, he could not, after this motion had been finally adjudicated against him, move to set aside the verdict as a nullity because of his absence when the verdict was rendered. There is nothing in the Fourteenth Amendment to prevent a State from adopting and enforcing so reasonable a regulation of procedure.[19]

Frank's death sentence was commuted by Georgia Governor John M. Slayton on June 21, 1915, the day before he was to be executed. On August 16th, a masked party of armed raiders forcibly took Frank from the custody of the Georgia prison authorities and hanged him from a tree outside of Marietta. The *Frank* case has been the subject of at least two books and more recently a television mini-series.

The hypothetical case envisioned in *Frank v. Mangum* became a reality after a race riot in Phillips County, Arkansas. A white man

---

18 Id., 335-336.
19 Id., 339-340.

had been shot to death and five black men, members of an organization known as the "Progressive Farmers Association,"[20] were
tried and convicted of murder and sentenced to death. These
convictions and sentences were upheld by the Arkansas Supreme
Court[21] and on April 26, 1920, the Supreme Court of the United
States declined to hear their appeal.[22] On the eve of their sched-
uled execution they sought and obtained from the U.S. district
court a writ of habeus corpus. When that court later dismissed the
writ the condemned men appealed to the Supreme Court of the
United States, which this time decided to hear the case.

To say that local sentiment was inflamed is no overstatement.
It truly was the case of mob domination hypothesized by the court
in *Frank v. Mangum*. While affidavits of condemned men seeking a
last-minute reprieve are naturally suspect, they here received persuasive support from an attached copy of a resolution by the local
American Legion Post, which had the "emphatic approval" of the
Rotary and Lions Clubs. It was in the form of a petition to the Governor not to commute any of the sentences of the "Elaine Rioters":

> [A]t the time of this race riot the members of this Post were
> called upon to go to Hoop Spur and Elaine to protect life
> and property, and in compliance with this request, there
> were two American Legion members killed and one seri-
> ously injured, besides the other non-members who also per-
> ished, and when the guilty negroes were apprehended, a
> solemn promise was given by the leading citizens of the
> community, that if these guilty parties were not lynched,
> and let the law take its course, that justice would be done
> and the majesty of the law upheld.[23]

---

[20] Arkansas Gazette, October 3, 1919, "Negroes Inflamed by a White Man . . .
Progressive Farmers Association is alleged to have Stirred Blacks to Hatred."

[21] *Hicks v. State*, 143 Ark. 158 (1920).

[22] 261 U.S. 98.

[23] *Moore v. Dempsey, Keeper of the Arkansas State Penitentiary*, 261 U.S. 86, 100
(1923).

It would have been surprising if there had been a white person in Phillips County—and the jury was all white—who did not know what was required for "the majesty of the law to be upheld." It certainly supported the petitioners' allegation that "[t]here never was a chance for the petitioners to be acquitted; no juryman could have voted for an acquittal and continued to live in Phillips County and if any prisoner by any chance had been acquitted by a jury he could not have escaped the mob."[24]

In both *Frank v. Mangum* and *Moore v. Dempsey*, the defendants were convicted of murder and sentenced to death, after a trial by a court and jury which they contended had been impermissibly influenced by a mob. In the case of Leo Frank, the Court saw nothing in the record to lend substance to his bare assertions. In the Supreme Court of Georgia, free of any taint of intimidation, these charges had been considered and found baseless. While not bound by law to accept these findings, the Court found that the comity demanded by federalism required they be accorded a certain respect. Absent reasonable grounds to the contrary, they should stand; Frank, they held, had not met this test. The Arkansas case was a different proposition.

If ever a case cried out for a postponement and a change of venue it was that presented in *Moore v. Dempsey*. Yet the court-appointed counsel never asked for either. The trial was a trial in name only; from start to finish the case was tried and the verdict delivered in less than one hour. Nor was due process in the appellate courts much better. It does not inspire confidence that the Supreme Court of Arkansas, "by way of answer to the objection that no fair trial could be had in the circumstances, stated it could not say 'that this must necessarily have been the case.'"[25] Subsequently, when a writ of habeas corpus was issued by a lower state court, the Supreme Court of Arkansas, after dismissing the writ, added what sounds like a cry for

---

[24] Id., 89, 90.

[25] Id., 91.

help: "What the result would be of an application to a Federal Court we need not inquire."[26]

The U.S. Supreme Court upheld the decision of the federal district court refusing Frank a writ of habeus corpus because his constitutional claim had been fairly and adequately considered by the Georgia Supreme Court. It required a hearing on the merits for Moore, because the Arkansas Supreme Court had not. And so the rule developed with respect to the use of habeas corpus to collaterally attack state felony convictions, that as a matter of comity under our federal system the federal courts would defer to the findings of fact made by a state court where the questions were fairly and adequately heard and a corrective judicial process available to correct the alleged wrong.[27]

The Great Writ has not been conspicuously successful in wartime. The most notable example was the detention and relocation by executive order of President Franklin Roosevelt of many thousands of Japanese-Americans during World War II. Then there was the case of the German saboteurs. In June of 1942 seven English-speaking German marines, specially trained in sabotage, were landed by submarine on the East Coast of the United States. They brought ashore explosives, fuses and incendiary and timing devices. Burying this equipment along with their military uniforms they proceeded in civilian dress to predetermined areas. They were captured and brought to trial before a military commission for being unlawful combatants not entitled to prisoner of war status.

Convicted and sentenced to death, the Germans filed petitions for habeas corpus directly to the U.S. Supreme Court. The courts of the United States are open, they aver, and the public safety assured. The civil authority has nowhere been overthrown. Like Lambdin Milligan, they are entitled to a public trial, by an impartial jury, with all of the protections prescribed by the Sixth

---

[26] Id., 92.

[27] See also *Mooney v. Holohan, Warden*, 294 U.S. 103, 113 (1935) and *Waley v. Johnson, Warden*, 316 U.S. 101 (1942).

Amendment. During the summer recess of 1942 the Court met in a special term and heard argument.[28] *Milligan* was invoked to no avail. On August 6, 1942, Richard Quiren and five of his comrades were executed by a firing squad in the courtyard of an unnamed office building in Washington, D.C.

In war most things are judged not on their own merits but on how they affect the larger picture. That calmness in deliberation and discussion so necessary to the correct conclusion of a purely judicial question, which obtained in *Ex Parte Milligan*, may be an unaffordable luxury. To a nation whose sons have their lives on the line, all else pales. The law of war makes reference not to Blackstone but to Clauswitz.

---

[28] *Ex Parte Quiren*, 317 U.S. 1 (1942).

CHAPTER 5

THE FOURTEENTH AMENDMENT

O N DECEMBER 4, 1865, the first post-Civil War Congress convened. Unrepresented were the states of the late Confederacy whose troops had laid down their arms eight months before. The first order of business was their "Reconstruction" and the Speaker of the House of Representatives, Thaddeus Stevens, introduced a resolution to create a "Joint Committee on Reconstruction." It was adopted on December 15, and thus was born the "Committee of Fifteen," nine Representatives and six Senators who would write the Reconstruction legislation and constitutional amendments.

The first bill to come out of the Committee, the Freedman's Bureau Bill, was passed by Congress in February of 1866. It applied only to the former Confederate states, and created certain rights and immunities for the new Freedmen, the interference with which was to be made a crime to be tried and punished under martial law. The bill was vetoed by President Andrew Johnson and an attempt to override his veto failed in the Senate.

A second bill then was drafted which protected the civil rights and immunities of all persons in all parts of the country. It was to be enforced by the federal courts rather than by military tribunals. On April 9th, the first anniversary of Lee's surrender at Appomattox Court House, the 39th Congress passed the Civil Rights Bill of 1866. The President vetoed it on constitutional grounds, but this time his veto was overridden.

Vexed by the constitutional vulnerability of the Civil Rights Bill, the Committee drafted, and in June Congress passed—thus proposing to the states for ratification—the Fourteenth Amendment to the Constitution of the United States. Its aims and purposes were summarized a quarter of a century later by Woodrow Wilson, Ph.D. and LL.D., at the time President of Princeton University.

Not wholly undisturbed, it would seem, by the President's constitutional objections to the Civil Rights bill, Congress proposed to the States in June, 1866, the Fourteenth Amendment to the Constitution, *to incorporate the principles of the bill in the fundamental law* . . . The acceptance of this Amendment by the southern States was to be regarded as a condition precedent to their recognition by Congress.[1]

The purpose of the Civil Rights Law of 1866, and the Fourteenth Amendment passed two months later, was to limit the power of the states—particularly the former Confederate states—in dealing with their citizens, particularly the new Freedmen. The *raison d'etre* of the amendment was to place the rights guaranteed by the civil rights law beyond the reach of a mere majority.

The Fourteenth Amendment made no reference to the Bill of Rights, the first ten (sometimes said to be the first eight) amendments to the Constitution enacted 75 years before. Yet, the recurring question has been whether or not the Fourteenth Amendment incorporated the Bill of Rights so as to make their provisions applicable to the states.

For almost a century the answer was a resounding "no." In case after case, the Supreme Court held undeviatingly that the Bill of Rights were limitations only on the powers of the federal government and did not apply to the several states. In the *Anarchists*

---

[1] Woodrow Wilson, *Epochs of American History, Division and Reunion*, 1829-1909. New York: Longmans, Green and Co. 1893 (1909 Ed.), 265 (emphasis added). (CK name.)

case—*Spies v. Illinois*—decided some 20 years after the Civil War, the Supreme Court was unequivocal on this point.

That case began in May of 1886, in Chicago, Illinois, when a bomb was hurled into the ranks of policemen whose leader had just read the "riot act" and ordered a mob of anarchists to disperse. Seven policemen were killed in what became known as the "Haymarket Riot." On the morning after the bombing, Chicago police raided the office of the International Workingmen's Association (IWA), an organization founded by Karl Marx, and, on the desk of August Spies, the leader of the Chicago organization, found two dynamite bombs encased in round iron shells. Inside a desk drawer was a letter to Spies which outlined in the minutest detail the ingredients and the procedure to be used in constructing these "Czar bombs." The seizure of this letter and its use in cross-examining him, Spies contended, not only violated the Fourth Amendment's guarantee against unreasonable search and seizure, it compelled Spies, in a criminal case, to be a witness against himself in violation of that provision of the Fifth Amendment.

When the Supreme Court of Illinois upheld their convictions, Spies and his comrades appealed to the Supreme Court of the United States. On November 2, 1887, in a packed courtroom, Chief Justice Morrison R. Waite delivered the opinion of a unanimous Court stating once again that the Fourth and Fifth Amendments, like the rest of the Bill of Rights, apply only to the federal government and not to the individual states:

> That the first ten Articles of Amendment were not intended to limit the powers of the state governments in respect to their own people, but to operate on the National Government alone, was decided more than a half century ago, and that decision has been steadily adhered to since.[2]

For three-quarters of a century, in case after case, this principle remained inviolate. The first article of the Fifth Amendment,

---

[2] *Spies v. Illinois*, 123 U.S. 131, 166 (1887).

for example, makes a constitutional mandate of the common law institution of the grand jury. Military cases aside, it says that before the federal government may try someone "for a capital, or otherwise infamous crime," that person must have been indicted by a grand jury. The alternative way to commence a criminal trial is through an "information," the name given a written accusation or criminal charge filed by the prosecuting attorney.

In 1884 James Wilson was convicted of passing counterfeit United States bonds and sentenced to a term of 15 years. He had been tried on an information sworn out by the United States Attorney and not upon "a presentment or indictment by a grand jury" required by that amendment if his crime was "infamous." In prison, Wilson sought release on a writ of habeas corpus, being held in custody, so he claimed, in violation of the Fifth Amendment.

> Deciding nothing beyond what is required by the facts of the case before us, our judgment is that a crime punishable by imprisonment for a term of years at hard labor is an infamous crime, within the meaning of the Fifth Amendment of the Constitution; and that the District Court, in holding the petitioner to answer for such a crime, and sentencing him to such imprisonment, without indictment or presentment by a grand jury, exceeded its jurisdiction, and he is therefore entitled to be discharged.[3]

This would not have been the result had Wilson been convicted of a state crime in a state court. The previous year the Court had reviewed a California case in which the defendant had been convicted of murder and sentenced to death. While Joseph Hurtado had been tried and convicted by a petit jury, he had not been indicted by a grand jury. As permitted by California law he had been accused in an information signed by the prosecutor. There was no question that if charged in a federal court, Hurtado

---

[3] *Ex Parte Wilson*, 114 U.S. 417, 429 (1885).

could not have been tried for murder except on a grand jury indictment. The Fifth Amendment requires no less in a capital case.

While the Fifth Amendment does not apply to the states, argued Hurtado, the Fourteenth certainly does, and the "due process of law" to which it refers is the American counterpart of Magna Charta's "law of the land." Since a grand jury indictment was a requirement under English common law for centuries, it is a "process of law" "due" a defendant tried for murder in a state court. This, said the Court, by no means follows.

> The Constitution of the United States was ordained, it is true, by descendants of Englishmen, who inherited the traditions of English law and history; but it was made for an undefined and expanding future, and for a people gathered and to be gathered from many nations and of many tongues. And while we take just pride in the principles and institutions of the common law, we are not to forget that in lands where other systems of jurisprudence prevail, the ideas and processes of civil justice are also not unknown.[4]

To hold that the customs and usages which were the law of the land of England, when we went our separate ways, is what "due process of law" requires in this country, would be to lock ourselves in the past. It "would be to deny every quality of the law but its age, and to render it incapable of progress or improvement. It would be to stamp upon our jurisprudence the unchangeableness attributed to the laws of the Medes and Persians."[5] Hurtado's second argument was that the phrase "due process of law," as used in the Fourteenth Amendment, was meant to require of the states that which the first eight amendments, our Bill of Rights, require of the federal government, the Fifth Amendment's requirement of grand jury indictment being one of them. California therefore,

---

4 *Hurtado v. California*, 110 U.S. 516, 530, 531 (1884).

5 Id., 529.

like the United States Government, cannot try Hurtado for murder except upon an indictment.

The objection to this argument is the text of the two amendments. It seems natural to assume that what is forbidden to the states in the Fourteenth Amendment by the words *nor shall any state deprive any person of life, liberty or property, without due process of law*, is precisely the same thing forbidden to the federal government under the Fifth Amendment by the words that *no person shall . . . be deprived of life, liberty, or property, without due process of law*. Looking to the Fifth Amendment we see it consists of one sentence conveying five prohibitions. They are, in order of appearance: (1) the requirement of grand jury indictment; (2) double jeopardy; (3) self-incrimination; (4) due process; (5) the taking of private property for public use without just compensation. These provisions, said the Court, must be all construed together.

> According to a recognized canon of interpretation, especially applicable to formal and solemn instruments of constitutional law, we are forbidden to assume, without clear reason to the contrary, that any part of this most important amendment is superfluous. The natural and obvious inference is, that in the sense of the Constitution, "due process of law" was not meant or intended to include, ex vi termini, the institution and procedure of a grand jury in any case. The conclusion is equally irresistible, that when the same phrase was employed in the Fourteenth Amendment to restrain the action of the States, it was used in the same sense and with no greater extent; and that if in the adoption of that amendment it had been part of its purpose to perpetuate the institution of the grand jury in all the States, it would have embodied, as did the Fifth Amendment, express declarations to that effect.[6]

---

[6] *Hurtado*, 534, 535.

The "recognized canon of interpretation" referred to is known as *pari materia*. It requires that laws on the same subject be construed with reference to each other. It is a rule of human experience applied to contracts and statutes as well as to constitutions. Here it requires the five prohibitions of the Fifth Amendment be construed with reference to each other and, absent a command to the contrary, to be given equal weight. This means that the first prohibition, requiring that a person prosecuted for a felony must first be indicted by a grand jury, cannot be construed to fall within the Fifth Amendment's "due process" clause, because to do so would render the former superfluous. Since the employment of the term "due process of law" in the Fourteenth Amendment must be taken to be used "in the same sense and to no greater extent" than in the Fifth, it follows that the Fourteenth Amendment does not require indictments in state felony cases.

Hurtado stands for two propositions. One is that a procedure established in the common law of England is not for that reason required by due process of law in the United States. The second is that the due process of law required of the states by the Fourteenth Amendment does not incorporate the specific guarantees the first eight amendments imposes on the federal government. What must be remembered, before we pass on, is that by the command of the Fifth Amendment, counterfeiter Wilson "walked" from federal prison, while by due process of law murderer Hurtado was hanged by California.

⚜ ⚜ ⚜

The Sixth Amendment guarantees the accused in a federal case a trial by a "jury of the state and district wherein the crime shall have been committed." This tells us where the jury must be from, but not how many jurors there must be. While federal law has always provided for a petit jury of twelve, and that was the number used under the common law of England, does this mean the number twelve is a constitutional imperative?

The answer to this question might never have been known but for a cattle rustler named Lars Thompson. First tried in 1895, when Utah was still a federal territory, he was convicted by a jury of twelve. For reasons that do not appear, the conviction was set aside and Thompson was granted a second trial—two more, one might add, than a lot of less fortunate rustlers got in those days. In the meanwhile, in January of 1896, Utah had become a state. When Thompson was tried again he was tried in a state court to a jury of eight, the number prescribed by the Utah constitution. Convicted once again, he appealed to the Supreme Court of the United States, which framed the issue this way:

> [T]he word "jury" and the words "trial by jury" were placed in the Constitution of the United States with reference to the meaning affixed to them in the law as it was in this country and in England at the time of the adoption of that instrument; and that when Thompson committed the offence of grand larceny in the Territory of Utah—which was under the complete jurisdiction of the United States for all purposes of government and legislation—the supreme law of the land required that he should be tried by a jury composed of not less than twelve persons. And such was the requirement of the statutes of Utah while it was a Territory.
>
> Was it, then, competent for the State of Utah, upon its admission into the Union, to do in respect of Thompson's crime what the United States could not have done while Utah was a Territory, namely, to provide for his trial by a jury of eight persons?[7]

The Court's answer was no. "When Thompson's crime was committed, it was his constitutional right to demand that his liberty should not be taken from him except by the joint action of the court and the unanimous verdict of a jury of twelve persons."[8]

---

7 *Thompson v. Utah*, 170 U.S. 343, 350 (1898).

8 *Thompson*, 351.

"[T]he provision of the constitution of Utah providing for the trial . . . by a jury composed of eight persons is *ex post facto* in its application to felonies committed before the Territory became a State."[9] Thompson's conviction was therefore reversed. *Thompson v. Utah* tells us that when the Sixth Amendment speaks of a jury, it means a jury of twelve.

In 1899 Charles Maxwell was in the Utah State Prison serving an 18-year sentence for armed robbery. Like Thompson before him Maxwell had been convicted by a jury of eight instead of a jury of twelve. The robbery, however, was committed in 1898 after Utah was admitted to the union so that he cannot make a federal case of it.

Maxwell, however, came up with a new argument not previously addressed by the Supreme Court. It was the intention of the 39th Congress—The Reconstruction Congress—in passing the Fourteenth Amendment, urged Maxwell, to thereby make applicable to the states the entire Bill of Rights, including, of course, the Sixth Amendment. In support of this position he quoted from a speech made by Senator Jacob M. Howard of Michigan which spoke precisely to this point:

> Such is the character of the privileges and immunities spoken of in the second section of the fourth article of the Constitution. To these privileges and immunities, whatever they may be—for they are not and cannot be fully defined in the entire extent and precise nature—to these should be added the personal rights guaranteed and secured by the first eight amendments of the Constitution; such as the freedom of speech and of the press; the right of the people peaceably to assemble and petition the Government for a redress of grievances, a right appertaining to each and all the people; the right to keep and to bear arms; the right to be exempted from the quartering of soldiers in a house without the consent of the

---

[9] *Thompson*, 355.

owner; the right to be exempt from unreasonable searches and seizures, and from any search or seizure except by virtue of a warrant issued upon a formal oath or affidavit; the right of an accused person to be informed of the nature of the accusation against him, and his right to be tried by an impartial jury of the vicinage; and also the right to be secure against excessive bail and against cruel and unusual punishments.

The purpose of reducing a matter to writing is so that the document, and it alone, stands as the arbiter of all prior understandings on the subject. For this reason the law does not favor the use of extrinsic evidence to interpret a written document. In the case of a contract, for example, a party will not be permitted to introduce evidence of prior oral understandings. All previous declarations are deemed to have merged in the writing, and a court will determine its import by what the contract says on its face. The rule barring the use of extrinsic evidence as an aid to the construction of a document is known as the "parole evidence" rule. There is no equivalent rule of statutory or constitutional construction which bars the use of such evidence, or any evidence, for that matter, which a judge may consider pertinent. But while the parole evidence rule may not apply, its logic surely does.

Both the rule and its rationale admit of an exception. Extraneous evidence is admissible to explain a *latent* but not a *patent* ambiguity. A patent ambiguity is a provision which can be seen on the face of the writing to be ambiguous. With respect to the Constitution the best example is "due process of law." It would not make sense to attempt to clarify its meaning by reference to the specific understanding of some senators, no matter how unequivocally expressed, when the Senate as a body elected to make it vague. Due process of law is ambiguous because the people who enacted it into law chose to make it ambiguous.

When a document containing a latent ambiguity is read, it appears on its face to be clear and capable of but one meaning.

The ambiguity arises from the later discovery of extraneous facts. A will leaving "my farm to my son John," for example, appears to be unambiguous until it is learned the testator had more than one farm. Parole evidence will be permitted to explain which farm was meant. The same rationale, argued Charles Maxwell, will support Senator Howard's understanding that the 39th Congress intended to include, among the "privileges and immunities" which a state shall not abridge, the personal rights guaranteed and secured by the first eight amendments of the constitution. This was the case presented in *Maxwell v. Dow, Warden*, argued before and decided after the turn of the century.

> In order to limit the powers which it was feared might be claimed or exercised by the Federal Government, under the provisions of the Constitution as it was when adopted, the first ten amendments to that instrument were . . . intended as restraints and limitations upon the powers of the General Government, and were not intended to and did not have any effect upon the powers of the respective States. This has been many times decided . . . It is claimed, however, that since the adoption of the Fourteenth Amendment the effect of the former amendments has been thereby changed and greatly enlarged. It is now urged in substance that all of the provisions contained in the first ten amendments, so far as they secure and recognize the fundamental rights of the individual as against the exercise of Federal power, are by virtue of this amendment to be regarded as privileges or immunities of a citizen of the United States, and, therefore, the States cannot provide for any procedure in state courts which could not be followed in a Federal court because of the limitations contained in those amendments.[10]

---

10 *Maxwell v. Dow, Warden*, 176 U.S. 581, 586-587 (1900).

In the years to come, Maxwell's argument will be referred to as "incorporation": The theory that the Fourteenth Amendment was meant to incorporate, as Senator Howard put it, "the personal rights guaranteed and secured by the first eight amendments of the Constitution," so as to make them applicable to the states as "privileges and immunities" which no state may "abridge." But one Senator does not speak for the entire Senate, much less the House of Representatives and the states which ratified the Fourteenth Amendment.

> What individual Senators or Representatives may have urged in debate, in regard to the meaning to be given to a proposed constitutional amendment, or bill or resolution, does not furnish a firm ground for its proper construction, nor is it important as explanatory of the grounds upon which the members voted in adopting it.
>
> In the case of a constitutional amendment it is of less materiality than in that of an ordinary bill or resolution. A constitutional amendment must be agreed to, not only by Senators and Representatives, but it must be ratified by the legislatures, or by conventions, in three-fourths of the States before such amendment can take effect. The safe way is to read its language in connection with the known condition of affairs out of which the occasion for its adoption may have arisen, and then to construe it, if there be therein any doubtful expressions, in a way so far as it is reasonably possible, to forward the known purpose or object for which the amendment was adopted.[11]

The right to a jury of twelve in a state criminal trial, held *Maxwell v. Dow*, is not required by the Fourteenth Amendment simply because it is required in a federal trial by the Sixth. It is a matter for state and not federal law to decide "whether there shall be a jury of twelve or a lesser number, and whether the verdict must

---

[11] Id., 602.

be unanimous or not. These are matters which have no relation to the character of the Federal Government."[12]

❦ ❦ ❦

The holding of *Maxwell v. Dow* and the Incorporation issue lay quiescent for more than forty years until resurrected in 1947 by Justice Hugo Black, at the time the ranking member of the Supreme Court liberal bloc of four. In *Adamson v. California*, Black contended as an historical fact that the framers of the Fourteenth Amendment, when it was passed in 1866, intended thereby to incorporate the Bill of Rights and make them applicable to the states.

> My study of the historical events that culminated in the Fourteenth Amendment, and the expressions of those who sponsored and favored, as well as those who opposed its submission and passage, persuades me that one of the chief objects that the provisions of the Amendment's first section, separately, and as a whole, were intended to accomplish was to make the Bill of Rights applicable to the states ... This historical purpose has never received full consideration or exposition in any opinion of this Court interpreting the Amendment.
>
> In construing other constitutional provisions, this Court has almost uniformly followed the precept of *Ex parte Bain*, 121 U.S. 1, 12, that "It is never to be forgotten that, in the construction of the language of the Constitution . . . as indeed in all other instances where construction becomes necessary, we are to place ourselves as nearly as possible in the condition of the men who framed that instrument."[13]

One contention of Justice Black was quite correct. The only case in which the legislative history of the Fourteenth Amendment had ever been considered was *Maxwell v. Dow* in 1900, and

---

12 Id., 605.

13 *Adamson v. California*, 332 U.S. 46, 71, 72 (1947).

there it was but that one speech by Senator Jacob Howard which had been brought to the attention of the Court. Black attached to his dissenting opinion an appendix containing over 30 pages of extracts from the debates of the 39th Congress which he claimed supported his position.

It is bizarre, to say the least, to contend 80 years after the event that a new study of the historical events culminating in the passage of the Fourteenth Amendment now reveals a constitutional truth of the greatest magnitude. That this could have eluded scholars and judges, particularly those contemporary to the Civil War and Reconstruction, seems incredible. This is all the more so when the question has been considered and explicitly rejected by the Court no less than a dozen times and the opinions of the Court, as Justice Felix Frankfurter pointed out, had almost all been unanimous.

> Between the incorporation of the Fourteenth Amendment into the Constitution and the beginning of the present membership of the Court—a period of seventy years—the scope of that Amendment was passed upon by forty-three judges. Of all these judges, only one [the first Justice John M. Harlan], who may respectfully be called an eccentric exception, ever indicated the belief that the Fourteenth Amendment was a shorthand summary of the first eight Amendments theretofore limiting only the Federal Government, and that due process incorporated those eight Amendments as restrictions upon the powers of the States.[14]

To Justice Frankfurter, the short answer to the question was that if his predecessors on the Court had held this belief, they had a very strange way of saying it: "Those reading the English language with the meaning which it ordinarily conveys, those conversant with the political and legal history of the concept of due process, those sensitive to the relations of the States to the central government as well as the relation of some of the provisions

---

[14] *Adamson, 62.*

of the Bill of Rights to the process of justice, would hardly recognize the Fourteenth Amendment as a cover for the various explicit provisions of the first eight Amendments."[15]

> Some of these are enduring reflections of experience with human nature, while some express the restricted views of Eighteenth-Century England regarding the best methods for the ascertainment of facts. The notion that the Fourteenth Amendment was a covert way of imposing upon the States all the rules which it seemed important to Eighteenth Century statesmen to write into the Federal Amendments, was rejected by judges who were themselves witnesses of the process by which the Fourteenth Amendment became part of the Constitution.[16]

Two professors of law at Stanford University, scholars of renown, undertook to examine the historical evidence and legal arguments advanced by Hugo Black in the *Adamson* case. It took them two years and the results were published in the *Stanford Law Review* in 1949 under the title "Does the Fourteenth Amendment Incorporate the Bill of Rights?"[17] "The Original Understanding," written by Charles Fairman, dealt with the historical evidence. "The Judicial Interpretation" by Stanley Morrison, "analyzed the Court's treatment of the cases, taking into account the arguments of counsel and views of the individual Justices." Professor Fairman examined all of the debates of the 39th Congress on the amendment. He also did what Justice Black did not, which was to examine the understanding of the state legislatures to whom the amendment was submitted for ratification.

Black's venture into the world of legal history was a disaster. To the extent the Fourteenth Amendment was understood to

---

15 *Adamson*, 63.

16 *Adamson*, 63, 64.

17 Fairman and Morrison, *Does the Fourteenth Amendment Incorporate the Bill of Rights?*, 2 Stanford Law Review, 1-173, Dec. 1949.

incorporate anything it was the provisions of the Civil Rights Bill of 1866. The main purpose of the Fourteenth Amendment, to those on either side of the debate, was to place the rights guaranteed by that bill beyond the reach of a mere majority vote:

> I voted for the civil rights bill, and I did so under a conviction that we have ample power to enact into law the provisions of that bill. But I shall gladly do what I may to incorporate into the Constitution provisions which will settle the doubt which some gentlemen entertain upon that question.[18] *Senator Thomas D. Eliot, Republican of Massachusetts.*
>
> If we are already safe with the civil rights bill, it will do no harm to become the more effectually so, and to prevent a mere majority from repealing the law and thus thwarting the will of the loyal people.[19] *Congressman John M. Broomall, Republican of Pennsylvania.*
>
> This section of the joint resolution [the proposed Fourteenth Amendment] is no more nor less than an attempt to embody in the Constitution of the United States that outrageous and miserable civil rights bill.[20] *Congressman Andrew Jackson Rogers, Democrat of New Jersey.*

No more to the point could a statement be than this by Congressman James A. Garfield, Republican of Ohio, formerly a General in the Union Army, and a future President of the United States.

> I am glad to see this first section here which proposes to hold over every American citizen, without regard to color, the protecting shield of law. The gentleman who has just taken his seat [Mr. Finck] undertakes to show that because we propose to vote for this section we therefore acknowledge that the civil rights bill was unconstitutional. He was anticipated in that objection by the gentleman from Pennsylvania. [Mr.

---

[18] Id., 48.

[19] Id., 46.

[20] Id., 49.

Stevens] The civil rights bill is now a part of the law of the land. But every gentlemen knows that it will cease to be a part of the law whenever the sad moment arrives when that gentleman's party comes into power. It is precisely for that reason that we propose to lift that great and good law above the reach of political strife, beyond the reach of the plots and machinations of any party, and fix it in the serene sky, in the eternal firmament of the Constitution, where no storm of passion can shake it and no cloud can obscure it. For this reason, and not because I believe the civil rights bill unconstitutional, I am glad to see that first section here.[21]

The only statement to the contrary was that of Senator Jacob Howard discussed by the Court in *Maxwell v. Dow*. While it most definitely expressed his belief that the proposed amendment would incorporate the Bill of Rights, it was the only statement that did. Professor Fairman's article laid waste to Hugo Black's exegesis into the Reconstruction debates. The speeches made by both the proponents and enemies of the Fourteenth Amendment, while it was undergoing ratification by the state legislatures, were replete with statements evincing the belief that the purpose of the amendment was to place the Civil Rights Bill beyond any future constitutional attack, and produced absolutely nothing to support the thesis that it was intended to incorporate the first eight amendments.

Even more damning to the cause of incorporation was the restoration of the congressional representation of the former Confederate States. In 1867 Congress laid down the terms on which they would be entitled to send representatives to Congress. One condition was that these states ratify the Fourteenth Amendment; among the others were that a state "shall have formed a government in conformity with the Constitution of the United States in all respects," and that "such [state] constitution shall have been

---

[21] Id., 45.

submitted to Congress for examination and approval, and Congress shall have approved the same."[22]

To meet these requirements, Louisiana and Georgia, among other former Confederate states, adopted new constitutions before they applied for readmission to Congress. The constitutions of both states contained provisions which stood in violation of the Fifth and Sixth Amendments, had these Amendments been deemed applicable to the states. Louisiana, for example, permitted prosecution for infamous crime without grand jury indictment; and in Georgia a felony case could be tried to a jury of seven. In addition Georgia provided for trial without a jury in civil cases where the Seventh Amendment required a jury.

The constitutions of these states were scrutinized to the extent that Senator Howard, the leader of the few incorporationists of the 39th Congress, found in Georgia's Constitution a section limiting the enforcement of a debt the consideration of which was a slave. Senator Howard concluded this violated Article I, Section 10 of the United States Constitution in that it was a law impairing the obligation of a contract. At his insistence the Senate required the Georgia legislature to rectify this situation. Senator Howard found nothing else in the constitutions of Louisiana and Georgia not in conformity with the constitution of the United States in all respects. If we are to "place ourselves," as Justice Black says we must, "as nearly as possible in the condition of the men who framed that instrument," what does all of this tell us of their contemporary understanding?

Most assuredly it says that: Louisiana and Georgia did not understand when they adopted their constitutions and ratified the Fourteenth Amendment, that the amendment incorporated, and thereby made applicable to the states the first eight amendments. For if that had been the case, their new constitutions would not have been in conformity with the Constitution of the United States in all respects, and therefore they would not have been

---

[22] Id., 126.

eligible for readmission to Congress. Congress was of the same understanding, or else it would not have readmitted Louisiana and Georgia. The contemporary understanding of the intellectual prowess of Senator Jacob M. Howard of Michigan is best attested by this eulogy to him by the Chief Justice of the Supreme Court of Michigan, memorialized in Volume 20 of the Michigan Reports after Howard's death in 1871:

> If he did not, as has been suggested, possess that sort of intellect that would enable him to wield the slender sci-meter (sic) of Salidin to sever the gauzy veil that was not worth severing, he was able to wield the ponderous battle-ax of the Lion-Hearted, before which iron and steel went down like wood.[23]

When Louisiana and Georgia applied to Congress for readmission after ratifying the Fourteenth Amendment, and submitted their new constitutions for examination and approval, Congressman John A. Bingham of Ohio (whom Justice Black said "may, without extravagance, be called the Madison of the first section of the Fourteenth Amendment"[24]), was on his feet urging the readmission of these two southern states, whose constitutions were, he said, "in accordance with the spirit and letter of the Constitution of the United States, as it stands amended."[25]

In 1918 Professor Dudley O. McGovney had posed this problem to those who advocate the incorporation theory: "If this had been the intention of the framers of the privileges and immunities clause it is strange that very clear and direct language did not occur to them. How easily it might have been said, the limitations imposed by the first eight amendments upon the central government are hereby extended to the states."[26] This point

---

23 Cited by Fairman at 134.

24 *Adamson*, 74.

25 *Fairman*, 128.

26 McGovney, "Privileges or Immunities Clause, Fourteenth Amendment," 4 *Iowa Law Bulletin* 219, 233 (1918) 159.

was left unanswered by Hugo Black and the other three dissent-ers. Professor Morrison's summation in the *Stanford Law Review* article speaks as much to their intellectual honesty as to their scholarship:

> The disturbing thing is not that this piece of judicial research was not more exhaustive, but that such inadequate research should be made the pretext for one of the most far-reaching changes in constitutional interpretation to be seriously pro-posed in our constitutional history. If long-established con-stitutional law is to be upset, some better reason should be found than exists here. While it is altogether unlikely that the views of the dissenting judges in the *Adamson* case will ever be accepted by the majority of the Supreme Court, the dissent remains critical as an illustration of judicial tech-nique. The real significance of *Adamson v. California* is that four of the judges are willing to distort history, as well as the language of the framers, in order to read into the Constitu-tion provisions which they think ought to be there.[27]

In 1949, in *Wolf v. Colorado*, decided two years after *Adam-son*, the Court pronounced the "issue" of incorporation "closed." Julius Wolf was convicted of abortion, a felony under Colorado law. The police knew for a certainty that an abortion had taken place and had the most probable of cause to believe that Wolf, a Den-ver doctor, had committed it. Without further ado, they went to his office and placed him under arrest. In the process they seized his appointment book, which was used at the trial to connect him with a woman on whom an abortion had been performed.

State authorities had always proceeded on the assumption that the Fourth Amendment and the exclusionary rule established in the 1914 case of *Weeks v. United States* applied to the federal gov-ernment alone, and that they had only to satisfy the Fourteenth Amendment's guarantee of due process. So that if a felony, in

---

[27] Id., 162.

fact, had been committed and state officers, without using excessive force, made a search and seizure based on probable cause, they had not deprived any person of his liberty or property without due process of law simply because they had not gotten a warrant beforehand.

After Benjamin Cardozo's death in 1938, Felix Frankfurter took his seat on the Supreme Court. With it he assumed Cardozo's mantle as the Court's leading opponent of the incorporation theory. His bouts with Justice Hugo Black on this subject were legendary.[28] In his opinion in *Wolf*, Frankfurter went to great pains to smite the "notion" of incorporation. It is hard to see how he could have been more explicit:

> Unlike the specific requirements and restrictions placed by the Bill of Rights (Amendments I to VIII) upon the administration of criminal justice by federal authority, the Fourteenth Amendment did not subject criminal justice in the States to specific limitations. The notion that the "due process of law" guaranteed by the Fourteenth Amendment is shorthand for the first eight amendments of the Constitution and thereby incorporates them has been rejected by this Court again and again, after impressive consideration. See, e.g.; *Hurtado v. California*, 110 U.S. 516; *Twining v. New Jersey*, 211 U.S. 78; *Brown v. Mississippi*, 297 U.S. 278; *Palko v. Connecticut*, 302 U.S. 319. Only the other day the Court reaffirmed this rejection after thorough reexamination of the scope and function of the Due Process Clause of the Fourteenth Amendment. *Adamson v. California*, 332 U.S. 46. The issue is closed.[29]

No one ever doubted that the basic rights protected from federal abridgement by the Fourth Amendment were comprehended in the "liberty" protected by the Fourteenth Amendment from

---

[28] Simon, *The Antagonists*. 173-175.

[29] *Wolf v. Colorado*, 338 U.S. 25-26 (1949).

deprivation by the state. To say the Fourteenth Amendment does not incorporate the Fourth Amendment and make it applicable to the states is not to say that a state is constitutionally free to do all that which the Fourth Amendment forbids. To use a worst case example by way of illustration, a state may not issue *lettres de cachet* and general warrants, cordon off a town block-by-block and conduct a house-to-house search in the middle of the night. Frankfurter put it less dramatically: "[W]e have no hesitation in saying that were a State affirmatively to sanction such police incursion into privacy it would run counter to the guarantee of the Fourteenth Amendment."[30]

One would have thought that this would have been the end of the incorporation theory. Not only had it been discredited by 70 years of constitutional interpretation; a painstaking examination had now demonstrated, to any fair and impartial judge, that the historical events culminating in the Fourteenth Amendment, and the expressions of those who sponsored and favored that amendment, as well as those who opposed its submission and passage, were *not* intended to make the Bill of Rights applicable to the states.

Before 1947, incorporation had been perceived as an academic question of interest only to constitutional scholars rather than an issue charged with political implications. And this seems natural enough; after all, why should people feel passionate about whether or not the Fourteenth Amendment incorporated the first eight? Yet it became *the* constitutional issue that eclipsed all others, and its most ardent proponents were those on the left.

> These efforts [for incorporation] have come largely from what may roughly be called the left wing of the Court, namely Justices Black and Douglas, and the late Justices Murphy and Rutledge. Mr. Justice Black has been a leader in this movement, and . . . is undaunted by any number of past decisions or with their supposedly settled

---

[30] *Wolf v. Colorado*, 28.

character . . . [*S*]*tare decisis* means little—and in [the Adamson] this case nothing—to Justice Black and his colleagues.[31]

When *Adamson* was decided, the political issue of the day was the treatment of those the left deemed victims of political persecution. One cannot help but think that this had a lot more to do with Justice Black's opinion than did his "study of historical events that culminated in the Fourteenth Amendment." Whether silence in the face of an accusation is, as Appleton said, "tantamount to confession" was a question of great consequence not only to those their detractors called "Fifth Amendment Communists" but their liberal supporters as well.

Frank Murphy and Wiley Rutledge died during the summer recess of 1949 before the Fairman-Morrison article was published. Hugo Black and William O. Douglas, the fourth dissenter, would live on to be octogenarians, their willingness to distort history, as well as the language of the framers, unabated by time or revelation. President Dwight Eisenhower will appoint to the Court two like-minded men in the persons of Earl Warren and William J. Brennan Jr. The Eisenhower legacy will be a Court with a left-wing not at all averse to another attempt to amend the Constitution by judicial fiat. Incorporation is not a matter of history to them, it is an ideological imperative, *stare decisis* be damned.

---

31 Fairman and Morrison, 140-142.

CHAPTER 6

FUNDAMENTAL FAIRNESS

MUCH OF AMERICAN JURISPRUDENCE can be traced back to Henry Plantagenet, King Henry II of England (1133–1189), the progenitor of that dynasty which was to rule England for more than three centuries. He was, through his mother Matilda, the great-grandson of the Norman King William I, the "Conqueror," and the grandson of Henry I. He married Eleanor of Aquitaine whose previous marriage to the King of France, Louis VII, had been dissolved for her failure to produce a male heir.

His domain at one time included what is approximately the western one-half of France as it exists today as well as the British Isles except Scotland and Wales. French was Henry's native tongue, and like most educated people of his time he knew Latin. He spoke other European languages as well, but not English. Born, bred and buried in the Loire Valley, this Frenchman, for such he was, is ironically the "Father of the English Common Law."

Before Henry II justice was dealt by an absolute monarch, and his appointees, more or less on the basis of their instincts. The status of the parties in feudal society was the most important factor. Who you were, and whom you knew, rather than the merits of the controversy, most often determined the outcome. To promote impartial justice, Henry II attempted to codify the law.

He assembled a group of scholars who, after exhaustive study, categorized, so they thought, all the wrongs one human being could inflict on another. Each was given a label and the status of a "writ." A writ in this sense was a formal complaint setting forth

a general proposition which, if fulfilled, the scholars felt constituted a legal wrong. The scholars drafted some forty-three writs
that were written into the law as statutes. If you felt aggrieved by
something someone did to you, you went to the King's Court and
selected the writ that best fit your case. This writ constituted your
major premise, and the facts in your case, the minor. It was all a
matter of dialectics; justice did not matter.

> To sum up, by the second half of the fifteenth century,
> the Common Law had been administered, developed,
> and refined by a small group of highly trained professional
> lawyers, who were determined to make out of a bundle of
> ancient writs, a handful of statutes, and a heap of prece-
> dents, a judicial system which would stand comparison as a
> monument of legal science with the Law of Rome and the
> Canon Law. With the best intentions they had sought to ren-
> der it more efficient by making it progressively more and
> more complicated. It could not be accepted that the answer
> ultimately arrived at by strict adherence to the intricate rules
> of process and procedure, coupled with the skilled interpre-
> tation of relevant precedents, would not always be the right
> one. If it was right legally it did not matter that it was often
> obviously unjust, any more than it mattered to the dialec-
> tician that his conclusion was practically absurd if it was, or
> appeared to be, syllogistically sound.[1]

The writ system would have been an enormous success had
not perverse people kept committing acts in combinations the
scholars hadn't foreseen. "Such a system, wholly deductive in its
essence, could not be upset by the necessity for considering the
unforeseeable vagaries of human affairs and conduct. The operation of conscience was anathema."[2] This did not daunt the practi-

---

[1] Charles Ogilvie, *The King's Government and the Common Law*, Oxford: Basil
Blackwood (1958). Republished in 1978 by Greenwood Press, Inc., Westport, Connecticut, 32.

[2] Id., 30.

tioners and judges of the common law. After all, there were many writs to choose from. If what had been done to you in your case did not meet the specifications of one of them, well then, obviously you had not suffered a legal wrong.

> The medieval student knew nothing of historical or comparative scholarship, nor was he concerned with observation. . . . The key to all knowledge was to be found in the existing pronouncements of recognized authorities. The instrument used for their detailed investigation was dialectic, based on Aristotelian logic . . . Generally speaking, all knowledge was deductive . . . conducted in accordance with the strictest syllogistic method—major premise, minor premise, conclusion—was the intellectual passion of the age. The absolute reverence for written authority made the syllogistic method readily practical and satisfying. It was necessary to have an authority regarded as axiomatic, behind which one could not go, or at least a statement clearly deducible from such an authority, as the foundation of one's major premise. . . In time the most admired feat of the dialectician was to demonstrate by syllogism—or rather by a concatenation of syllogisms—the truth of what to the untutored reason was obviously false or absurd. . .[3]

> It may be said that the root cause of the failure of the Common Law was the application of Aristotelian dialectic to what was regarded as established authority as the method of arriving at decisions without observation of the circumstances of the case under consideration. Direct observation was considered to be a delusion and a snare.[4]

It was not just the text of a statute from which a decision was to be deduced, but case law as well. "A mass of commentary, packed with legal learning, refined distinctions, and ingenious

---

[3] Id., 15,16.
[4] Id., 94.

reconciliations, grew up around each writ."[5] According to English legal historian Frederic Maitland, unless something was done the "Law of England . . . might well become . . . 'an occult science, a black art, a labyrinth of which the clue has been lost.'"[6] The most trivial deviation from a technical rule required the dismissal of a case.

The result was that the outcome of a case depended not so much on the text of a statute, or its underlying purpose, as upon "case law." Prior decisions became axioms from which future cases would be argued and decided. A point of law decided in one case became a precedent binding in future cases. This was called the doctrine of *stare decisis*. This judge-made law became the common law of England.

Law, it has been said, is the point where life and logic meet. Neither law nor man can function by logic alone; nor can they function without it. Experience is logic's essential complement. In attempting to reduce the law to immutable principles, Henry II and his scholars had attempted the impossible. The only thing immutable were the results. Henry could no more codify the law than the Saxon King Canute could hold back the tide.

There are in any legal system two approaches to the resolution of a case. In the jurisprudence of the English-speaking peoples these two approaches are called "Law" and "Equity." In logic they are known as analysis and synthesis. Analysis is objective. To keep a principle inviolate it lays down the law and lets the chips fall where they may. Sometimes, however, the chips fall where they were not expected to fall and a miscarriage of justice is the result. Synthesis, on the other hand, is subjective. It guards against unforeseen consequences by delegating power to judge a case according to its circumstances. It accomplishes this by couching its commands vaguely, hedging them by such words as "just," "fair," "due," "necessary," "proper," "reasonable" or "probable."

---

5 Ogilvie, 13.

6 Id., citing Pollock and Maitland, *History of English Law*, 1911.

Men have been trying to codify the law since Hammurabi, four millennia ago. Where they have attempted to accomplish this by purely objective commands they have failed for lack of flexibility. Government by untrammeled subjectivity, on the other hand, might well be the road to tyranny. The solution, to the extent there is a solution, is to counterpoise objectivity with subjectivity and keep the balance true.

In his *Commentaries on Equity Jurisprudence*, Joseph Story, the American legal scholar and Supreme Court Justice, wrote that "Equity is synonymous with justice . . . Equity must have a place in every rational system of jurisprudence, if not in name, at least in substance. It is impossible that any code, however minute and particular, should embrace or provide for the infinite variety of human affairs, or should furnish rules applicable to all of them."[7] Statutes were drawn more with a view toward delegating authority to judges of a later day to deal with a question of law in the context of their own times and according to the circumstances of the case before them.[8]

Law—the common law—and Equity were at first jealous rivals. As civilization advanced, they became recognized as the two essential components of any valid jurisprudence. Neither is superior to the other; they are complementary, and, in the proper mix, mutually supportive. It is worthy of note that Article III of the United States Constitution, in establishing the judicial branch of government, extends the "judicial power" to "all cases, in law and equity, arising under this Constitution."

Those drafting a constitution designed to endure for centuries must balance consistency with flexibility. In their polarities these

---

7 Joseph Story, *Commentaries on Equity Jurisprudence as administered in England and America*. Boston: Little, Brown & Co., 1886, [13th Edition], Vol. 1, 6.

8 At this point illustrate by using Venn circles named after John Venn who first used them. "Venn, John. 1834-1923. English logician and man of letters; teacher of logic and author of *The Logic of Chance* (1866), *Symbolic Logic* (1881), and *The Principles of Empirical Logic*" (1889). Webster's Biographical Dictionary. Springfield, Mass: G. & C. Merriam Co. (1963).

two competing considerations are sometimes characterized as a "government of laws" versus a "government of men." Clichés notwithstanding, to function and be just, a society must be governed by a proper mix of both. Were it possible to empanel a select group of all wise and virtuous people, we could simply let them decide our controversies on the merits of each individual case as they deemed just and proper. There would be no necessity of being bound by laws written by men long since dead, who could not possibly have foreseen the world in which we live, much less the circumstances surrounding a case which must now be adjudged. In its ultimate form this is a government not of laws but of men.

At the opposite pole is the quest for perfect objectivity by means of a principle of law couched in terms so unequivocal as to prevent its future compromise or dilution. Inflexible constitutional commands, when applied to the cases produced by the unlimited permutations of circumstances and human behavior, will inevitably produce inequities which the judges of another day, deprived of discretion, will be unable to ameliorate.

Thus where a draftsman elects to express a principle in immutable terms, he does so with the knowledge it may result in injustice under some future circumstances he cannot foresee in their specifics. He considers this an acceptable price to pay for the principle to be preserved inviolate. Where he opts for flexibility, it is so that the cases he cannot envision in a world he may never know, will be decided on their own facts and circumstances in a manner consistent with justice and equity.

The original, unamended Constitution created the system and structure under which our unique system of federalism operates. Ninety-nine percent of its text tells us what is ordained in terms so clear as to brook no question. It is the other one percent which makes it flexible. For example, after enumerating the powers of Congress, Article I, Section 8 concludes with the power: "To make all laws which shall be necessary and proper for carrying into execution the foregoing powers." When legislation is before Congress at some future date, it will be the congressmen of that day who will decide whether or not it is necessary and proper given the problems and needs of their time. No one questions that it was the original intention of the Framers of the Constitution to invest them with the power to do so autonomously.

The most important, for our purposes, is this clause of the Fourteenth Amendment: "No person shall . . . be deprived of life, liberty or property, without due process of law." Virtually all of the constitutional questions of the day respecting our criminal justice system focus on the four words "due process of law." What do they mean and what do they require?

With regard to state action due process of law became a phrase malleable enough to meet the needs of justice in a particular case. This jurisprudence was called "fundamental fairness"; "equity" would have done as well. It was ad hoc. It applied not to a hypothetical case, but to the case before the court, the case "at bar." The only question was whether that which was done by the state, in the case at bar, however it might be categorized or labeled, was "consistent with the fundamental principles of liberty and justice."

> The due process of law clause in the Fourteenth Amendment does not take up the statutes of the several States and make them the test of what it requires . . . What it does require is that state action, whether through one agency or another, shall be consistent with the fundamental principles of liberty and justice which lie at the base of all our civil and political institutions and not infrequently are designated as "law of the land."[9]

Law, as contradistinguished from equity, protects a value by rule. No rulemaker can foresee all the permutations of human behavior and circumstance, and it is inevitable that the application of a rule will result in injustice in some cases. Those who

---

9 *Hebert v. Louisiana*, 272 U.S. 312, 316-317 (1926).

write the rule accept this fact of life as the price of protecting the value. Equity protects a value, but one case at a time. To prevent injustice in the case at bar, it looks behind the words of a rule to its purpose. In his Commentary No. 61, Sir William Blackstone gave us what remains the classic illustration of why this is so—an example, known as Cicero's Case, first put forth by that Roman philosopher in the first century B.C.

> There was a law, that those who in a storm forsook the ship should forfeit all property therein; and that the ship and lading should belong entirely to them who staid in it. In a dangerous tempest all the mariners forsook the ship, except only one sick passenger, who by reason of his disease, was unable to get out and escape. By chance, the ship came safe to port. The sick man kept possession and claimed the benefit of the law. Now here all the learned agree, that the sick man is not within the reason of the law; for the reason of making it was to give encouragement to such who should venture their lives to save the vessel. But this is a merit which he could never pretend to, who neither staid in the ship upon that account, nor contributed any thing as to its preservation.

The Law would say that a vessel is a ship and a tempest is a storm; the only question we have here is whether the claimant is a person who did not forsake the ship. This rule, notes the Law, does not distinguish between mariners and passengers, nor between the sick and the well. It guarantees the rights of all who stayed, able-bodied seamen and sick passengers alike. Judgment for the claimant, says the Law, banging down its gavel. The ship and its lading have been forfeited by the owners and must be awarded to the sick passenger. Whether this is unjust or absurd is beside the point. It is the Law.

Law and Equity, it must be emphasized, are not contradictory terms. The affirmation of one is not the denial of the other. That which the Law requires by virtue of a rule may also be what is fair and equitable under the facts and circumstances of the case at bar. Unlike Cicero's case, for example, a storm-battered ship will most often be brought safely to port by the able-bodied passengers and mariners who stayed in it. Their claim cannot be disputed. The ship and its lading will be awarded to them at dockside, and the learned will not be called upon to venture an opinion. Law and Equity should coincide in the vast majority of cases. If they do not, a nation has either very bad laws or very unlearned judges.

With respect to criminal procedure the words "due process of law" had come to mean "fundamental fairness." What it required of state criminal trials is that they be fair. A process of law unfair to a defendant in a state case also may be one which would be prohibited by a specific article of the Bill of Rights were it a federal case. In the former it is unconstitutional because it is unfair; in the latter it is unconstitutional because it is forbidden. Most of the time, but not always, it will be both.

For example, take the law of confessions we inherited on our independence, restated in *Wilson v. United States, supra*. "The true test of admissibility," held *Wilson*, "is that the confession be made freely, voluntarily, and without compulsion." Not only was this proposition the Law, it was just and equitable as well. How we got from there to the iniquity perpetrated in the case of Robert Williams, the murderer of Pamela Mason, we shall see shortly. In the meanwhile, keeping in mind that we are applying different constitutional standards to federal and state cases, we move on to other examples.

The Sixth Amendment provides that "the accused shall enjoy the right . . . to be confronted with the witnesses against him." To deny to a defendant in a federal criminal case the right to be personally present at his trial would be a clear violation of this article. Due process of law guarantees a fair trial. Can a trial be fair, if the defendant is excluded from any part of the trial? Would not a defendant in a state case, to which the Sixth Amendment does not apply, be entitled to the same right of confrontation he would have in a federal court? This was the question before the Court in the 1934 case of *Snyder v. Massachusetts*. Justice Benjamin Cardozo wrote the Court's opinion:

> On April 9, 1931, James M. Kiley was shot to death at a gasoline station at Somerville, Massachusetts. Three men, Garrick, Donnellon and the petitioner Snyder, joined in the murder and in the attempted robbery that led to it. Garrick confessed to his part in the crime and became a witness for the state. Donnellon and Snyder were tried together and sentenced to be put to death. The jury found upon abundant evidence that the guilt of each had been established beyond a reasonable doubt. At the trial and on appeal Snyder made the claim that through the refusal of the trial judge to permit him to be present at a view there had been a denial of due process of law under the Fourteenth Amendment of the Constitution of the United States. The Supreme Judicial Court of Massachusetts affirmed the conviction.[10]

The view was of the gasoline station which was the scene of the murder. An entourage led by the trial judge took the jury through the view. Counsel for both defendants were present throughout, but the defendants themselves were not. "Counsel for Snyder moved that his client be permitted to view the scene with the jury, invoking the protection of the federal constitution.[11] The motion was denied for security reasons.

> The defendant took the stand and admitted that he was at the gasoline station at the time of the crime. He tried to reduce the grade of his wrongdoing by testifying that the shot had been fired by his codefendant Donnellon and that larceny, not robbery, was the aim of the conspiracy.*

---

*Under the law of Massachusetts, homicide is murder in the first degree when committed "with deliberately premeditated malice aforethought" or in

---

[10] *Snyder v. Massachusetts*, 291 U.S. 97, 102-103, (1934) (emphasis added).

[11] *Snyder*, 103.

the commission or attempted commission of a crime that would be punishable, if there were no homicide, with imprisonment for life. Robbery by one armed with a dangerous weapon is a crime so punishable, but not larceny or attempted larceny.[12]

The defendant's contention was that the confrontation guaranteed a defendant in a federal case was a fundamental right made applicable to the states by the Fourteenth Amendment. This fundamental right was abridged by Massachusetts, so he argued, by the trial court's refusal to permit him to be present during the view. The Court assumed "in aid of the petitioner that in a prosecution for a felony the defendant has the privilege under the Fourteenth Amendment to be present in his own person whenever his presence has a relation, reasonably substantial, to the fullness of his opportunity to defend against the charge."[13]

This, however, was not the case. Snyder had not been prejudiced; his defense, such as it was, went not to his innocence, but to the degree of his guilt to which the view was immaterial. "The least a defendant must do . . . is to show that in the particular case in which the practice is exposed to challenge, there is a reasonable possibility that injustice has been done."[14] "Due process of law requires that the proceedings shall be fair, but fairness is a relative, not an absolute concept. It is fairness with reference to particular conditions or particular results . . . What is fair in one set of circumstances may be an act of tyranny in others."[15]

Due process addresses only the case at bar: "Nor is there need for us to hold that conditions can never arise in which justice will be outraged if there is a view in the defendant's absence. Enough for present purposes that they have not arisen here."[16] And justice, we also must remember, is a two way street; "justice, though due to the accused, is due to the accuser also. The

---

[12] *Snyder*, 109, *footnote in original.

[13] *Snyder*, 105, 106.

[14] *Snyder*, 113.

[15] *Snyder*, 116, 117.

[16] *Snyder*, 115.

concept of fairness must not be strained till it is narrowed to a filament. We are to keep the balance true."[17] Snyder's conviction and death sentence were affirmed.

⁑ ⁑ ⁑

The "double jeopardy" clause of the Fifth Amendment provides that no person shall be "subject for the same offense to be twice put in jeopardy of life or limb." It was at issue when, in 1873, Edward Lange was convicted of stealing U.S. Post Office mailbags of a value less than $25, a federal crime punishable by a term of not more than one year in prison or a fine of not more than $200. The trial judge inadvertently sentenced him to one year in prison and a fine of $200. Lange immediately paid the fine and sought a writ of habeas corpus to secure his release.

Before the return of the writ, the trial judge, now aware of his error, vacated the first sentence and imposed a new sentence of simply one year in prison. The race was to the swift. The $200 had passed into the public treasury and was thus an accomplished fact. To uphold the second sentence would be "to punish him twice for the same offence. He is not only put in jeopardy twice, but put to actual punishment twice for the same thing."[18] By command of the Fifth Amendment, Lange walked out of the federal courthouse a free man happy to be $200 poorer.

Some 65 years later another case of double jeopardy was before the Court. The issue was whether the Fourteenth Amendment prohibits a state, as the Fifth Amendment prohibits the federal government, from twice putting in jeopardy the life of a defendant in a capital case. The story, told here by the Connecticut Supreme Court of Errors, began in Bridgeport.

Late in the evening of September 29, 1935, the accused, taking with him a revolver which he had possessed since obtaining it from Ryan's Tavern several months before, with

---

[17] Snyder, 122.

[18] *Ex Parte Lange*, 85 U.S. (18 Wall) 163, 175 (1873).

Frank Burke, left their apartment at No. 590 Fairfield Avenue in Bridgeport, and going to Gilman's Music Store at No. 243 Fairfield Avenue, just after midnight, broke into the show window thereof, from which each seized and carried away a radio, departing by different routes on the return to their apartment. In breaking the plate glass window with the revolver, the grips thereof were broken off and found there shortly after. When the accused had reached a point on the southerly side of Golden Hill street, an officer stepped out from each side of a police car which had drawn up to him, the one on the left laying his hands on him and asking where he was going with the radio. Thereupon the accused, who was carrying his revolver in the sleeve of his coat, let it drop down into his hand and fired one shot into this officer, and then, turning as the other came near, fired a shot into him . . .

Wilfred Walker, one of the officers shot, and Thomas J. Kearney, the other, for whose murder the accused was on trial in this proceeding, each died within a few hours from his wound inflicted by the accused. At the time of the killing the accused was on parole from Elmira Reformatory where he had been sentenced for rape.[19]

Frank Palko was indicted and tried on a charge of murder in the first degree, punishable by death, and was convicted of murder in the second degree, a crime punishable by life imprisonment. At the first trial the judge had charged the jury that in considering whether the murder of the policeman was premeditated, they could consider only the events immediately preceding the homicide, never mind that Palko had armed himself with a pistol before he set forth on his felonious foray. On the ground that this constituted an error of law to the prejudice of the prosecution, the state appealed—as it was permitted to do under Connecticut law—and was granted a new trial. At the second trial, Palko was convicted of

---

[19] *State v. Palko*. 186 Atl. 657, 658 (1936).

murder in the first degree and sentenced to death, whereupon he appealed to the Supreme Court of the United States. Once again Justice Cardozo wrote the Court's opinion:

> The argument for appellant is that whatever is forbidden by the Fifth Amendment is forbidden by the Fourteenth also. The Fifth Amendment, which is not directed to the states, but solely to the federal government, creates immunity from double jeopardy. No person shall be "subject for the same offense to be twice put in jeopardy of life or limb." The Fourteenth Amendment ordains, "nor shall any State deprive any person of life, liberty, or property, without due process of law." To retry a defendant, though under one indictment and only one, subjects him, it is said, to double jeopardy in violation of the Fifth Amendment, if the prosecution is one on behalf of the United States. From this the consequence is said to follow that there is a denial of life or liberty without due process of law, if the prosecution is one on behalf of the People of a State.[20]

In a federal case the question would be whether what was done to Palko was a species of the genus called "double jeopardy." If the answer was in the affirmative, his conviction for first-degree murder would have to be set aside. Whether or not he was guilty of premeditated murder would have been irrelevant. But this is a state case to which the Fifth Amendment does not apply. It is the Fourteenth Amendment with which we are dealing, and due process, as the Court explained, concerns itself not with labels but with justice:

> Is double jeopardy in such circumstances, if double jeopardy it must be called, a denial of due process forbidden to the states? The tyranny of labels, Snyder v. Massachusetts, 291 U.S. 97, 114, must not lead us to leap to a conclusion

---

[20] *Palko v. Connecticut*, 302 U.S. 319, 322 (1937).

that a word which in one set of facts may stand for oppression or enormity is of like effect in every other.

We have said that in appellant's view the Fourteenth Amendment is to be taken as embodying the prohibitions of the Fifth. His thesis is even broader. Whatever would be a violation of the original bill of rights (Amendments I to VIII) if done by the federal government is now equally unlawful by force of the Fourteenth Amendment if done by a state.[21]

Palko's claim was that Connecticut was depriving him of his life without the due process of law required by the Fourteenth Amendment. This is not, Cardozo said, to be determined by reference to the Fifth Amendment or whether what Connecticut did can be labeled double jeopardy. Call it anything you wish, there is but one question to be answered. Is it unfair, or is it unjust, under the circumstances of this case, to execute Frank Palko?

Does it violate those "fundamental principles of liberty and justice which lie at the base of all our civil and political institutions"? Hebert v. Louisiana, supra. The answer surely must be "no." What the answer would have to be if the state were permitted after a trial free from error to try the accused over again or to bring another case against him, we have no occasion to consider. We deal with the statute before us and no other.[22]

The holding of *Palko* was that it mattered not what process of law is forbidden by the Fifth Amendment under its double jeopardy clause. The Court assumed the federal government could not, as did Connecticut, try Palko a second time for murder in the first-degree. But this is a state criminal case to which the Fifth Amendment does not apply. The test therefore is not whether this constituted double jeopardy but whether what was done to Palko, whatever label one chooses to put upon it, "violate[d]

---

[21] Id., 323.

[22] Id., 328.

those 'fundamental principles of liberty and justice which lie at the base of all our civil and political institutions'"? This is anything but a specific guarantee.

Frank Palko did not come to the Supreme Court seeking justice denied him by Connecticut, he came invoking a Law which in his case was a mere technicality. Palko did not contend that he did not commit first degree murder; only that Connecticut may not execute him for it. Like the sick man who stayed on the ship and rode out the tempest in Cicero's case, Palko was not an intended beneficiary of the Law. Since it was "a merit which he could never pretend to," the "learned" put their law books aside, and got out their scales of justice.

On one scale was the murder of not one but two policemen; for what he did to them and their families, he must pay. What does justice require? No doubt Cardozo, who lived in neighboring Westport, knew better than most. On the other scale sat Frank Palko, convicted murderer and rapist, confessed robber and career criminal.[23] Why should the people of Connecticut foot the bill to succor this brute for the rest of his miserable life while his victims lie in an early grave and their widows and orphans suffer their loss?[24]

Those who made the Fifth Amendment law in the eighteenth century feared the newly created federal government might some day stand in loco tyrannis to the Stuarts of the seventeenth century or the recently departed minions of George III whatever the color of their coats. They passed the Bill of Rights to see that this should not happen. The power and the duty to deal with the enemy within—the common criminal—they left with the individual states.

---

[23] Palko had a prior felony conviction for rape in New York. He had served a prison sentence and was out on parole when he murdered the policemen. He fled from Bridgeport to Buffalo, New York, where he committed an armed robbery to which he confessed after he was apprehended. See *State v. Palko*, 186 Atl. 657 (1936).

[24] According to the front page of the *Bridgeport Times Star* of October 6, 1935, Sergeant Kearney left a widow and two children and Patrolman Walker a widow and three sons.

Those who made the Fourteenth Amendment law after the Civil War could have selected all or any of the first eight amendments, or any of their specific articles individually. They chose only due process of law as a limitation on the procedures the states must follow in criminal cases. In the seven decades that intervened between the adoption of the Fourteenth Amendment and the *Palko* decision the Court had equated due process of law with fundamental fairness. In the field of criminal procedure due process of law had become "if not in name, at least in substance," the "Equity" which Story said every "system of jurisprudence" must have to be "rational."

What due process of law owed Frank Palko was not a judgment made deductively through analysis, it was a judgment of equity arrived at inductively by synthesis. "After the wearisome process of analysis has been finished," wrote Cardozo, "there must be for every judge a new synthesis which he will have to make for himself. The most that he can hope for is that with long thought and study, with years of practice at the bar or on the bench, and with the aid of that inward grace which comes now and again to the elect of any calling, the analysis may help a little to make the synthesis a true one."[25] Cardozo had always insisted that jurisprudence must "maintain a relation between law and morals":

> What really matters is this, that the judge is under a duty, within the limits of his power of innovation, to maintain a relation between law and morals, between the precepts of jurisprudence and those of reason and good conscience . . . The constant insistence that morality and justice are not law, has tended to breed distrust and contempt of law as something to which morality and justice are not merely alien, but hostile.[26]

---

[25] Benjamin N. Cardozo, *The Nature of the Judicial Process*. New Haven: Yale University Press (1921), 162, 163.

[26] Id., 133-134.

The law often distinguishes between acts that are *mala in se*, defined in *Black's Law Dictionary* as "wrongs in themselves; acts morally wrong; "offenses against conscience," and those *mala prohibita*, acts innocent or indifferent in themselves, the commission of which are only wrong because a law forbids them. All that is morally wrong could not be prohibited by law without creating an all intrusive state.

On the other hand, legal prohibitions cannot be limited simply to what is immoral. In some areas of life and commerce people must know what is required so they can act accordingly. But in the majority of cases, the ambits of *mala in se* and *mala prohibita* overlap and occupy common ground, so that which is immoral is also prohibited, and that which is prohibited is also immoral.

Frank Palko was not executed pursuant to any constitutional command written by men of another century. In deciding whether or not something done in the case before him is "fair" a judge does not ask what men of another time would have done. The Supreme Court permitted Connecticut to deprive Frank Palko of his life by due process of law because, in the minds of Benjamin Cardozo and seven of his brethren[27], there was nothing unfair, immoral, unjust or inequitable about executing the murderer of Wilfred Walker and Thomas J. Kearney. Their synthesis was a true one.

---

[27] The Court consisted of Chief Justice Charles Evans Hughes and Associate Justices James C. McReynolds, Louis D. Brandeis, George Sutherland, Pierce Butler, Harlan F. Stone, Owen J. Roberts, Hugo L. Black and Benjamin Cardozo. It was Butler who dissented and he did so without writing an opinion.

CHAPTER 7

THE END OF
FUNDAMENTAL FAIRNESS

BEFORE 1961 THE TEST of what due process of law required of the states in criminal trials was called "fundamental fairness." If the defendant's conviction was "fair," it was "constitutional," and it was upheld. If it was "unfair," it was "unconstitutional" and would be reversed. In the context of due process of law the words "fair" and "constitutional" were interchangeable. In 1961, in two murder cases arising out of Connecticut, fundamental fairness came to an end.

Dorothy Kennedy was shot and killed on November 21, 1953, in the West Shore Package Store at 143 Ocean Avenue in West Haven. She and her husband owned and operated the store. She was alone in the store at 7:30 p.m. on the day in question, and within a space of minutes thereafter the tragedy had taken place and the cash register was rifled, about $60 being taken. On January 9, 1954, the New Haven police were seeking to arrest the defendant on charges of attempted robbery, breaking and entering and theft committed that day at the Travelers Hotel in New Haven. That evening, officers located the defendant, sitting in his car on Oak Street in New Haven. He had in his possession a .38 caliber Smith and Wesson revolver . . . On January 30, 1954, the revolver which had been taken from him was turned over to the state police for testing, and it was found to have fired the bullets which killed Mrs. Kennedy. Thereafter, the defendant made statements to the police and to the coroner in which he admitted that he had killed Mrs. Kennedy. These statements were free and voluntary. Their truth was not disputed by any witness at the trial.[1]

Harold Rogers did not deny that his admissions were true, only that they were voluntary. On the day the police learned the gun taken from Rogers was used to murder Mrs. Kennedy, they took him to the Office of the State's Attorney. The interrogation commenced at approximately 2:00 p.m. of that day and continued throughout the afternoon and evening. During the interrogation Rogers was allowed to smoke, was brought a sandwich and coffee, and was at no time subjected to violence or threat of violence.

What happened thereafter was disputed. According to Rogers the police threatened to bring his wife in for questioning. The poor woman suffered from arthritis, said Rogers, and to spare her from this ordeal, he confessed to murdering Mrs. Kennedy. He confessed again the next day at a coroner's hearing. What is not disputed is that Rogers shot and killed Mrs. Kennedy with this particular .38 caliber revolver in the course of his robbery of the liquor store and that his confession in this regard is true. But according to the Supreme Court of the United States, speaking through Justice Felix Frankfurter, that is beside the point. The point is the Connecticut trial court erred in charging the jury that:

> No confession or admission of an accused is admissible in evidence unless made freely and voluntarily and not under the influence of promises or threats. The fact that a confession was procured by the employment of some artifice or deception does not exclude the confession if it was not calculated, that is to say, if the artifice or deception was not calculated to procure an untrue statement. The motive of a person in confessing is of no importance provided the par-

---

[1] *State v. Rogers*, 143 Conn. 167, 120 A 2d 409, 411, (1956).

ticular confession does not result from threats, fear or promises made by persons in actual or seeming authority. The object of evidence is to get at the truth, and a trick or device which has no tendency to produce a confession except one in accordance with the truth does not render the confession inadmissible . . .[2]

The Supreme Court of the United States set aside the conviction for the reason that "while the trial judge ruled that each of petitioner's confessions was 'freely and voluntarily made and accordingly was admissible in evidence, he reached that conclusion on the basis of considerations that undermine its validity. He found that the pretense of bringing Rogers' wife in for questioning 'had no tendency to produce a confession that was not in accord with the truth.'"[3]

From a fair reading of these expressions, we cannot but conclude that the question whether Rogers' confessions were admissible into evidence was answered by reference to a legal standard which took into account the circumstance of probable truth or falsity. And this is not a permissible standard under the Due Process Clause of the Fourteenth Amendment. The attention of the trial judge should have been focused, for purposes of the Federal Constitution, on the question whether the behavior of the State's law enforcement officials was such as to overbear petitioner's will to resist and bring about confessions not freely self-determined—a question to be answered with complete disregard of whether or not petitioner in fact spoke the truth.[4]

The test of whether a confession was voluntary always had been whether the psychological pressure applied to the defendant might have made him—as an innocent man—confess falsely.

---

[2] *Rogers v. Richmond*, 365 U.S. 534, 542 (1961).

[3] *Rogers*, 541-542.

[4] *Rogers*, 543-544.

In the natural order of things this would be done by empathy. A judge or juror would ask himself whether what was done to the defendant might have made him, the judge or juror, confess to a crime he did not commit. He would then size up the defendant's ability to withstand pressure, compare it to his own, and thereupon make his decision.

This will be the law no longer. The test now will be whether the psychological pressure applied would have made a guilty man confess truly. The ordinary person would be nonplused. How could he imagine himself holding up a liquor store and shooting someone, much less how much pressure it would take to make him to admit it if he did?

And if truth is irrelevant, juries can no longer take into consideration the defendant's guilt, and what it bespeaks of his character and credibility. A majority of the Supreme Court may accept Rogers' story, but you couldn't find a jury who would. They would believe the police chief, who said Rogers made up the whole story about interrogating his wife just to save his skin.

Truth and volition had always been considered mutually supporting elements of a confession. They both stand or fall together, so to speak. The more detailed and truthful a confession is, and the more it can be corroborated by extrinsic evidence, the more voluntary it is apt to be. A confession short on detail, or partially false, suggests that it may have been coerced. Truth and volition are to a confession what "across" and "down" are to a crossword puzzle. Each comes to the aid of the other, and for any solution to be valid, both must jibe.

Now if a judge or juror cannot consider the truth of a confession, as evidenced by subsequent corroboration, and if he cannot consider the defendant's reputation for truth and veracity, and whether he has a good reason to lie, as did Rogers, how is he to judge whether it is voluntary? To exclude from consideration in a problem that which is most relevant to its solution is irrational. On June 19, 1961, the Supreme Court dropped the other shoe in

Culombe v. Connecticut. Once again it is the Connecticut Supreme Court of Errors which tells the story.

> On December 15, 1956, the bodies of Edward J. Kurpiewski and Daniel J. Janowski were found in Kurp's gasoline station on Stanley Street in New Britain. An autopsy revealed that both had died from bullet wounds in the head. In the afternoon of February 23, 1957, the defendants were taken into custody by the state police. Columbe, on February 27, and Taborsky, on March 1, confessed to robberies at the gasoline station and to the two homicides. Each confession corroborated the other in the main. A general summary of the facts contained in them follows: About 6 p.m. on Saturday, December 15, 1956, the defendants drove in Culombe's Oldsmobile from Hartford to New Britain. They were armed and they intended to hold up a gasoline station. They stopped at Kurp's station. The proprietor, Kurpiewski, serviced their car. Taborsky left the car to go, as he said, to the toilet in the station. After Culombe had paid for the gasoline, he ordered Kurpiewski, at gun point, into the boiler room of the station, shot him, and took his wallet. Meanwhile, Taborsky was searching the main office of the station for money. Culombe joined him and they found and took money from the cash register and the desk. During this search Janowski, who had his eighteen-month-old daughter with him, drove up and stopped by the pumps. Taborsky and Culombe waited in the station, but when Janowski did not drive away they came out. Culombe pretended to service Janowski's car. Taborsky pointed a gun at Janowski, took his wallet and ordered him into the station and then into the toilet room, where Taborsky shot him twice in the left side of the head above the ear. Taborsky and Culombe then drove to Culombe's house in Hartford and divided the money.[5]

---

[5] *State v. Taborsky, State v. Culombe* 147 Conn. 194, 158 Atl. 2d 239, 241-242.

Culombe and Taborsky were arrested by Hartford police on a Saturday evening. With their consent, or at least without their objection, the two had spent most of that afternoon accompanying police on a trip to stores where other robberies and other murders had recently occurred. They were questioned intermittently over the next four days. They were not, nor did they contend that they were, physically mistreated or threatened. They were properly fed and never questioned in such a way or for such a length of time as to exhaust them. At one point Culombe's wife, at her request, was brought to see him. "Mrs. Culombe asked Culombe if he were responsible for the New Britain killings and told him that if he were he should tell the police the truth . . . Culombe was upset by the scene with his family and choked up or sobbed."[6] On Wednesday, Culombe confessed:

> Culombe then agreed to show the officers where the guns were. Lieutenant Rome, Sergeant Paige, Detective Murphy and Detective Vincent O'Brien went with Culombe in a police car to Culombe's house. On the way Culombe related the facts substantially as contained in his confession outlined hereinbefore, except that he claimed that Taborsky, and not he, had shot Kurpiewski in the boiler room of the gasoline station. At Culombe's house, the officers removed the medicine cabinet from the wall in the toilet room and found, in a brief case between the walls, a gun and two blackjacks. They also found, in a safe, a metal box with some parts of a gun. At Culombe's direction, they recovered from a swamp at Dexter and Reed Avenues in Hartford a raincoat with human bloodstains on it. Culombe stated it belonged to him and was worn by Taborsky on the night they went to New Britain. While at his house, Culombe said to his wife that he had told a true story to the police and that he might get life but Taborsky would get the chair. The offi-

---

[6] *Culombe v. Connecticut*, 367 U.S. 568, 643 (1961).

cers, at Culombe's suggestion, then went with Culombe to the intersection of Newfield and Dexter Avenues in Hartford. Pointing to a pond, he said that two guns could be found there and that the gun parts in the metal box would fit one of the guns. Culombe directed the officers to a service station, where he pointed out a 1949 black Oldsmobile which he said was previously owned by him and was used the night he and Taborsky went to New Britain.[7]

The following day Taborsky was arraigned. The court told him he need make no statement "and that any statement which he did make could be used against him. The next day, Friday, March 1, Taborsky's mother came to state police headquarters at her own request. She told Taborsky that she wanted him to tell the truth and that he should tell his part of the story, because Culombe had put the blame on him. Taborsky then, in the presence of Lieutenant Rome and Officer Reimer, told his mother that at the Kurp gasoline station the other fellow killed the station attendant, that they both robbed him and that he, Taborsky, killed the customer and robbed him."[8]

Culombe had been arraigned on Thursday, February 28, and warned of his right to remain silent. On Saturday night, March 2, the day after Taborsky confessed, Culombe was in his cell and called over the officer who was watching him: "and offered to give the police some further information concerning the New Britain affair. He then admitted that it was he who followed Kurpiewski into the service station, forced him at gun point into the boiler room and shot him."[9]

The Culombe case was argued a month before the thunderbolt in *Rogers v. Richmond* came down, so that Connecticut could not have anticipated its holding. Even had they been able to reargue the case, it's difficult to see how they could have met the new

---

[7] 158 Atl. 2d 245.

[8] 158 Atl. 2d 246.

[9] Id.

criteria. Being told that the truth of a confession is irrelevant in determining whether it is voluntary left most people stunned. Arthur Culombe, we are told, is entitled to an hearing solely on whether or not his confession was voluntary. This issue must be decided strictly on its own, free of any taint of its truth or the guilt of its maker. Irrelevant matters like finding guns in ponds and bloody raincoats in swamps must be banished from one's mind. This is a touchy business, for knowing for an absolute certainty that a defendant executed the owner of a gas station—KGB style—could easily prejudice a jury. It might well inflame their passions and turn them against the defendant so that they do not approach the question of volition calmly and deliberately.

It is clear Connecticut has deprived Arthur Culombe, as it did Harold Rogers before him, of a fair hearing, unprejudiced by emotion, on the discrete issue of the volition of his confession. One need look no further than the decision of its highest appellate court, in a unanimous opinion, to see they have again beclouded the issue of voluntariness with extraneous facts leading to the absolute but irrelevant feeling of certitude that the accused is guilty of the crime to which he confessed:

> The sign on Kurp's gasoline station was as described by Taborsky in his confession. The body of Janowski was found in the toilet room; there were two bullet wounds in his head. This corroborated Taborsky's description of the shooting. The body of Kurpiewski was found in the boiler room with one bullet wound in his head. The statements of both Taborsky and Culombe included these details of the crime. Janowski's car was found at the pumps in front of the station, facing south. Taborsky's statement put the car in that position. In this car was Janowski's little daughter. This fact corroborated statements made by both Taborsky and Culombe as to the presence of a child in the car. Taborsky stated that Kurpiewski was wearing a cap with a black visor. There was independent testimony that Kurpiewski

had been wearing such a cap, and one was found with Kurpiewski's body in the boiler room. Both defendants said, when they were taken to the gasoline station after their confession, that the location of the desk and the cash register had been changed. Other evidence confirmed it. Two guns were retrieved from the pond where Columbe said he had disposed of the guns used in the shootings, Taborsky having directed him to do so. One of the guns was identified by evidence independent of the confessions as the one from which certain parts found in Culombe's house had been removed. The other was identified by Taborsky as the gun he used to shoot Janowski. A raincoat with human bloodstains on it was found in a swamp where Culombe said he had thrown it.[10]

While the validity of the confession is contested, the facts surrounding it are not. Let us see first what the police did *not* do. At the outset Justice Frankfurter, who once again wrote the Court's opinion, put aside "physical brutality, threats of physical brutality . . . the keeping of prisoners unclothed or standing on their feet for long periods during questioning. No such obvious, crude devices appear in this record."[11] He also ruled out cases where the prisoner was deprived of sleep or food and turned to Culombe's interrogation.

Finally, we may put aside cases of gruelling, intensely unrelaxing questioning over protracted periods. Culombe's most extended session prior to his first confession ran three and a half hours with substantial respites. Because all of his questioning concerned not one but several offenses, it does not present an aspect of relentless, constantly repeated probing designed to break concentrated resistance. Particularly, the sustained four-and-a-half hour interview that preceded the Wednesday-midnight confession was almost wholly taken

---

10 158 Atl. 2d 247, 248.

11 367 U.S. 622.

up with matters other than Kurp's, and at that time, far from resisting, Culombe was wholly cooperating with the police.[12]

Culombe contested the validity of the confession made orally in the police car the Wednesday afternoon he showed the police where he had thrown away the bloody raincoat and the guns. Culombe did not contest the validity of the confessions he made after Taborsky confessed. The earlier was the Saturday night confession when he told the guard it really was he, and not Taborsky, who shot Kurp. The next day, it was incorporated into a written statement Culombe signed.

The first confession was held involuntary and Culombe's conviction set aside. Precisely what made the confession involuntary we are not told. Taking what is stated, and adding it up, we see that the defendant at one time said he wanted a lawyer and the police did not offer to get one. This was a factor, but in the opinion of Justice Frankfurter, not a controlling one. The use made by the police of Culombe's family was called into question. "By Lieutenant Rome's arrangement, Mrs. Culombe was permitted— indeed asked—to confront her husband and tell him to confess. Culombe's thirteen-year-old daughter was called upon in his presence to recount incriminating circumstances."[13] Culombe's wife was not at all supportive; she did not stand by her man in his hour of need. The use of Culombe's family sapped his powers to resist. It certainly caused him terrible emotional distress. We are told no less than three times that the episode with his wife and daughter left him choked up and sobbing.

The Connecticut police were confronted with this situation: "At the scene of the killings of Kurpiewski and Janowski no physical clues were discovered. The bullet slugs removed from the brains of the two victims were split and damaged."[14] No witnesses—no clues; the slugs cannot be tied by ballistics to any

---

12 367 U.S. 623.

13 367 U.S. 632.

14 367 U.S. 569.

gun or to its owner. But there had been other robbery-murders in the greater Hartford area with the same *modus operandi*.

> In the last week of February 1957, for reasons which do not appear in this record, suspicion in connection with at least two of the holdups under investigation, holdups of a country store in Coventry and of a package store in Rocky Hill, focused on two friends, Arthur Culombe and Joseph Taborsky. On the afternoon of February 23, the two were accosted by teams of officers and asked to come to State Police Headquarters.[15]

There is no denying that a request by a policeman to come to headquarters for a chat is not a social invitation. Nor should it be casually dismissed. Policemen are suspicious people who, if you spurn their invitations, are apt to think you have something to hide. For this reason, people generally accept, as did Culombe and Taborsky after each was "accosted" by a "team" of two officers. It was to allay the suspicions of the police that they agreed to visit the two stores, figuring that they would be better off if they did than if they didn't. For a while it looked as if they had made the right decision. As far as they knew they had not been identified, and their relations with the officers were friendly.

In fact, they got along so well they were taken to dinner. Maybe they thought it was a peace offering to make up for the trouble they had been put to. Things were going well for the two friends; they had put one over on the cops, or so they thought. Later Culombe told the officers of his gun collection and took them to his house to see it. That's when things took a turn for the worse. When they left, one member of the team waited outside with Culombe, while the other talked to Culombe's wife. After a talk at headquarters, suspicion had ripened into probable cause, and according to the Connecticut Supreme Court, the police were justified in apprehending them and holding them in custody.

---

15 367 U.S. 570, Douglas, J., concurring.

Culombe was questioned for a total of twelve and one-half hours over the next two and one-half days, never for a session of more than three and one-half hours with substantial respites. During this period of incarceration we may assume the police played Culombe and Taborsky off one against the other; that information received from other sources, perhaps Mrs. Culombe, was put to Culombe in such a manner that he would think it came from Taborsky, and vice-versa. We may assume also that the police convinced Mrs. Culombe that Taborsky was the "heavy," and her husband his pawn. No doubt they called her attention to the fact that if they were forced to release Taborsky for lack of evidence he would be a threat to her and her family. It appears she disliked and feared Taborsky and accepted this as a realistic appraisal. Mrs. Culombe cooperated with the police, and told her husband he should tell them the truth. Her daughter did the same.

Assuming the police did do these things, what is wrong about that? No doubt there are murderers smart enough to see through the police and their ploys, and well-advised and canny enough to remain silent. Does this mean equal justice under law requires that Arthur Culombe get away with the murder of Edward Kurpiewski, because Culombe is less intelligent, less wary or less well-advised than some other murderer?

What the police did was to get first Mrs. Culombe, and then Culombe, to believe it in their interest to tell the truth. This was done by playing on their fear of Taborsky. It was he who had gotten the Culombes in all this trouble. Saturday's pal became Wednesday's enemy. Culombe made his motives clear when he said to his wife that he had told a true story to the police, and that he might get life but Taborsky would get the chair.

Much is stated of the situation with which the Connecticut police were faced, but no weight given to its exigency. To solve the case the police had to get one of the murderers to lead them to the evidence. Finding the guns and the raincoat by themselves would not have been sufficient. It is Culombe's guilty knowledge that condemns him. There was nothing the officers could have done by being more scientific, professional or simply better policemen. They had to get one of the murderers to speak without using duress or coercion. They did their duty and did it well, for which they should have been commended.

¥ ¥ ¥

Watts v. Indiana and *Turner v. Pennsylvania* were ambiguous cases. The findings of fact in the state courts were given lip service by the Court's majority and then ignored. The defendant's version of controverted events was then accepted in each case over that of the police, when the trial court and jury, who heard the testimony, did the opposite. But *Watts* and *Turner* did not change the law, they simply twisted some facts. Whatever was lost in these two cases was retrieved in *Stein v. New York*—made possible, one might add, by the passing of liberal Justices Murphy and Rutledge during the summer recess of 1949.

But the law was changed in 1961 by *Rogers* and *Columbe*. In *Culombe*, the conviction of a confessed murderer was set aside. His guilt was presumed by the Court and then presumed to be irrelevant. Now it is one thing to overturn the conviction of a person because his guilt is open to doubt, and quite another to set free a proven murderer like Culombe. In the former case one truly can say the freedom of all has been enhanced by an additional protection against an innocent man being convicted. The price that some guilty men may escape justice must be accepted by a free society.

But what freedom emerges from *Culombe*? The right not to be psyched by the police into telling the truth? Of what value is that to the law-abiding citizen who has nothing to hide? The flipside of this so-called freedom is that people like Rogers and Culombe walk the street, robbers and murderers whose liberty is inimical to the freedom of the law-abiding. "Fear and freedom are mutually exclusive," said Eric Hoffer—particularly, one might add, to such targets of opportunity as people who run package-stores and gasoline stations.

On their own, *Rogers* and *Columbe* will not bring about significant change. For one thing, it is unrealistic to think that juries in the United States will follow a judge's instruction that the volition of a confession is "a question to be answered with complete disregard as to whether or not [the accused] told the truth." Defendants must perforce take the witness stand. To spare his arthritic wife the ordeal of being questioned by the police, a defendant like Rogers testifies, he confessed to murdering someone like Mrs. Kennedy. His criminal record will become known to the jury.

Having received these instructions from the trial judge, the jury will retire, deliberate, and decide the defendant is not only a murderer, but a perjurer as well. They will return and find a Harold Rogers guilty of murdering a Dorothy Kennedy a second time, or as many times as he is tried. On what grounds can a Rogers appeal a second conviction? Connecticut will have done everything the Supreme Court required of it. Who is to presume the jury disregarded the explicit instructions of the trial judge? Rogers's second conviction will stand and the Court's ukase will be nullified.

In writing a constitution, a great nation must balance two conflicting considerations. There must be sufficient unity of purpose and command so its fundamental principles and aims are not compromised; but this object must be accomplished in such a manner that its agents have sufficient latitude to deal with the problems they must face. This is especially true of the United States where the commands emanate from a constitution that is difficult of change, and was written by men of another era. They were men of great foresight, however, who set up a system, with respect to criminal justice, whose balancing of these considerations had served us well.

A command may be framed so comprehensively and definitively as to deprive the agent who must enforce it of all discretion in the subject matter. The paradigm of such an agent is an amanuensis. Conversely, a command may be so vaguely worded as to give an agent sufficient authority to judge a case as he thinks it should be decided under the facts and circumstances which attend it. In international affairs a person invested with full authority to act for his government is called a plenipotentiary. A plenipotentiary may make a judgment on the spot without further reference to the source of his power. An amanuensis, should you question what he has done, will not attempt to defend its wisdom. Whatever he did, he will tell you, he did under superior orders. He is not, in his own mind at least, in any way blameworthy for the consequences. It is quite the opposite with the plenipotentiary. The results of his decision, good or bad, lie squarely on his shoulders.

In applying a specific, categorical constitutional command a justice reasons deductively, from the general to the particular. The command gives him his major premise, the general proposition, and the case at bar his minor. It remains only for him to determine whether the particular, that is, what was done in the case at bar, falls within or without the ambit of the general. Either way his conclusion is compelled. This is a process of classification or "labeling." The judge who "finds" the law must be a logician— an Aristotle.

A vague constitutional command calls for the opposite process of reasoning. In applying "due process of law" a judge reasoned inductively, from the particular to the general, drawing from the facts and circumstances in the case at hand his own conclusion as to such matters as whether or not a confession was voluntary. The scales of justice, not the syllogism, were his tool; conscience, not logic, his guide. "The law which is the resulting product," wrote Cardozo, "is not *found* but *made*."[16] The judge who "makes" the law must be wise—a Solomon.

---

16 Benjamin N. Cardozo, *The Nature of the Judicial Process*, (New Haven: Yale University Press (1921), 113-115 (emphasis added).

In certain matters the Framers spoke in language so inflexible as to deprive their posterity of any discretion in their interpretation. Take, for example, those parts of the original unamended Constitution which requires that the President of the United States must be at least 35 years of age, United States Senators, 30, and members of the House of Representatives, 25. Under certain circumstances this might debar the person most qualified, someone whose election would be a great boon to the body politic. Why should the right of the living to elect their own representatives be restrained by the dead hand of the past? But those considerations are unavailing in the face of a clear constitutional command. This is the price the Framers were willing to pay to insure that only the mature will guide the ship of state. Headstrong young men shall never be at the helm—someone like George III, for example, who at the age of 22 succeeded to the throne of England.

The same is true of Article III, Section 3, which provides that: "No person shall be convicted of treason unless on the testimony of two witnesses to the same overt act, or on confession in open court." This is so clear and inflexible a command as to make the judge who must apply it an amanuensis. That treason may thereby go unpunished is neither fair nor just, but nevertheless it is "the law." The traitor goes free, if he must, but it is the law that sets him free—the Framers' law.

Due process of law, on the other hand, is as vague and indefinite a phrase as the Framers could devise. They drew no line between that "process" which is "due" and that which is not, so that "due process of law" is incapable of being used as a major premise. In our jurisprudence it had branched into two equally nebulous standards. As to substantive rights, protected from state abridgement were those freedoms "basic to our free society," or "implicit in the concept of ordered liberty"; criminal procedure had to be "fundamentally fair." Neither are precise, nor were they intended to be.

In deciding whether a procedure was fair or a freedom basic to a free society, a judge did not refer to preestablished rules and then proceed to determine whether what happened in the case at hand came within their purview, the mental process of classification known as analysis. To the contrary, in making such a decision, a judge, like anyone else, took all of the facts and circumstances of a case into consideration, weighed them in the light of all of his knowledge and experience and rendered his decision on what *he* thought was fair and just. This is a balancing process called synthesis.

A person can be highly intelligent and well-schooled, and be a fanatic or a fool nevertheless. On the other hand, he can be of limited intelligence and little education, and yet be wise and successful. The difference does not lie in the sum total of a person's knowledge, or his acuity, but in the weight that person attaches to the facts and circumstances around him. He or she must be able to tell what is important from what is not, and to what degree this is so. To be successful in life or in law one must be "well-balanced." The ability to synthesize successfully is known in the vernacular as "having common sense." You can learn a lot of things from books, but this is not one of them.

The very purpose of using such terms in a constitution as "due process of law," "necessary and proper," "reasonable," "probable cause," and other words or phrases as call for an independent judgment, is to give a judge of another day, in the context of his times, under the facts and circumstances of the case before him, the power to do what that judge thinks liberty and justice demand. It is he who must make the call. The results of his decision, good or bad, lie squarely on his shoulders.

An analogy can be found in the game of American football. The rule book prescribes the layout of a football field in terms which brook no deviation. It is the form of a gridiron in which there are sidelines and goal lines of great significance in the contest. The team that gets the ball has four plays in which to advance it ten yards. If they succeed they get another four plays to gain another ten yards, if they fail the ball goes over to the other team. On the sidelines are officials with poles connected to each other by chains which measure exactly ten yards.

Where there is a doubt as to whether the offensive team has gained the necessary yardage the officials must call for a measurement. The chains provide them with the major premise and all depends on whether the ball lies within or without their embrace, by how much or how little does not matter. The chains must be held taut; the officials cannot stretch them nor permit them to be slack. In taking the measurement an official has no discretion; he is in effect an amanuensis.

Football is a contact sport in which men's bodies collide with great force. It is a rough game in which players often get angry and do and say things they should not. There are rules proscribing certain types of conduct. While they are found in the same rule book that prescribes how the gridiron should be laid out, these proscriptions are couched in less definitive terms such as "unnecessary roughness" and "unsportsmanlike conduct."

There are no lines that demark, nor chains that measure, when roughness becomes "unnecessary" or conduct "unsportsmanlike." The force with which one player hits another is not determinant; that he did not hit him harder still is rarely out of compassion. To leave your adversary prone and senseless ranks among the highest traditions of the game provided—and this is an important proviso—that the hit be "clean."

Mens rea and *scienter* have a lot to do with "personal fouls" in the game of football. They can be read in the body language of accuser and accused, the demeanor and gesticulations by which malice is imputed and at the same time denied. Whether roughness is "unnecessary" or conduct "unsportsmanlike" is not a judgment an official arrives at by deduction. It is a synthesis he must make according to the facts and circumstances of the case at hand in the light of all of his knowledge and experience. He must "make the call."

A football referee carries out his mandate by two distinct and opposite processes of reasoning. From a clear command he proceeds *a priori*. The chains and the fixed lines of the gridiron provide him with a major premise, the ball and the ball carrier his minor. The judgment whether the latter lies within the former is reached dispassionately and mechanically. It is a process in which considerations of "justice" or "fairness" have no place. The result was ordained by those who framed the rules of football.

Whether roughness is "unnecessary" or conduct "unsportsman-like" is determined *a posteriori* from the circumstances of the case. It is a process of reasoning in which justice and fairness are not just considerations, they *are* the question which must be decided. A referee must "make the call" in the light of his knowledge and experience. If his synthesis is not a true one, the fault lies with him. He cannot lay the blame on Walter Camp, the Father of Football, or those who wrote the rules, for a "bad call."

Under fundamental fairness, the analogy to football was apropos. The due process clause was deemed to have invested in judges the same autonomy the rules of football repose in referees. When it came to such questions as to whether a confession was voluntary, they had to "make the call." Nor would a judge ever be bound by the doctrine of *stare decisis* to permit a miscarriage of justice in the case before him. "What due process requires in one situation may not be required in another—and this, of course, because the least change of circumstances may provide or eliminate fundamental fairness."[17]

One would think this gave those who wished to change our jurisprudence sufficient autonomy to meet what they considered to be the problems of their time. Indeed, that is the whole idea of using vague precepts. But therein lies the problem: with autonomy so also goes accountability. The judicial revolutionists did not want to increase a judge's latitude to meet changing conditions, they wanted to constrict it. They must always be able to say that

---

[17] *Crooker v. California*, 357 U.S. 433, 441 (1958).

the criminal goes free, not by any exercise of discretion on their part, but by virtue of a rigid constitutional command. They must not "make" the law, they must feign to "find" it. Their hands must be tied, or so it must appear, in order that they may be washed of injustice with appropriate sanctimony.

Under fundamental fairness, the Court had taken the intentionally vague guarantee of due process of law as a delegation of power to them to render justice, as does a court of equity, according to fairness and conscience. With respect to the case before them, the case at bar, the justices were plenipotentiaries. The competing concerns were the right of the defendant to a "fair trial," on one side, weighed against something on the other called the "rights of society."

It was clear to the revolutionists that "fundamental fairness" must be abolished and replaced by rules framed so comprehensively and definitively so as to make a judge who must administer them an amanuensis. Then, when they are confronted with the consequences of their decisions, they need only respond that they are simply enforcing "the law." This, the American people will be told, is the "price we pay for freedom." It used to be called "the rights of society."

CHAPTER 8

THE LIBERALS

THE VAST MAJORITY OF CITIZENS have always taken for granted that the purpose of a criminal trial is to determine the truth of the accusation against the defendant. The innocent must be exonerated and the guilty convicted. They believe not only that punishment deters crime, but that society should exact from the criminal a penalty for the harm he has done.

Opposed to them is a well organized and close-knit minority that misses no opportunity to decry our historic legal process. The belief that a criminal trial ought to be a search for the truth is anathema to them. A crime that is committed bespeaks to this group the culpability of society, rather than that of the perpetrator, whose personal guilt they find of little interest. These people wage an incessant campaign to make it as difficult as possible to try, convict and punish criminals; the idea that we can have a fair and effective system of criminal justice which will convict the guilty and free the innocent must never be permitted to prevail.

This school of thought and its advocates may with justice be called the Amicus Criminalis, the "Friend of the Criminal." They are a core constituency of the American left, who, were they Europeans, would call themselves Socialists or Social Democrats. In the United States today they are known generically as liberals, and when it comes to criminal justice they speak through the mouth of the American Civil Liberties Union. To the liberals the real criminal is our capitalist society; those who transgress the penal code are but some of its victims. As the year 1961 began, they knew that if they were to change the criminal justice system they had to act now.

Sitting on the United States Supreme Court were four doctrinaire liberals. Two, Hugo Black and William O. Douglas, were Democrats who had been appointed by President Franklin Roosevelt in the late 1930's. "The two of them became identified as the Court's most liberal and activist members during the more than three decades they served together."[1] While the antics of Douglas both on and off the bench were highly controversial, they pale in comparison to the political pedigree Hugo Lafayette Black brought to the Supreme Court.

During FDR's first term there had been no vacancies on the Supreme Court. Then, in August of 1937, a seat became vacant and to fill it the President chose Black, the then junior United States senator from Alabama. Quickly confirmed by his Senate colleagues, Black took the oath of office and immediately embarked on a European vacation. While he was abroad it came to light that the newly appointed justice had been a member of the Ku Klux Klan. This fact was known to some of his Alabama constituents but not to the country at large. Besieged abroad by reporters, Black declined any comment until he returned to the United States. Then, on October 1, 1937 he made a statement broadcast on national radio.

> My words and acts are a matter of public record. I believe that my record as a Senator refutes every implication of racial or religious intolerance. It shows that I was of that group of liberal Senators who have consistently fought for civil, economic and religious rights of all Americans, without regard to race or creed . . . I did join the Klan. I later resigned. I never rejoined . . . Before becoming a Senator I dropped the Klan. I have had nothing whatever to do with

---

[1] *The Douglas Letters*, Melvin L. Urosky, Editor, Adler & Adler: Bethesda, Maryland (1987), 106.

it since that time . . . When this statement is ended, my discussion of this question is closed.[2]

And so it was. Black refused comment on the subject of the Klan forever after. He had made his statement and that was that. Today it would be called "stonewalling." But Black's membership in the Klan was not just nominal nor at age 40 was it a youthful indiscretion. "Black's involvement in Klan activities was extensive and ardent. One of his law partners, Crampton Harris, was cyclops of the largest Birmingham Klavern . . . Alabama's Grand Dragon, James Esdale, actively managed Black's senatorial campaign in 1926, and there is no doubt that the Klan's massive support supplied him with the margin of victory in that election. Indeed, Black himself did not doubt it at the time."[3] At a Klan rally celebrating Black's victory in the 1926 Democratic primary, then tantamount to election, Senator-elect Hugo Black breathed his

> undying prayer that this [Klan] will carry on, sacredly true to the real principles of American manhood and womanhood, revering [the] virtue of the mother of the race, loving the pride of Anglo-Saxon spirit—and I love it—true to the heaven-born principles of liberty which were written in the Constitution of this country, and in the great historical documents, straight from the heart of Anglo-Saxon patriots.[4]

President Roosevelt, on September 14, 1937, after Black's appointment but before Black's radio statement, told a press conference "that he had not known of any Klan link" when he appointed the Alabama Senator to the Court. "I only know what I have read in the newspaper,"[5] Roosevelt declared. And Black's

---

2 *New York Times*, October 2, 1937, p. 1.

3 *Hugo Black and Modern America*, Tony Freyer, Ed., Tuscaloosa: University of Alabama Press (1990) 141-142, J. Mills Thornton, Author.

4 Id., 146.

5 Id., 126.

statement that he had resigned from the Klan must be taken with a grain of salt.

> Black *was* a Klan member, but in July (1925) he submitted a letter of resignation. The Alabama Grand Dragon replied: "I'll keep [the resignation] in my safe against the day when you'll need to say you're not a Klan member. Thus, as Professor Hamilton shrewdly has observed, "Black had all the advantages of Klan support and none of the disadvantages of membership."[6]

Hugo Black's midlife conversion from Klu Klux Klansman to activist liberal Supreme Court Justice must be viewed as an example of his propensity to sail with the prevailing political winds. It was certainly expedient. For had he strayed from the liberal line, Justice Black would have been savaged. Political cartoonists could have cut him to pieces. The imagery of white sheet to black robe made him a sitting duck. Black's legal opinions, particularly his championship of the incorporation doctrine, must always be viewed in this light.

Liberalism served Black well in 1945 when he was accused of a violation of judicial ethics by casting the deciding vote in a five-to-four decision in which Crampton Harris, his former law partner (and cyclops of the largest Birmingham Klaven of the Klu Klux Klan), represented the successful litigant.[7] The affair caused a furor not only in the press but within the Court as well, after Associate Justice Robert H. Jackson made public a letter he had written to the chairmen of the House and Senate Judiciary Committees. But with some help from the liberal press Black weathered the storm. The *New York Post*, for example, "saluted Black's 'sterling liberalism' and criticized Jackson's 'personal pique.'"[8]

---

[6] Id., citing V. Hamilton.

[7] *Jewell Ridge Coal Corp. v. United Mine Workers*, 325 U.S. 897 (1945).

[8] James F. Simon, *The Antagonists: Hugo Black, Felix Frankfurter and Civil Liberties in Modern America*. New York: Simon and Shuster (1989), 167-168.

When Dwight D. Eisenhower left office in January of 1961, five of his appointees sat on the Supreme Court. Two were Republicans appointed to pay off political debts Eisenhower had incurred at the 1952 Republican Convention. The first of these was Governor Earl Warren of California, who in 1953 was nominated for Chief Justice. "It had been Warren . . . who was primarily responsible for swinging all but eight of California's 70-member delegation at the Nominating Convention to Eisenhower rather than Senator Robert A. Taft."[9] Another chit was picked up in 1958 when Eisenhower chose Potter Stewart as an Associate Justice. Stewart and his family were from Taft's home town of Cincinnati, Ohio, and had always been steadfast Taft supporters.

> The Stewarts had long been prominently active in Ohio Republican politics as part of the political retinue of Senator Robert A. Taft—for whose Presidential aspirations young Potter campaigned assiduously in the late 1940s. In mid-1952 . . . he transferred his allegiance to Eisenhower. He was convinced that Ike could win, and he was, in fact, more comfortable with Eisenhower's political stance than he was with Taft's.[10]

A third politically inspired appointment took place in October of 1956, when Eisenhower chose New Jersey Supreme Court Judge William J. Brennan, Jr., to fill a recent vacancy. With the election a month away Ike saw the political wisdom of picking "a Democrat who also happened to be a Roman Catholic. It might well avoid a 'return home' by the Eisenhower Democrats of 1952, buttressing the non-political or bipartisan atmosphere in which he felt most comfortable."[11] In the event this proved quite unnecessary when Eisenhower swamped former Illinois Governor Adlai

---

9 Henry J. Abraham, *Justices and Presidents: A Political History of Appointments to the Supreme Court*. New York: Oxford University Press (1985), 252-253.

10 Id., 267.

11 Id., 263.

Stevenson nationally and took New Jersey by a margin of almost two-to-one. Brennan, along with Chief Justice Warren, soon joined Black and Douglas to form a liberal bloc of four.

In 1957, Eisenhower appointed Charles Evans Whittaker of Kansas City, Missouri, to the high court. Whittaker was a friend of Ike's brother, Arthur,[12] a Kansas City banker, and turned out to be an unmitigated disaster. Whittaker suffered from an affliction which in judges is terminal. He simply couldn't make up his mind. "For Whittaker, the agonizing he had gone through in making decisions had been unbearable . . . Now the strain had proved too much."[13] After suffering a nervous breakdown in early 1962, the dithering Whittaker resigned in the midst of the so-called "judicial revolution."

John Marshall Harlan was the least liberal of Eisenhower's choices. According to one observer, Harlan "was a lifelong, solid Republican, but he had always kept a low political profile and was widely regarded as non-partisan."[14] In a letter to his friend, Judge Learned Hand, Justice Felix Frankfurter diagnosed Harlan's low-profile non-partisanship as lack of knowledge and timidity:

> With all his judicial aims and character, he really has not had the appropriate intellectual background of reading and reflection for the ultimate task, that of passing on constitutionality . . . Moreover, he is not meant for battle, represents at its best what I'm told (by an esteemed Princetonian) is the dominant Princeton ideal, to be nice . . .[15]

Felix Frankfurter was the remaining holdover from the New Deal. While Frankfurter is not a man you mention just in passing, age and infirmity will limit his part in this story. The enigmatic Frankfurter, it is safe to say, was by far the best mind on

---

[12] *Abraham*, 266-267.

[13] Bernard Schwartz, *Super Chief: Earl Warren and His Supreme Court, A Judicial Philosophy*. New York: New York University Press (1983), 427.

[14] *Abraham*, 259.

[15] Felix Frankfurter to Learned Hand, June 30, 1957, Learned Hand Papers, Harvard Law School Library, cited by Hirsch at 181-182.

the Court. A founding member of the ACLU in 1920,[16] he nevertheless was the justice most effective in opposing their machinations. And therein lies an irony.

As a young man Frankfurter had taken an abiding interest in what liberals then called "labor unrest" and had a proclivity for taking the side of labor leaders accused of violence. Appointed by Woodrow Wilson in 1917 to a Mediation Commission to settle labor disputes harmful to the war effort, he took up the cause of Tom Mooney, an organizer for the International Workers of the World (IWW) who had been convicted of the bombing of a 1916 "Preparedness Day" parade in San Francisco which killed 10 people and wounded many more. Many Americans, Theodore Roosevelt among them, could not see what this had to do with labor mediation. Moreover, in 1919, as a Harvard law professor, Frankfurter had led protests against the measures the Wilson Administration had taken to oppose the Bolsheviks in the Russian Civil War. When Felix Frankfurter was nominated for the Supreme Court in 1939, conservatives were horrified. In their minds Frankfurter was, if not a Red, then at least, in the vernacular of the day, a "parlor pink."

Frankfurter was concerned that the liberals might exert an undue influence over Harlan. "The non-judicial twain of Justices," he wrote of Black and Douglas, "are crafty on the job— I'm watching their effort on John [Harlan]. It's hard for a decent man to realize how indecent people operate."[17] In his declining years FF saw the liberals for what they were. "Frankfurter was convinced that his opponents did not really believe in their judicial philosophy; that they only wanted to appear 'liberal' in law reviews and in history. Frankfurter would often pour out his anger at them to Learned Hand."[18]

Look at them. Hugo [Black] is a self-righteous, self-deluded part fanatic, part demagogue, who really disbelieves in law,

---

[16] ACLU Annual Report No. 1 (January 1920-August 1921), at 31, shows Felix Frankfurter to be a national committeeman.

[17] FF to LH, April 2?, 1954, Learned Hand Papers (cited by Hirsch at 182).

[18] Hirsch, 180.

thinks it is essentially manipulation of language. Intrinsically, the best brain in the lot, but [only as] . . . an instrument for supporting a predetermined result, not a means for responsible inquiry . . . Bill [Douglas] is the most cynical, shamelessly immoral character I've ever known. With him I have no more relation than the necessities of court work require. He is too unscrupulous for any avoidable entanglement.[19]

Had the liberal agenda in 1961 gone according to plan, June 19th would have seen them win a double-header. *Columbe v. Connecticut* and *Mapp v. Ohio* are consecutive cases in Volume 367 of the United States Reports and were decided on the same day. But for Justice Frankfurter the liberals would have succeeded in not only foisting a Fourth Amendment exclusionary rule on state criminal procedure, but a Fifth Amendment exclusionary rule as well. And at the time this seemed to be the most likely outcome.

In 1958, Potter Stewart took the seat of retiring Justice Harold Burton. In two cases decided at the end of the 1957/58 term, Burton had voted with the five-man majority in upholding the validity of confessions made in the absence of legal counsel.[20] Stewart did not take long to announce his opinion to the contrary. Concurring in a New York case, decided unanimously, Justice Stewart added this statement. "While I concur in the opinion of the Court, it is my view that the absence of counsel when this confession was elicited was alone enough to render it inadmissible under the Fourteenth Amendment."[21] If Potter Stewart is of the opinion that such confessions, regardless of circumstance, are inadmissible, this as a practical matter means all custodial confessions.

Potter Stewart would have given the liberals the necessary fifth vote in Columbe had not Felix Frankfurter thrown a monkey

---

[19] FF to Learned Hand, November 17, 1954, Learned Hand Papers (cited by Hirsch at 182).

[20] *Crooker v. California*, 357 U.S. 433 (1958) and *Cicenia v. Lagay*, 357 U.S. 504 (1958).

[21] *Spano v. New York*, 360 U.S. 315, 326 (1959).

wrench into the works. Justice Frankfurter wrote an opinion of 67 pages which Chief Justice Earl Warren in his dissent aptly characterized as a "lengthy and abstract dissertation" which was "in the nature of an advisory opinion." The only thing it established with any certainty was that Culombe and Taborsky did, in fact, murder Kurpiewski and Janowski and that their confessions in this regard were true. The Chief Justice also pointed out, quite correctly, that "while three members of the Court agree to the general principles enunciated by the opinion, they construe those principles as requiring a result in this case exactly the opposite from that reached by the author of the opinion."[22]

Frankfurter's opinion was rambling and obfuscating. It was a dumb opinion and Felix Frankfurter was anything but dumb. It conceded to the police the right to interrogate a suspect in the absence of counsel without cautioning him. "Indeed, even to inform the suspect of his legal right to keep silent will prove an obstruction. Whatever fortifies the suspect or seconds him in his capacity to keep his mouth closed is a potential obstacle to the solution of crime."[23] His ruling that the voluntariness of a confession is a question to be answered with complete disregard as to whether or not the accused told the truth, created an exclusionary rule that was utterly unworkable.

Somehow he was able to persuade Potter Stewart to join him. Had Stewart adhered to the view that the absence of counsel alone was sufficient to invalidate a confession he would have joined Warren, Black, Douglas and Brennan and *Columbe v. Connecticut* would be to the law of confessions today what *Mapp v. Ohio* is to the law of search and seizure. June 19, 1961 was a black day in the history of American constitutional law, but it could have been blacker still.

In April of 1962, Felix Frankfurter suffered a stroke that left him incapacitated. Justice Frankfurter never returned to the Court and resigned the following August. To replace him, President John

---

[22] 367 U.S. 635-6, Warren, C.J. dissenting.

[23] *Columbe* at 580.

F. Kennedy chose Secretary of Labor Arthur Goldberg, formerly General Counsel of the AFL/CIO, a man of impeccable liberal and leftist credentials, membership in the ACLU and the National Lawyers Guild among them.[24] The departure of Frankfurter left the quartet of Warren, Brennan, Black and Douglas without effective opposition. With Frankfurter gone, and Goldberg in his place, it appeared that there was a left wing bloc of five justices "willing," to use the words of Professor Morrison, "to distort history, as well as the language of the Framers, in order to read into the Constitution provisions which they think ought to be there."[25]

Under the specific commands of the Bill of Rights, addressed to the federal government, and it alone, a procedure is unconstitutional if it is thereby forbidden, regardless of whether this be "fair" or "just" in a particular case. Under the Due Process Clause of the Fourteenth Amendment, which applies to the states and the states alone, a procedure is constitutional if it be "fair" or "just" in a particular case, regardless of whether it is one forbidden the federal government by one of the specific commands of the Bill of Rights. In the former, it is unconstitutional because it is forbidden; in the latter, it is unconstitutional because it is unfair. In the first instance a judge "finds" the law, in the latter he "makes" it.

The liberals were aware that if they were to avoid political responsibility for a fundamental change in the law of confessions which would benefit only the guilty, that they must "find" the Exemption from Compulsory Self Incrimination clause of the Fifth Amendment within the Fourteenth. This passage by Justice Douglas, joined by Justice Black, in a dissenting opinion in 1951, pointed the way:

> As an original matter it might be debatable whether the provision in the Fifth Amendment that no person "shall be compelled in any criminal case to be a witness against himself" serves the ends of justice. Not all civilized legal proce-

---

[24] Edward B. Shil, *Arthur Goldberg: Proof of the American Dream*.
[25] *Supra*, __.

dures recognize it. But the choice was made by the Framers, a choice which sets a standard for legal trials in this country. The Framers made it a standard of due process for prosecutions by the Federal Government. If it is a requirement of due process for a trial in the federal courthouse, it is impossible for me to say that it is not a requirement of due process for a trial in the state courthouse . . . [The evidence in this case is] inadmissible because of the command of the Fifth Amendment.[26]

One can see how this posture would absolve liberal judges of political accountability for the consequences of such decisions. If a murderer goes free because his confession, voluntary and true as it may be, is excluded from evidence, that judge is not responsible. It is not given to him to decide whether such a decision is fair or serves the ends of justice. The choice was made by the Framers when they wrote the Fifth Amendment and it is a judge's duty not to reason why, but to uphold and enforce the commands of the Constitution as written.

But the application of the Fifth Amendment to the states is an affirmation of the theory of Incorporation rejected by the Court time and time again in an unbroken line of decisions going back to the passage of the Fourteenth Amendment itself. In *Wolf v. Colorado*, decided only a short two years before, after "impressive consideration," the Court had pronounced the "issue" "closed." But even if one assumes the validity of the Douglas dicta, there remained what seemed to be an insurmountable barrier.

The Fifth Amendment specifically states that no person "shall be compelled in any criminal case to be a witness against himself." This is the problem. Obviously, a person who makes a voluntary confession is not compelled to say anything, much less be a witness against himself. When, therefore, a confession is proffered, the prosecution will introduce along with it evidence that it

---

26 Dissenting in *Rochin v. California*, 342 U.S. 165, 178-9 (1951) [footnote omitted].

was made voluntarily. The facts and circumstances that surround the confession will become known not only to the jury, but to the public as well.

Nor was there any need to caution a prisoner being interrogated that he has the right to remain silent or advise him that he is entitled to a lawyer. "We feel no urge," said a unanimous Second Circuit Court of Appeals in 1959, "to elevate to the dignity of a constitutional right a practice which perhaps even as a matter of etiquette, may, in the present condition of society, be an unwarranted extravagance."

> It is not an evil thing for one accused of crime to voluntarily admit his guilt. It is a good thing. It removes his crime from the list of unsolved crimes and enables the police to get about the task of solving other crimes on the list. It enables the criminal courts and their juries to reach decisions free from the uncertainties which trials involving principally circumstantial evidence involve. It brings down upon the accused no worse than his due, the punishment prescribed by law for his crime.[27]

In the minds of most Americans it is unfair, unjust, and manifestly immoral, once his guilt is proved to be an incontrovertible fact, to send a vicious criminal back to the streets to prey upon the law abiding. If they were to survive politically, liberals knew that the moral responsibility for such judgments must never rest on them. They must never be seen as "soft on crime." It was not only criminals who had to be shielded from public accountability but their amici as well. The liberals already knew what they wanted. Senate Bill 3325 introduced by Oregon Senator Wayne Morse on February 21, 1958, was right on the mark:

> 3051. Caution to accused persons
>
> No officer or employee of the United States Government or of the municipal government of the District of Columbia

---

[27] *United States v. Wilson*, 264 Fed 2d 104, 106 (1959).

shall interrogate, or request any statement including a confession from a person accused or suspected of an offense, without first informing him—

(a) of the nature of the offense;

(b) that he does not have to make any statement regarding the offense of which he is accused or suspected;

(c) that he has the right to have legal counsel present at all times while he is being questioned or is making any statement; and

(d) that any statement made by him may be used as evidence against him in a criminal prosecution.

3501. Admissibility of statements

No statement, including a confession of guilt, shall be admissible in evidence in a criminal prosecution in any district court of the United States or in the municipal court for the District of Columbia until there is established proof that the provisions of section 3051 of this title have been complied with.

The trouble with the Morse Bill was that it could not be passed. Congress was overwhelmingly against it. In 1958 it was considered by the Senate Judiciary Committee along with other legislation bearing on the admissibility of self-incriminating statements and then passed over in favor of H.R. 11477, the Willis-Keating Bill, which would have abolished the *McNabb-Mallory* rule and reestablished voluntariness as the test of admissibility in federal courts. This bill, which had passed the House by a vote of 294 to 79, passed the Senate by a margin of 65 to 12. Then, according to the Congressional Record of August 23, 1958, in the closing minutes of the 85th Congress, the Willis-Keating Bill was blocked by a parliamentary maneuver by Senator John Carroll of Colorado.[28] No one who voted for the Willis-Keating Bill, it is reasonable to

---

[28] "The *McNabb-Mallory* Rule: Its Rise, Rationale and Rescue." James E. Hogan and Joseph M. Snee, 47 Georgetown Law Journal (1958), 45-46.

assume, would have voted for the Morse Bill, and had the liberals been so rash as to make its exclusionary rule applicable to the
individual states, the vote would have been even more lopsided.

The Morse Bill would give the liberals a pulpit from which
to pontificate. And it is far more noble to wrap yourself in the
Bill of Rights than to argue cases like Culombe or Rogers on
guilt or innocence. If you play your role correctly, as does the
ACLU, you can equate any attack on you, or your legal scholarship, into an attack on the Bill of Rights. You can then portray
yourself as the defender of the Constitution, making the tough
decisions in the hard cases, and your adversaries as the mis-
guided, who would sacrifice our most cherished institutions on
the altar of expediency. Moreover, the Morse Code would give
the liberals a sally-port from which they could venture forth to
flay those Neanderthals who still thought that truth and justice
mattered in criminal cases.

The facts in the Pamela Powers murder case were recited in
the Introduction to this book. On Christmas Eve of 1968, Robert
Williams murdered a 10-year-old girl in Des Moines, Iowa, after
sexually attacking her. He then fled to Davenport, Iowa, some
160 miles east where he decided to surrender to the police. On
the day after Christmas, Williams was taken in a police car back
to Des Moines and on the way, in a pang of conscience, led the
police to the culvert where he had hidden her body. He gave them
a detailed description of how he murdered her. He did so after no
fewer than five warnings of his rights to silence and to counsel.

But this is immaterial. The police had agreed, so we are told,
that they would not question Williams on the way back to Des
Moines. They really hadn't, but like the Court, we will pretend
they did anyway. Detective Leaming reneged on this agreement,
it is claimed, through his poignant Christian Burial Speech. Leaming knew that Williams was deeply religious so that the speech,
while posing no questions, was so "evocative" as to be tantamount
to interrogation. A footnote led to a second trial.

While neither Williams' incriminating statements them-selves nor any testimony describing his having led the police to the victim's body can constitutionally be admitted into evidence, evidence of where the body was found and of its condition might well be admissible on the theory that the body would have been discovered in any event, even had incriminating statements not been elicited from Williams.[29]

This time the prosecution introduced evidence that at the time Williams led officers to the child's body, 200 volunteers were mak-ing a systematic search of the area. The trial court concluded that the state had proved by a preponderance of the evidence that, if the search had not been suspended and Williams had not led the police to the victim, her body would have been discovered anyway. While Williams' guilty knowledge was not admitted into evidence, the girl's body was, so that Iowa was at least able to prove that she had been murdered. His second trial ended in a second convic-tion and Williams again appealed. In 1984, sixteen years after the murder, the murder conviction of Robert Williams was upheld.[30]

Justices Brennan and Marshall dissented. They were not satis-fied Williams got a fair hearing on the discrete issue of whether the child's body would have been discovered in a short enough time to be in the state of preservation in which it was actually found. Brennan and Marshall would have made the prosecution satisfy a "heightened burden of proof" before it is allowed to use as evi-dence the corpse of Pamela Powers. "I would require clear and convincing evidence before concluding that the government had met its burden of proof on this issue." wrote Justice Brennan.[31]

Justice Stevens wrote a separate opinion taking Detective Leaming to task. "Thanks to Detective Leaming, the State of Iowa has expended vast sums of money and countless hours of professional labor in his defense." He concluded that "the

---

[29] 430 U.S. 407.

[30] *Nix v. Williams*, 467 U.S. 431, 459-460 (1984).

[31] Id., 459.

responsibility for that expenditure lies not with the Constitution, but rather with the constable." Justice Thurgood Marshall,
concurring separately, laid out the enormity of this "knowing
and intentional police transgression of the constitutional rights
of a defendant."

> Undoubtedly Leaming realized the way in which that infor-
> mation would be conveyed to the police: McKnight would
> learn it from his client and then he would lead police to the
> body. Williams would thereby be protected by the attorney-
> client privilege from incriminating himself by directly
> demonstrating his knowledge of the body's location, and
> the unfortunate Powers child could be given a "Christian
> burial" . . . The detective demonstrated once again "that the
> efficiency of the rack and the thumbscrew can be matched,
> given the proper subject, by more sophisticated modes of
> 'persuasion.'"[32]

Marshall reminded us of what really was at stake here with an
excerpt from Justice Brandeis' opinion in the 1928 case of *Olmstead v. United States*: "[T]o declare that the Government may
commit crimes in order to secure the conviction of a private criminal—would bring terrible retribution."[33] The cases of *Olmstead*[34]
and *Williams*, however, are not exactly analogous. One involved
a bootlegger whose phone was illegally tapped by Prohibition
agents, while the other "crime" consisted of making an "evocative" statement to the man who raped and murdered 10-year-
old Pamela Powers.

---

[32] Brewer, *Warden v. Williams*, 430 U.S. 387, 408 (1977).

[33] Id., 409.

[34] *Olmstead v. United States*, 277 U.S. 438 (1928).

THE RANSOM
OF CHARLES NOIA

U NDER THE ENGLISH COMMON LAW habeas corpus had never
been available to any person serving a sentence under a criminal conviction imposed by a court of competent jurisdiction. This
rule was adopted in the United States well before the Civil War. In
1830, Tobias Watkins, convicted of fraud in the District of Columbia, sought release on a writ of habeas corpus. The writ of habeas
corpus, held the Supreme Court, cannot be used in lieu of an
appeal.

> Can the court, upon this writ, look beyond the judgment,
> and reexamine the charges on which it was rendered. A
> judgment, in its nature, concludes the subject on which it
> is rendered, and pronounces the law of the case. The judg-
> ment of a court of record whose jurisdiction is final, is as con-
> clusive on all the world as the judgment of this court would
> be. It is as conclusive on this court as it is on other courts.
> It puts an end to inquiry concerning the fact, by deciding it
> . . . An imprisonment under a judgment cannot be unlaw-
> ful, unless that judgment be an absolute nullity; and it is not
> a nullity if the court has general jurisdiction of the subject,
> although it should be erroneous.[1]

A court is a court of competent jurisdiction when it has jurisdiction over the person and the subject matter. Jurisdiction over

---

[1] *Ex Parte Tobias Watkins*, 28 U.S. 193, 202-203 (1830).

the person is obtained by having the defendant physically present at the trial. Jurisdiction over the subject matter means, in this context, that the court is vested by statute with the legal right and power to try the defendant for the crime of which he stands charged, and to punish him if he is found guilty. All courts in the cases we will examine are courts of unquestioned competent jurisdiction.

In a civil action a plaintiff sues a defendant for money or property. One party or the other prevails in the trial court and is awarded a judgment that becomes final unless the loser chooses to appeal. Either litigant has a specific limitation of time in which to appeal a judgment against him. That party must appeal to a higher court within that time or the judgment becomes final. The vast majority of civil cases are terminated not by a decision of the court of last resort, but at a lower level when the unsuccessful party throws in the towel by simply letting an appeal period expire. He accepts the judgment against him by default.

Thereafter it is final, and neither side will be permitted to litigate the matter anew. This doctrine is known as *res judicata*, which *Black's Law Dictionary* defines as the "rule that a final judgment rendered by a court of competent jurisdiction on the merits is conclusive as to the rights of the parties, and an absolute bar to a subsequent action involving the same matter." *Res judicata* is a fundamental principle of the law of the English-speaking peoples.

Now while a judgment in a civil case, right or wrong, may be final, this can never be so in a criminal case. If at a later date it is discovered that the defendant is innocent the judgment must be set aside and he must be set free. So whenever the words "finality" and *res judicata* are used in this discussion, it is with this implicit caveat. A criminal judgment is never truly final because justice may require it be undone.

Nothing in the Habeas Corpus Act prohibits a federal court from reviewing and overturning a conviction in a state court. The limitations on their power to do so are self-imposed as a matter of comity under our federal system. "Comity" is the respect and deference due the decisions of state courts. Too little would be an abdication of their mandate under the Habeas Corpus Act; too much would unduly interfere with the administration of criminal justice in the states. A balance must be struck.

In 1885 the Supreme Court established as a rule of comity that no application for habeas corpus should be granted unless the "applicant has exhausted the remedies available in the courts of the state."[2] In 1948 Congress incorporated this requirement into the Habeas Corpus Act.[3] The exhaustion rule eliminated the vast majority of felons who had acquiesced in their convictions by failing to appeal. It limited the use of habeas corpus in a federal forum to reverse a state criminal conviction to those who had pursued their appellate remedies to the state court of last resort.

Only a defendant whose appeal had been denied by a state court of last resort could appeal his conviction to a federal court, and the only federal court to which he could appeal was the Supreme Court of the United States. While there is only one United States Supreme Court there were hundreds of federal judges, each of whom, but for the comity required by federalism, had the power to undo through habeas corpus the conviction of a state felon. The exhaustion requirement prevented a convicted defendant from accomplishing collaterally, by way of habeas corpus, what Congress had forbidden him to do directly by appeal.

Take the case of someone tried for the crime of armed robbery in a state court. The prosecution offers into evidence a confession said to have been made by the defendant. The defense objects on the ground the incriminating statement was involuntarily made, so that its admission into evidence would be a violation of the defendant's constitutional rights. The trial judge orders the jury

---

2 *Ex Parte Royal*, 117 U.S. 241 (1885).

3 28 U.S.C. 2254.

to retire and hears the evidence going to this discrete issue outside of their presence.

The prosecution produces a number of witnesses, including
policemen, who testify to the circumstances surrounding the confession. Their testimony, if true, would show it was made freely
and voluntarily. These witnesses are cross-examined by defense
counsel and their testimony remains unshaken. The defense then
produces witnesses, including perhaps the defendant, who testify to facts that, if true, call for a finding that the confession was
coerced. The trial judge decides to accept the testimony of the
witnesses for the prosecution as being true and reject that of the
defense as being false. He finds the confession to be voluntary
and admits it into evidence.

The jury is recalled, the trial resumes, and the same testimony
with respect to the circumstances of the confession is repeated
by both sides. At the conclusion of the trial the judge charges the
jury that before considering the confession at all, they must first
determine that it was voluntary. The jury retires, deliberates, and
returns a verdict of guilty. The judge sentences the defendant to
a term in prison. The time in which he may appeal elapses so that
his conviction becomes final.

Now this defendant has had his day in court. The judge and
jury heard him testify, if he chose to testify, as well as those who
testified against him, and found him guilty beyond a reasonable
doubt. To do so required they believe that the prosecution witnesses told the truth. The recurring question is under what circumstances, and to what extent, will a federal habeas court permit
this convicted felon to reopen and relitigate the facts going to the
validity of his confession.

In *Daniels v. Allen*, decided in 1953, the defendants had missed
the deadline in which to file their appeal to the North Carolina
Supreme Court. By not making a timely appeal, they had not
exhausted available state remedies and so lacked standing. "A failure to use a state's available remedy, in the absence of some inter-

ference or incapacity . . . bars federal habeas corpus. The statute requires that the applicant exhaust available state remedies. To show that the time has passed for appeal is not enough to empower the Federal District Court to issue the writ."[4]

> The writ of habeas corpus in federal courts is not authorized for state prisoners at the discretion of the federal court. It is only authorized when a state prisoner is in custody in violation of the Constitution of the United States. 28 U.S.C. 2241. That fact is not to be tested by the use of habeas corpus in lieu of an appeal. To allow habeas corpus in such circumstances would subvert the entire system of state criminal justice and destroy state energy in the detection and punishment of crime.[5]

The default was the result of a most curious lapse on the part of defense counsel. Bennie and Lloyd Daniels were tried and convicted of first-degree murder and sentenced to death. Under North Carolina law, they had 60 days in which to prepare an appeal and serve it on the state solicitor. The trial record was voluminous and 50 days passed before defendants' counsel received the typed transcript from the court stenographer. This in itself was more than adequate grounds for the defense to request an extension of time. The granting of such an application would have been pro forma. No prosecutor in the country would have opposed it and no judge would have denied it. Yet, no extension or waiver of time to serve the statement was made, and none was requested.[6]

A copy of the papers filed in court by an attorney for one side in a case must be served on the attorney for the other side. Customarily such service is done by mail. The original document is filed in court together with an affidavit stating that a copy has been mailed

---

[4] *Daniels v. Allen* decided *sub.nom.* (under the name of) *Brown v. Allen*, 344 U.S. 443, 487 (1953).

[5] Id., 485.

[6] *State v. Daniels*, 231 N.C. 17, 56 S.E. 2d, 2, 3 (1949).

to the opposing counsel. Such documents are usually enclosed in a cover sheet on which there are preprinted forms of "Affidavit of Service by Mail" which may be completed by inserting in the blanks the date of mailing, and the name of the addressee and the affiant. It is the date upon which the paper is mailed, and not the date upon which it is received, that controls. All of this is common practice in the legal profession.

By his own statement defense counsel Herman L. Taylor of Raleigh completed the necessary papers for appeal on Thursday, August 4, 1949, one day prior to the deadline. The following day, Friday, he telephoned the Solicitor's office in Greenville, and was told the Solicitor had taken his family to the beach for the weekend, and would not return until Monday. At this point all Taylor had to do was to place the appeal papers in an envelope addressed to the Solicitor's office, with sufficient postage affixed, and deposit the same in the U.S. mail. The appeal would have been served on time and the deadline met.

But Mr. Taylor did not avail himself of this expedient. Instead, he let the day pass and the appeal period lapse. On the next day, a Saturday, now in default, and knowing the Solicitor was away for the weekend, Mr. Herman Taylor journeyed the 70 miles to Greenville and personally handed the appeal papers to the Solicitor's secretary.

It is a grievous matter for a lawyer to miss such a deadline, and have the rights of his client foreclosed by default. It is unthinkable in a case of life and death. Nor was it an oversight. Either Mr. Taylor was the most inept of lawyers, or he deliberately was trying to set up a scenario in which the Supreme Court of the United States would be forced to choose between the exhaustion rule or the execution of two defendants whose rights had manifestly been prejudiced by inadequate legal counsel. This casual handling of the matter is especially intriguing given that Herman L. Taylor, Esq. was an ACLU "Cooperating Attorney."[7]

---

[7] A roster of "Cooperating Attorneys of the American Civil Liberties Union" dated June 1, 1966 lists seven such attorneys in North Carolina of whom one is

✿   ✿   ✿

While the attorney for the Daniels brothers did not succeed in overturning their conviction, he had succeeded in delaying their execution for almost three years and there was nothing to prevent him from doing the same thing over and over again. Apparently the abuse of habeas corpus as a dilatory tactic had proliferated to such an extent that Justice Jackson, in a concurring opinion, described it as a "caricature of the great writ." "Certainly the use of the federal courts as aids to such delaying tactics as are evidenced here does not elevate the stature of the writ of habeas corpus. We have no mythical abuse here but a very real problem of harassment of the state."[8] A few months before the decision in *Daniels v. Allen*, in fact between the time that case was argued and the time it was decided, a conference of the Chief Justices of the States of the Union took place and the following resolution was adopted:

> Conference of Chief Justices—1952, 25 State Government, No. 11, p. 249 (Nov. 1952).
>
> Whereas it appears that by reason of certain principles enunciated in certain recent federal decisions, a person whose conviction in a criminal proceeding in a State Court has thereafter been affirmed by the highest court of that State and, whose petition for a review of the State Court's proceedings has been denied by the Supreme Court of the United States, may nevertheless obtain from a Federal district judge or Court, under a writ of habeas corpus, new, independent, and successive hearings based upon a petition supported only by the oath of the petitioner and containing only such statement of facts as were, or could have been, presented in the original proceedings in State Courts;

"Herman L. Taylor, P.O. Box 1923, Greensboro, North Carolina [telephone] 275-3065."

8 *Daniels v. Allen, supra,* 538.

And whereas the multiplicity of these procedures available in the inferior Federal Courts to such convicted persons, and the consequent inordinate delays in the enforcement of criminal justice as the result of said Federal decisions will tend toward the dilution of the judicial sense of responsibility, may create grave and undesirable conflicts between Federal and State laws respecting fair trial and due process, and must inevitable lead to the impairment of the public confidence in our judicial institutions;

Now therefore be it resolved that it is the considered view of the Chief Justices of the States of the Union, in conference duly assembled, that orderly Federal procedure under our dual system of government should require that a final judgment of a State's highest court be subject to review or reversal only by the Supreme Court of the United States.[9]

There is something wrong with a system in which a single federal district judge has the power to reverse the judgment of the highest appellate tribunal of a state by overruling on the same evidence the facts found against the petitioner by the jury and judge who tried the case and heard the testimony. This power, say the Chief Justices of the States of the Union, should be vested only in the Supreme Court of the United States.

The overwhelming majority of the prison population is composed of felons who have either pleaded guilty or failed to appeal their conviction. In the limited sense with which these words may be used in the field of criminal justice, the judgments against them are final and *res judicata*. Assuming a state's procedures for review are fair and adequate, they would not be subject to collateral attack in a federal court in a habeas corpus proceeding. Only those who had pursued their appeal to the state court of last resort were eligible.

---

[9] Id., 539.

This situation was not to the liking of Justice William J. Brennan, Jr. In October of 1961, four months after *Culombe v. Connecticut* and *Mapp v. Ohio* had been decided, Justice Brennan, always a farseeing man, delivered a lecture at the University of Utah Law School, advocating, in effect, the abandonment of the "exhaustion" rule. He cited the Daniels case as a prime example of inequity.

> The case was this: Two boys, 17 and 18 years old and illiterate, were convicted of murder and sentenced to death. State procedures required the filing of the prisoners' appeal within 60 days of the conviction. Counsel did not receive from the court stenographer any of the trial record until 30 of the 60 days elapsed, and the last 200 pages of the 500-page record were not received until a mere 10 days remained. The 60th day was a Friday, and the appeal was ready on Thursday. Friday morning, counsel phoned the state officer on whom the appeal had to be served, but that officer could not be reached because he had gone to the beach for the weekend. If counsel mailed the appeal on Friday, the 60th day, the state requirement of timeliness would have been satisfied. Instead, he delivered it personally on Saturday morning, the 61st day, and although that personal delivery was at least as early as the mail would have been, and although the state officer did not return to see the material until Monday morning, the State Supreme Court refused to hear the appeal on the ground that it was out of time.[10]

But things have changed since *Daniels*, said Justice Brennan, "when release on habeas corpus required a showing that the proceeding in the state court was void for want of jurisdiction . . . Perforce as the Supreme Court brings state criminal proceedings more and more within the protection and limitations of the Federal Bill

---

[10] Brennan, *Federal Habeas Corpus and State Prisoners: An Exercise in Federalism*, 7 Utah Law Review, 423, 430 (1961).

of Rights, federal habeas corpus jurisdiction will correspondingly expand."[11]

> But now . . . under one formulation or another the Supreme Court has extended to state prisoners many of the procedural safeguards of the Federal Bill of Rights. Violations of these safeguards may be redressed in federal habeas corpus since the statute reaches not merely convictions void for lack of jurisdiction in the tribunal, but convictions secured in violation of constitutional rights.[12]

As Brennan spoke, the case that will expand habeas corpus, to meet the emerging needs of the new jurisprudence he has in store for us, was being concocted in New York, where, so it appears, an ogre from Brooklyn had imprisoned Charles Noia, and was holding him for ransom. Twenty years earlier, in 1942, Noia, along with Santo Caminito and Frank Bonino, had been convicted by a Kings County jury of the robbery and murder of a jeweler. Used against them at their trial was a confession obtained under questionable circumstances.

First the trio was interrogated by police over an extended period during which no incriminating statements were elicited. Then Noia, Caminito and Bonito were faced with three individuals who identified them as the perpetrators. This was a ruse. These "eye-witnesses" in fact were detectives and they had not been present when the crime was committed. A few hours after this confrontation, individually and as a group, the three defendants confessed to the murder. Later they recanted, claiming they had been beaten and deprived of food and sleep.

Caminito and Bonino appealed, and their convictions were upheld by New York's highest appellate court. By so doing they had exhausted their remedies in the courts of the state, one of

---

[11] Id., 440.

[12] Id.

the preconditions of federal habeas corpus. Noia did not appeal. When the jury had found the three defendants guilty of felony murder they had included in their verdict a recommendation of mercy. This meant that the judge was permitted, but not obliged, to sentence them to life-imprisonment instead of death.

Noia had confessed to being the triggerman and the statements of his two co-defendants had corroborated this admission. Before imposing sentence the judge told Noia that he originally had decided to disregard the jury's recommendation as to him, and to sentence Noia, but not Caminito and Bonino, to death. Noia was lucky, the judge told him, that he had changed his mind that morning. Noia knew if he appealed and won, he would be retried. If convicted once again he could be sentenced to death.

Ten years later Caminito sought a writ of habeas corpus and in 1955 the Second Circuit Court of Appeals, overruling the federal district court, held that his confession had been obtained in violation of the Fourteenth Amendment.[13] In an impassioned opinion Circuit Judge Jerome Frank characterized the treatment of Caminito as "satanic"[14] and analogized the behavior of American policemen in general to that of the Russian N.K.V.D.[15] Judge Frank described himself as an "old-fashioned liberal."

> It will not do to say—as some do—that deep concern with such problems of the humble is the mark of an "old-fashioned liberal." For repeated and unredressed attacks on the constitutional liberties of the humble will tend to destroy the foundations supporting the constitutional liberties of everyone. The test of the moral quality of a civilization is its treatment of the weak and powerless.
>
> Reversed.[16]

---

13 *Caminito v. Murphy, Warden*, 222 F.2d 698 (1955).

14 Id., 701.

15 Id., 702-703.

16 *Id.*, 706.

The career of Jerome Frank was closely intertwined with that of William O. Douglas. Both had been professors at Yale Law School. Frank, "high-strung, intellectual, fiercely liberal . . . helped to found the school of jurisprudence known as Legal Realism. In his 1930 book, *Law and the Modern Mind* . . . Frank suggested that most legal rules were little more than the arbitrary imposition of shifting prejudices manufactured by fallible and sometimes irrational judges."[17]

With the advent of the New Deal both men went to Washington, Frank to the Agricultural Adjustment Administration and Douglas to the Securities and Exchange Commission. Douglas was Chairman of the SEC when he was named to the Court in 1939. It was on the recommendation of William O. Douglas that FDR appointed Frank to succeed him at the SEC.[18] Jerome Frank also owed his seat on the Second Circuit Court of Appeals to Justice Douglas, who had lobbied the President on his behalf. "Jerry," Douglas wrote Roosevelt, "would really be 'tops' in CCA."[19]

After Caminito's success, Bonino reargued his case before the New York Court of Appeals and that court, positing their decision on the opinion of Judge Frank, set aside his conviction.[20] With Caminito and Bonino now free, Noia applied for a writ of *corum nobis* to the court which had originally convicted him, praying his conviction be vacated on the ground that his confession was coerced as well. Kings County Judge George J. Joyce granted his petition:

> Here we have this defendant Noia sitting out a life sentence
> in one of the state prisons on a conviction on a state of facts
> and law which it is conceded are identical with those of his

---

[17] Michael E. Parrish, *Felix Frankfurter And His Times: The Reform Years*, New York: The Free Press (1982), 227.

[18] Douglas Letters, See commentary at p. 31.

[19] Douglas Letters, January 3, 1941, William O. Douglas to Franklin D. Roosevelt, 215.

[20] *People v. Bonino*, 1 N.Y.2d 752, 135 N.E. 2d 51 (1956).

codefendants Caminito and Bonino, on a conviction that our highest courts held in the Caminito and Bonino decisions to be an unlawful one and in violation of due process.

This Court is convinced that it would be a travesty of justice to withhold from petitioner the relief he seeks in view of the tainted antecedents of the conviction entered against him. To withhold the relief because of the procedural technicality would compound the injustice and on any conception of constitutional law it would be unthinkable to condemn petitioner to serve out a life sentence on the palpable illegal conviction . . . [21]

Noia was released on bail and was at liberty for almost two years, during which time he married and fathered a child.[22] In the meanwhile, however, Assistant District Attorney William I. Siegel, who handled the case throughout, had appealed Judge Joyce's ruling on a technicality having to do with the nuances of the writ of *corum nobis* and was successful in having it reversed. Noia was remanded to state prison to serve out his life sentence.[23] After the Supreme Court declined to hear his appeal,[24] Noia sought a writ of habeas corpus in federal court. He was being held in custody by Edwin M. Fay, Warden of Green Haven Prison, he alleges, in violation of the Constitution of the United States. The District Attorney did not dispute this; in fact, he entered into this astonishing stipulation.

It has been stipulated between counsel herein that: "For purposes of this proceeding, the District Attorney of Kings County concedes that the coercive nature of the confession

---

21 *People v. Noia*, 3 Misc. 2d 447, 158 N.Y.S. 2d 683, 686 (1956).

22 Transcript of Record, *Edwin M. Fay, as Warden of Greenhaven Prison, State of New York*, and *The People of the State of New York, Petitioners, against Charles Noia, Respondent*, filed in the Supreme Court of the United States November 30, 1962, Docket No. 84, Petition for Writ of Habeas Corpus, 24.

23 3 N.Y. 2nd 596, 601, 148 N.E. 2d 139 (1958).

24 357 U.S. 905.

elicited from the respondent and introduced in evidence against him at the trial in Kings County Court was established and, therefore, the record of trial need not be printed."[25]

The District Attorney's position was not that Noia was not being held in custody in violation of the Constitution, only that the federal courts were powerless to intervene. On oral argument he had this exchange with Federal District Judge John W. Cashin:

THE COURT: Let me interrupt you here.

MR. SIEGEL: Yes, Sir.

THE COURT: Do you stand here and tell me that because this man did not take an appeal the Court is powerless to do anything about it?

MR. SIEGEL: Absolutely.

THE COURT: That is a situation where our Court of Appeals said that this confession was unconstitutionally obtained . . .

THE COURT: Do you mean to say then that this particular man is powerless to do anything because he did not take an appeal from the conviction?

MR. SIEGEL: In a nutshell, yes . . .

THE COURT: Do you admit that what Mr. Edelbaum said that there was not any evidence in this case except the confession?

MR. SIEGEL: Oh, yes . . .

THE COURT: You had none then and of course you have none now?

MR. SIEGEL: Yes. I am urging that you do not have the power.

THE COURT: I do not know whether I have or not, but if I have, I am going to exercise it.

MR. SIEGEL: I think you will.

[25] Transcript, *Respondent's Brief*, 15.

THE COURT: There is no question about that.[26]

Like all federal courts, the Supreme Court is limited in its jurisdiction to deciding "cases" or "controversies" arising under the Constitution or laws of the United States. The Court may not initiate action, but only may decide cases brought before it by litigants. It may not render advisory opinions at the behest of private parties or other branches of government. A decision by the Supreme Court on a point of law necessary to the determination of a case, under *stare decisis*, becomes an axiom in the adjudication of future cases.

The doctrine rests on the implicit assumption that a case on which a precedent is based was a genuine "case" or "controversy" honestly arrived at. To put it another way, our jurisprudence will be subverted if precedents can be created by means of bogus cases argued by lawyers masquerading as adversaries when they are really allied in achieving the same end. The validity of *stare decisis* therefore depends on both sides of a legal argument being fairly represented by counsel. Anything less than the most skilled and dedicated advocacy before the nation's highest court is inadequate. Anything short of arm's length dealing, in the utmost good faith, is unfair. To suborn the selection, or to collude or connive in the prosecution of a case, strikes at the very heart of our jurisprudence.

What militates against *Fay v. Noia* being a genuine "case" or "controversy" is the otherwise inexplicable behavior of Kings County Assistant District Attorney William I. Siegel. It is hard to believe a prosecutor could be so satanic as Mr. Siegel, much less admit it in open court. Forty years later, the distinct odor of mackerel lingers. So let us do what people do when they are suspicious, and entertain a hypothesis more in accord with human experience.

Let us postulate that Charles Noia, Santo Caminito and Frank Bonino were in fact guilty of the first degree murder of jeweler Murray Hammeroff and that the district attorney was certain of

---

[26] Transcript, *Transcript of Hearing before USDC - SDNY*, March 8, 1960, 28-33.

this. The reason it did not trouble him to have Noia remanded to prison was not that William Siegel was a man without a conscience, it was that his conscience was clear. He knew Noia had shot the jeweler and that if he served another five years in prison justice would not be offended.

The Kings County Court which had convicted Noia in 1942 vacated its own judgment in 1956 because Noia's conviction was "manifestly unlawful" and "common decency and substantial justice" required it to be set aside. Why then did the district attorney appeal? What was it he was trying to prove? The streets of the Borough of Brooklyn, County of Kings, in the City of New York provide enough grist to keep the district attorney's mill in business. They are compromising cases every day that, given the resources, they would prosecute to the hilt. Why squander them fighting a seven-year appeal?

His argument in the federal court was monstrous. The charge against Noia we now agree is baseless, said Mr. Siegel in effect; we'll even stipulate his conviction is unconstitutional, and that Noia's petition is correct. New York is holding Noia in custody in violation of the Constitution of the United States. So what? We don't deny that; all we say is that the federal courts can't do anything about it. Judge Cashin could hardly believe his ears.

For a prosecutor to admit, as Siegel did of Noia, that there is no evidence against him but his confession, and then to stipulate that the confession was coerced, is nothing short of a stipulation in Noia's case that New York, for 18 years, had imprisoned a man whose innocence the law is bound to presume. One would think the highest priority of the district attorney's office would have been to set Noia free.

There had to be others involved besides Siegel. They, too, were aware that Caminito, Bonino and Noia were guilty of the murder for which they were convicted but were willing to set them free to further what they considered to be a greater good. The precedent established in *Fay v. Noia* was indispensable to the success of the judicial revolution for which they were striving and this was a once-in-a-lifetime scenario. Here are three defendants convicted of the same crime, in the same trial, on the same confession. One of them—Charles Noia—cannot avail himself of federal habeas corpus review because he did not appeal his original conviction to the highest appellate court of the state. If the convictions of Caminito and Bonino can be reversed, the Supreme Court would have to choose between upholding the "exhaustion" rule or condemning a presumptively innocent Charles Noia to life imprisonment on the basis of a confession clearly unconstitutional.

There was nothing to be gained by New York in the way of precedent. The law was, and always had been, that a convict in a state prison must have exhausted his appeals in the state courts before he would be permitted to reopen and relitigate his conviction in a federal habeas corpus proceeding. What the Brooklyn District Attorney did in *Fay v. Noia* was the legal equivalent of giving his adversaries what in the sports of hockey or soccer is called a "penalty shot." He himself could not score a point, the best he could do was to make a "save." In the event, he gave them their goal.

Justice Brennan announced the Court's decision. In an opinion of almost 50 pages he traced the history of the Great Writ back to the Middle Ages. On this side of the Atlantic, after being incorporated in our Constitution in 1789, habeas corpus was pressed into service to obtain the release of Bollman and Swartwout, Aaron Burr's agents in his seditious undertaking. Lambdin Milligan in 1866, and Richard Quiren in 1942, both sentenced to death by a military tribunal, made muster. *Frank v. Mangum* and *Moore v. Dempsey* were cited in due course. "This case," said Justice Brennan, "presents important questions touching the federal habeas corpus jurisdiction . . . in its relation to state criminal justice."

The narrow question is whether the respondent Noia may be granted federal habeas corpus relief from imprisonment under a New York conviction now admitted by the State to rest upon a confession obtained from him in violation of the Fourteenth Amendment, after he was denied state post-conviction relief because the coerced confession claim had been decided against him at the trial and Noia had allowed the time for a direct appeal to lapse without seeking review by a state appellate court.[27]

Fay v. Noia did not abolish the exhaustion rule, it simply held that the rule "is limited in its application to failure to exhaust state remedies still open to the habeas applicant at the time he files his application in federal court."[28] In other words, Noia's failure to appeal his conviction in 1942 does not prevent him from seeking to overturn it now, twenty years later, by way of federal habeas corpus, since his time to appeal to a state appellate court has long since expired and is no longer available.

This seems simple enough, indeed one wonders why no one had ever realized this before. Like the Supreme Court, for example, when it held in *Daniels v. Allen* that the validity of a conviction in a state court "is not to be tested by the use of habeas corpus in lieu of an appeal. To allow habeas corpus in such circumstances," said the Court, "would subvert the entire system of state criminal justice and destroy state energy in the detection and punishment of crime."[29] But to Justice Brennan, it was a simple matter of fundamental fairness.

> Surely no fair-minded person will contend that those who have been deprived of their liberty without due process of law ought nevertheless to languish in prison. Noia, no less than his codefendants Caminito and Bonino, is conceded to have been the victim of unconstitutional state action. Noia's case stands on its own; but surely no just and humane legal system can tolerate a result whereby a Cami-

---

[27] *Fay v. Noia*, 372 U.S. 391, 394 (1963).

[28] Id., 435 (emphasis added).

[29] 344 U.S. 485.

nito and a Bonino are at liberty because their confessions were found to have been coerced yet a Noia, whose confession was also coerced, remains in jail for life. For such anomalies, such affronts to the conscience of a civilized society, habeas corpus is predestined by its historical role in the struggle for personal liberty to be the ultimate remedy. If the States withhold effective remedy, the federal courts have the power and the duty to provide it. Habeas corpus is one of the precious heritages of Anglo-American civilization. We do no more today than confirm its continuing efficacy. Affirmed.[30]

To effective law enforcement *Fay v. Noia* was a disaster of epic proportions. It did wonders, however, to facilitate the reversal of convictions thought to be final. Whereas a defendant may appeal a decision of the highest appellate court of a state only to the Supreme Court of the United States, a habeas corpus application may be made to any federal judge. This opens up a lot more thoroughfares to convicted felons who want to take a "walk."

The irony is that the case of the not-proven-guilty-by-stipulation Charles Noia will be used as a precedent to free vast numbers of convicted criminals whose guilt had been proven beyond any doubt. Never again will we see a habeas corpus case reach the Supreme Court involving a conviction that all men acknowledge was fundamentally wrong. Quite to the contrary, the future petitioners will be convicts like Robert Williams, who all acknowledge, at least tacitly, murdered Pamela Powers. Their posture will be not that they are innocent, but that the Court must release them anyway because the evidence used to prove their guilt should have been excluded. Convictions sometimes will be reversed years later, when it is no longer possible to reassemble the case. In his 1976 book *Where the Money Was*, Willie Sutton—

---

[30] Id., 441.

a/k/a "Willie the Actor," bank robber, escape artist and jail-house lawyer—gave us an insider's view of *Fay v. Noia*:

> The question that came to the Court was this: Does a conscious and knowing failure of a state prisoner to "seek his remedies" [appeal] within the state system prevent him from asserting a Constitutional right forever after?
>
> For 175 years, the answer had been that it did. In *Fay v. Noia* 372 US 391 (1963), the Supreme Court said that maybe it did once but it sure as hell wasn't going to any longer . . .
>
> The most important from a philosophical and psychological point of view was that the Court had not only rejected the government's argument that Noia had made "an intelligent and understanding waiver" of his rights in preferring the life sentence to the risk of ending up in the electric chair, it turned the argument on its head by ruling that his fear of the electric chair had made it impossible for him to make an "intelligent and understanding" waiver . . .
>
> No case was ever dead, it was as simple as that.[31]

The author had gotten out of prison several times the old-fashioned way. But Willie was getting a little long-in-the-tooth for jailbreaks and he used *Fay v. Noia* to get out the easy way—to walk through the front gate. Before he did, he helped some of his fellow convicts to do the same. "Through it all, I had been continuing my growing legal practice . . . After I had walked a couple of guys out by drawing up the appropriate writs, everybody had begun to come to me for help. Boy, I'll bet I got a couple of dozen people out of there."[32]

Once Sutton was consulted by an inmate who had been convicted of murder. "He had made a full confession and then tried to withdraw it during his trial." The inmate claimed the police had "tricked" him into confessing. "He asked me a number of times

---

[31] William F. Sutton. *Where the Money Was*, New York: Viking Press, 1976, 291-292.

[32] Id., 295.

to look his case over and see whether I could find some kind of technicality for him." Sutton read the minutes of his trial. "When I had finished reading it I knew two things; I knew that he was the Buffalo Strangler and I knew that I could put him back out on the street."[33] But Willie had a code of ethics. "I wouldn't help a rapist, a drug peddler, or a psychopathic killer."[34] Real lawyers labor under no such constraints. This is what Sutton thought of criminal defense lawyers, the "dirty shirts" as he called them:

> And whatever they might say in the law schools, it also helps to have a grudge against society. The criminal lawyer, like the criminal, is the enemy of Law and Order. The criminal attacks society head on; the lawyer is trying to set you free after you have been caught so that you can go out and steal some more. Whether he succeeds or not, he profits from your crime. The only way you can pay him is out of the money you have got away with at one time or another, everybody knows that. It isn't called his share of the loot, of course. It's called "the fee."[35]

Fay v. Noia, the habeas corpus case we have just seen, will make it ever possible for a convicted felon to relitigate the validity of his conviction and the facts upon which it is based. The sun will never set on his day in court. We may now envision state penitentiaries as beehives of activity, swarming with inmates, transcripts in hand, consulting jail-house lawyers like W.F. Sutton, Esquire, in the hope that he can find a technicality which will put them back on the streets. The Legal Revolution, as Sutton put it, was underway.

---

[33] Id., 299.

[34] Id., 297.

[35] Id., 28.

CHAPTER 10

MALLOY v. HOGAN

N O JUSTICE HAS EVER SAT on the Supreme Court of the United States as long as William Orville Douglas. From his appointment in 1939 to his retirement in 1975, he was the subject of constant and severe criticism. It was not only his bizarre views on the law that came under attack, but his extra-judicial activities as well. But Bill Douglas had his admirers, and none were more ardent than his former law clerks. Upon his retirement a number of them published encomiums the obsequiousness of which would have sickened Uriah Heap. The winner in this toadying contest was Yale Law Professor Steven B. Duke.

> It was my life's greatest privilege to have served as the Justice's law clerk in the 1959 Term, and to have counted him a friend. Yet writing a tribute to him on his retirement is as difficult as some of the tasks he gave me as his clerk. One strains for words that can reflect his incandescence, his elan, his courage . . . His essence is elusive and cannot be captured in a conventional verbal harness. . .
>
> His is a highly disciplined mind that when at work moves at electric speed, devouring facts and ideas like a giant threshing machine . . . A raconteur of easy wit and charismatic charm, he makes all around him feel warm and worthy, when moments before they had felt slow and stupid, mesmerized by his dynamic drive and brilliance.[1]
>
> The cat-quick mind, the restlessness, the impish grin and the warm wit; the soft, boylike voice, the hint of shyness

---

[1] "A Tribute to Mr. Justice Douglas," *9 Akron Law Review*, 399 (1976).

and the awesome extrusions of power and fearlessness were intact in all their contradictory colorations. His gait had slowed a bit since we last hiked the C & O Canal, but his energy and zest were undimmed.[2]

In the same article Professor Duke tells us how awful things were in the United States before Justice Douglas took his seat on the Supreme Court. "Police regularly ransacked homes and convicted the occupants with what they found . . . The States were free to compel self-incrimination, to make unreasonable searches and seizures, to deny speedy trials, to inflict cruel and unusual punishments."[3] He repeated the litany in another venue. "Police and prosecutors could suppress and fabricate evidence," he said at Harvard, "self-incrimination could be compelled, and the accused denied access to defense witnesses . . . Trial could be without a jury or an unbiased judge; double jeopardy and cruel and unusual punishment could be imposed; a speedy trial could be denied."[4]

It must be a continuing source of amazement to a person of this mindset that so many Americans, in the first six years of his idol's tenure, no less, were willing to squander their lives for a civilization so unworthy of preservation. One doubts, however, that the Justice sans pareil would have demurred. Douglas thought well of Duke too although he was able to capture him in more conventional verbal harness. "Duke and Ares," wrote Justice Douglas, were clerks of "high caliber."[5]

Professor Charles Ares[6] teaches law at the University of Arizona Law School, of which he and Professor Duke are both alumni.

---

[2] Id., 401.

[3] Id., 400.

[4] 11 *Harvard Civil Rights-Civil Liberties Law Review*, 241 (1976).

[5] *The Douglas Letters*. Melvin I. Urofsky Editor, Bethesda, MD.: Adler & Adler, 1987. William O. Douglas to Stanley E. Sparrowe, Dec. 29, 1959 and commentary, 51.

[6] The ACLU *Report of Activities* for 1984-85 and 1986-87 lists Charles Ares as a member of the National Advisory Council.

Professor Ares clerked for Justice Douglas in the 1952 term. When they were singing the praises of William O. Douglas at Harvard in 1976, his two acolytes were there to pay tribute. Professor Ares spent quite a bit of time telling the faithful how their hero's Fifth Amendment dream came true. While no names were mentioned in this context, we may be sure the cognoscente there assembled knew enough to give credit where credit was due.

> But in many cases these seemingly implausible views took hold and became law. For example, from the time of *Brown v. Mississippi*, the Court attempted to deal with the admissibility of confessions under an amorphous due process standard of voluntariness. Douglas insisted that what was really at stake was the privilege against self-incrimination, a constitutional right that could be shown to have been waived only by proving that the suspect had known of his right and freely given it up.
>
> The privilege against self-incrimination had not yet been applied to the states, and moreover, prior decisions in confession cases, even in federal court, did not rest on the privilege. But as the Court struggled to decide cases filled with conflicting evidence regarding coercion, it became increasingly clear that a more administrable standard was required. Finally in *Malloy v. Hogan*, the Court, in deciding that the privilege against self-incrimination applies to the states, acknowledged it had implicitly accepted the privilege as the underpinning of the rule against coerced confessions. It was to protect that privilege that in . . . *Miranda v. Arizona* the right to counsel was made applicable in the station house.[7]

This is an accurate, incisive account of how the *Miranda* rule came about. But we are getting ahead of our story. It is now the

---

7 Ares, *Mr. Justice Douglas*, 11 Harvard Civil Rights-Civil Liberties Law Review, 229, 230-1 (1976). [citations omitted and emphasis added]

15th of June, 1964, a perfect day for what in the 1960's was the Court's annual June surprise. Justice William J. Brennan, Jr., will give us the official version of *Malloy v. Hogan*, the case which, as Professor Ares said, led to *Miranda v. Arizona*.

> The petitioner was arrested during a gambling raid in 1959 by Hartford, Connecticut police. He pleaded guilty to the crime of pool selling, a misdemeanor, and was sentenced to one year in jail and fined $500. The sentence was ordered to be suspended after 90 days, at which time he was to be placed on probation for two years. About 16 months after his guilty plea, petitioner was ordered to testify before a referee appointed by the Superior Court of Hartford County to conduct an inquiry into alleged gambling and other criminal activities in the county. The petitioner was asked a number of questions related to events surrounding his arrest and conviction. He refused to answer any question "on the grounds it may tend to incriminate me."[8]

For refusing to answer the questions put to him, Malloy was held in contempt and imprisoned. He sought his release by way of habeas corpus against his jailer, Patrick J. Hogan, the Sheriff of Hartford County. Since Malloy would be protected by a one year statute of limitations on misdemeanors, as well as by the defense of "double jeopardy," the lower court saw no real or appreciable danger that Malloy's answers might incriminate him. It therefore dismissed the writ. This decision was upheld by the Connecticut Supreme Court of Errors on the same ground, and Malloy appealed to the Supreme Court of the United States.

Now *Malloy v. Hogan* could be an honest attempt by Hartford County to crack down on the local purveyors of football pools and the like. If Malloy can be made to testify the law can put them out of business and in jail. Since Malloy is not civic-minded enough to do so voluntarily, pressure must be brought to bear. To use a

---

[8] *Malloy v. Hogan*, 378 U.S. 1, 3 (1964).

figure of speech, what Connecticut is doing to Malloy is holding his feet to the fire to make him talk.

On the other hand, we have good reason to be suspicious of cases involving petty gamblers. They seem to have a way of setting the precedents which are later used to overturn the conviction of those who commit more serious crimes—murderers like Robert Williams, for example. A case involving a "pool seller" is immediately suspect.

Let us postulate that *Malloy v. Hogan* was a mere colorable dispute in which the nominal parties were acting in concert to elicit from the Supreme Court a precedent which later could be used to the prejudice of the law-abiding people of this country who had no idea of what was going on and thus no opportunity of being heard in defense of their rights. Let us examine the hypothesis that *Malloy v. Hogan* was not a genuine "case" or "controversy" to which the "judicial power" of the Supreme Court "extends," but in fact a sham in which the lawyers for both parties were working to the same end.

Although the object of this hypothetical case is to elicit a precedent which can be used to exclude confessions made without the presence of a lawyer, it must, ironically, be a case in which no incriminating statements were ever made. As a practical matter, a confession case cannot be colluded. The usual modus operandi will not work; the police would hardly "sweat" a confession out of a lottery ticket peddler and, in cases of more serious crime, the confessions arrive freighted with corroboration bound to have a prejudicial effect on the jury.

Take as an example *Culombe v. Connecticut*. There, the jury already knew Arthur Culombe had led the police to the swamp where he had disposed of the bloody raincoat, and the pond in which he had thrown parts of the gun used in the robbery and murder. In their confessions both he and his accomplice had evinced a knowledge of the layout of the gasoline station, and other circumstances of the crime, which could have been known only by the perpetrators.

Can a jury with a mental image of a car, empty but for an infant child, parked by the gasoline pumps of a New England service station on a December night, while her father lies dead in the men's room with two slugs behind his ear, be depended upon to judge the discrete question of volition objectively? Are they not apt to be influenced by the absolute but irrelevant knowledge that the accused is guilty of the crime to which he confessed?

Whether a confession is voluntary can only be decided after the fact. To deal with confessions after they have been corroborated puts the defense in an embarrassing position. By the time the case has been argued everyone knows the defendant committed the crime of which he was convicted. They can only find the confession involuntary by accepting the testimony of the defendant and rejecting that of the prosecution, when the trial court and jury, who had the advantage of observing the witnesses, did exactly the opposite. As Professor Ares pointed out, "a more administrable standard was required."

Now there is another way besides a confession in which a person might be compelled in a criminal case to be a witness against himself. He may be called to testify before a grand jury. While he may decline to answer questions which might incriminate himself, he may not refuse to testify against other parties with whom he may be involved. Should the authorities have little interest in prosecuting the witness, but need his testimony to pursue another quarry, they may decide to grant him immunity. Had Malloy been granted immunity, his testimony could no longer have been used against him. As far as Malloy was concerned the privilege would no longer be applicable. He would have had to answer the questions or go to jail. Either way, there would have been no such case as *Malloy v. Hogan*.

Suppose a prosecutor asks a pool-seller questions about other pool-sellers, and the privilege is invoked. "I refuse to answer," says the pool-seller, "on the grounds it might tend to incriminate me." "Your Honor," responds the prosecutor, "this claim of privilege is frivolous. This man is in no real or appreciable danger of incriminating himself. He is just trying to protect his associates, and his refusal to answer is a contempt of this court. I move that you commit him to the county jail until he purges himself by answering the questions."

The first thing that would occur to a judge is that if the state truly does not wish to incriminate the witness, why haven't they granted him immunity? Why should a prosecuting attorney attack a claim of self-incrimination, when he has at hand the means of obviating it? "I have little doubt, Mr. Prosecutor," the judge would respond, "that you are correct in your evaluation of the situation. But why not place the matter beyond any doubt, and grant this witness immunity? He will then have a very clear choice. He will either tell us about the others, or I will put him in jail until he does."

On what grounds could the prosecutor object to so reasonable a request? A refusal to grant immunity would only cast doubt on his motives. If in truth he does not want to incriminate the witness, let him, as the saying goes, "put his money where his mouth is." Under these circumstances, a judge would most likely uphold the invocation of the privilege, and would not order the witness to answer until he was provided immunity. In this event, there would be no such case as *Malloy v. Hogan.*

Now suppose, for the sake of argument, that a judge agrees with the prosecutor's assessment and disallows the privilege. The witness persists in his refusal to answer and is jailed for contempt. His application for a writ of habeas corpus is denied by the state courts and he appeals to the Supreme Court of the United States. Only in this scenario can you have such a case as *Malloy v. Hogan.*

But what kind of a "case" or "controversy" would this be? Suppose the prosecutor prevails in the highest Court? What has he gained? The witness must now answer his questions or go to jail. But this is the same "square one" where the parties would have been had he been granted immunity in the first place. So if the prosecutor was sincere, and not really trying to incriminate the witness, the appeal was a complete waste of time and money.

The prosecutor's constituents would wonder why he had squandered the resources of his office on an expensive and protracted appeal, when the simple expedient of granting immunity would have served as well. People would wonder how a case which established such an important precedent could have come about for so trivial a reason. Why, they might ask, was there ever such a case as *Malloy v. Hogan?*

This could bring on a confrontation in which ugly charges of collusion might be bruited about. *Malloy v. Hogan*, the mean-spirited would say, was not a case in which a pool-seller was being made to talk about other pool-sellers. They would say *Malloy v. Hogan* was but a sham, a facade behind which the attorneys on both sides of the case were working in concert to establish a precedent for the theory of incorporation that Justice Douglas had been advocating. Such an inquiry could easily turn into a "witch hunt," in which other precedents and "hard won gains" might be threatened.

In Connecticut, however, a prosecutor had a plausible excuse he could fall back on. The Nutmeg State did not at the time have an immunity statute as it does now.[9] Neither the prosecutor nor the court, nor both of them together, could grant a witness immunity in exchange for his testimony.[10] This quirk in that state's law was a little known fact, one not known, as we shall see, to the National District Attorneys' Association. Connecticut was apparently the only state in which such a case as *Malloy v. Hogan* could have arisen.

---

[9] 54-47 (a) adopted in 1969. (CK)

[10] *State v. Roberts*, (year) 4 Conn. Cir. 271, 280 A. 2d 239, 241. (Need correct citation)

Two things in this case we may take as givens. John D. LaBelle, the State's Attorney for Hartford County, will not grant William Malloy immunity for his testimony, because Connecticut law does not permit him to do so. William Malloy will not answer John LaBelle's questions because the code by which he lives does not permit him to do so either. If *Malloy v. Hogan* was a sham, it was a well-planned sham, staged in just the right venue with just the right cast. Neither party could change position and prevent the case from going all the way.

It also provided a side issue, an escape hatch that the liberals could use to decide the case, should things not go their way. It is a moot question, one really incapable of resolution, whether a claim of privilege by someone in Malloy's situation should be allowed. It can be argued that a witness must give some inkling, where none is otherwise apparent, of the danger he apprehends. Otherwise it is the witness, and not the judge, who passes on his own claim. On the other hand, it is only the witness who can truly appreciate his own dilemma. Either an answer, or an explanation for his silence, might provide a link in a chain of evidence which could connect him to a more recent crime not barred by the statute of limitations, or a crime unrelated to the matter under investigation.

Malloy v. Hogan bears a certain resemblance to a type of proceeding before a tribunal that long ago used to convene in a room off the Great Hall at Westminster, the sky blue ceiling of which was adorned with gold stars. It came as close as one could get in the United States to replicating the situation of a political dissident or religious deviant hauled before the *Camera Stellata* for an inquisition into his political or religious associations.

The examinate was compelled to appear before the Star Chamber and to take the oath ex officio. If he refused to take the oath, or after taking it refused to answer the questions put to him, he could be jailed until he did. The inquisition was conducted in private and the suspect had no right to confront or question the witnesses against him.

William Malloy was ordered to appear before a referee[11] appointed by the Superior Court of Hartford County; if he did not, he could have been arrested and brought before it as a prisoner. If he refused to take the oath, or after taking the oath refused to answer the questions put to him, he could have been jailed until he did. The interrogation was held in private. Aside from the referee only the prosecutor and a stenographer were present. "Counsel was not permitted to be there," nor were members of the public.[12]

Upon first impression there is nothing unusual about this; much the same thing can be said about any other witness summoned before a grand jury in the United States today. There are only two differences, but they are vital. They are in fact what distinguishes a present day grand jury investigation from an inquisition before the Star Chamber. The first is that a grand jury is a panel of 12 to 23 individuals taken from the community at large. The *raison d'etre* of a grand jury is to interpose a buffer of ordinary citizens between someone suspected of a crime on one hand and those who wield official power on the other. The appointment by a local judge, at the request of the local prosecutor, of a retired judge to act as a referee—in effect, a one-man grand jury—defeated the very purpose of that institution.

The second distinction is that a grand jury may not compel a witness to incriminate himself. In situations where a witness refuses to answer on grounds of self-incrimination, the matter is handled quite simply. Either the invocation of the privilege is upheld and the witness dismissed, with the state retaining the right to prosecute him if it can, or the witness is granted immunity from prosecution and is compelled thereafter to answer questions

---

[11] "Referee. A person to whom a cause pending in a court is referred by a court, to take testimony, hear the parties, and report thereon to the court . . ." *Black's Law Dictionary*.

[12] Transcript: Oral Argument of Harold Strauch, Esq. on March 5, 1964, on behalf of Petitioner William Malloy, 3.

under the threat of imprisonment. The "inquisition" of William Malloy could have taken place only in Connecticut.

The people involved *nisi prius* were retired Judge Ernest A. Inglis, acting as a referee, Hartford County Superior Court Judge Frank Covello, who appointed him, and Hartford County State's Attorney John D. LaBelle. There were no nosey civilians about, jurors who might cock a quizzical eye and wonder about the order of priorities of those charged with the duty of enforcing the law in Hartford County.

The proceedings were remarkably expeditious. Subpoenaed on January 15 and questioned before Judge Inglis on January 16 and 25, 1961, William Malloy was jailed for contempt on January 26. His attorney applied for a writ of habeas corpus forthwith. The writ was dismissed and judgment entered on February 7. Considering the time allotted and the veniality of the offense Judge Covello wrote an uncommonly good opinion.

On February 8, Malloy's attorney made an application for a certification "that a question is involved in the decision that was made in the herein case that should be reviewed by the Supreme Court of Errors."[13] Judge Covello signed an order to that effect the same day. The following day Malloy, now free on bond, filed his appeal. On February 9, 1961, 23 days after the case began with the service of the subpoena on William Malloy, *Malloy v. Hogan* was before Connecticut's highest appellate court.

Malloy was at all times represented by Harold Strauch, a local attorney. On April 19, 1963, after the Connecticut Supreme Court ruled against Malloy, Strauch filed a petition for a writ of certiorari in the Supreme Court of the United States. The question presented was whether the Connecticut court erred in holding that the Fifth Amendment does not apply to state proceedings. On May 17, Assistant State's Attorney Harry W. Holtgren, Jr., filed a statement

---

13 Transcript of Record, *William Malloy, Petitioner* vs. *Patrick J. Hogan, Sheriff of Hartford County,* filed in the Supreme Court of the United States, April 19, 1963, Docket 110, Petition for Certiorari, Brief for Petitioner, 14, 15.

in opposition on behalf of the respondent Sheriff Hogan. It was most perfunctory. Certiorari was granted June 3, 1963.

On August 24 attorney Strauch filed a brief urging reversal. "Inasmuch as the Fifth Amendment is indissolubly entwined with the Fourth Amendment," says he, "it logically follows that the provision of the Fifth Amendment protecting any person in a criminal case from testifying against himself should be extended likewise by the Fourteenth Amendment to cover State proceedings, as it does Federal proceedings."[14] "The *Mapp* case cleansed a smudge from the escutcheon of Justice . . . Another smudge can be removed by a reversal of the decision of the State Court in this case . . . The right to become untrammeled in this area of constitutional guarantees is of no less standing and validity than in *Mapp*."[15] One has the impression here that Squire Strauch may be a decoy to mask the approach of the real adversary. We shall give Strauch and his heraldic metaphors free passage and wait for a foeman worthy of our steel. On September 20, 1963, the ACLU, with the consent of both parties, filed a brief amicus curiae. Its position was stated in the opening two paragraphs.

BRIEF FOR AMERICAN CIVIL LIBERTIES UNION AMICUS CURIAE

The American Civil Liberties Union is a private nonpartisan organization engaged solely in the defense of the Bill of Rights. Our interest in the case at bar revolves around the due process of law, specifically, the Fifth Amendment privilege against self-incrimination and its application to the states through the Fourteenth Amendment. We believe that the privilege should be held applicable to the states as part of the "fundamental law" of our nation. Due process requires nothing less than that *Twining v. New Jersey*, 211 U.S. 78 (1908) be overruled.

---

14 Transcript, Brief for Petitioner, 3, 4 (citations omitted).

15 Id., 14, 15.

Let us examine this brief and speculate on how a lawyer for the Connecticut sheriff might respond. The opening line of the ACLU argument—"When the barons wrested Magna Charta from King John at Runnymede in 1215"—tells us we are in for a lecture in history. The "rack and screw" of the Inquisition make their obligatory appearance. The point of law decided in *Maxwell v. Dow* is reargued as if it were an original proposition without that case ever being mentioned. Congressman John A. Bingham of Ohio and Senator Jacob M. Howard of Michigan are resurrected to reconstruct the passage of the Fourteenth Amendment for our benefit.

To prove that it is clear that the framers of the Fourteenth Amendment intended that Amendment to make the Bill of Rights binding on the states, the ACLU offered as proof the following: "In placing the proposed amendment before the Senate of May 23, 1865 (sic), Senator Howard spoke as follows: 'To these privileges and immunities . . . should be added the personal rights guaranteed and secured by the first eight amendments of the Constitution.'" There is no doubt Senator Howard's words evince an understanding that the Fourteenth Amendment was meant to incorporate the Bill of Rights. But this was the very argument made and rejected by the Supreme Court in 1900 in the case of *Maxwell v. Dow*:

> "What individual Senators or Representatives may have urged in debate, in regard to the meaning to be given to a proposed constitutional amendment, or bill of resolution, does not furnish a firm ground for its proper construction, nor is it important as explanatory of the grounds upon which the members voted in adopting it." This is all the more true in the case of a constitutional amendment which, as the Court pointed out, "must be agreed to, not only by Senators and Representatives, but must be ratified by the legislatures, or by conventions, in three fourths of the States before such amendment can take effect."[16]

---

[16] *Maxwell v. Dow*, 176 U.S. 581, 601-602 (1900).

We would not have to pore over dusty volumes of the Congressional Record to demolish the ACLU's argument. The exhaustive study by Professors Charles Fairman and Stanley Morrison gives us all the ammunition we need. The relevant statements of the legislators and leaders of the post-Civil War period are catalogued in this treatise. All but Senator Howard and Congressman Bingham expressed an understanding inimical to incorporation. Those two statements by Howard and Bingham are quoted in the ACLU brief without mentioning the fact that these two legislators later took positions irreconcilable to the position the ACLU attributes to them.

These would be among the points naturally occurring to someone seriously arguing the case for the state and for the people. Yet they go unmentioned in this brief filed on behalf of the respondent Sheriff Hogan, and the revisionist history of the ACLU and its incorporation argument was allowed to pass unchallenged. Uncited was *Maxwell v. Dow* and the Stanford study which would have put the lie in their teeth. Contrary words of Bingham and Howard as well as a host of others were likewise left unquoted.

The brief made not even a passing reference to the fact that under the Connecticut law then extant, neither the prosecutor nor the court had the power to grant Malloy immunity. It was imperative that this idiosyncrasy in Connecticut law be clearly stated so that anyone reading the brief would not assume, as did the National District Attorney's Association in their brief amicus curiae, that: "To honor these privileges [against self-incrimination] without sacrificing vital investigations of crime, all of the states have passed statutes that grant immunity from prosecution for any state crime revealed by a witness, in exchange for the witness's testimony."[17]

Few things can be more gratifying to a lawyer than to have his words immortalized in the United States Reports. Just seeing the

---

[17] Brief of National District Attorney's Association, dated October, 1963, *Amicus Curiae*, 2. (CK filing date)

numbered volumes sitting in a row on the library shelf gives him a warm feeling and a sense of accomplishment. It is a resource he can draw upon in time of trouble. At the end of a hard day he can always take that special volume and turn to the well worn pages that contain his contribution to American jurisprudence and thereby gain renewal.

Like most general propositions, this one needs to be qualified. Whether the quotation appears in the Court's opinion, or in a dissenting opinion usually makes a difference. To a client, it might make an even bigger difference. But what is most critical are the words which immediately precede the quotation. "As learned counsel for the respondent has so forcefully pointed out" gets top grades. Somewhere in the middle is "counsel for the respondent has argued that." This can go either way.

The world's worst record, the one that stands today, was set in *Malloy v. Hogan.* On pages 9 and 10 of that opinion are 137 words excerpted from the Respondent's Brief by Justice Brennan which became footnote 8 right after he wrote: "The respondent Sheriff concedes in his brief that under our decisions, particularly those involving coerced confessions, the accusatorial system has become a fundamental part of the fabric of our society and, hence, is enforceable against the States."

> Underlying the decisions excluding coerced confessions is the implicit assumption that an accused is privileged against incriminating himself, either in the jail house, the grand jury room, or on the witness stand in a public trial.
>
> . . . It is fundamentally inconsistent to suggest, as the Court's opinions now suggest, that the State is entirely free to compel an accused to incriminate himself before a grand jury, or at the trial, but cannot do so in the police station. Frank recognition of the fact that the Due Process Clause prohibits the States from enforcing their laws by compelling the accused to confess, regardless of where such compulsion occurs, would not only clarify the principles involved

in confession cases, but would assist the States significantly in their efforts to comply with the limitations placed upon them by the Fourteenth Amendment.[18]

This concession was unnecessarily broad and entirely gratuitous. *Malloy v. Hogan* was not a confession case, nor was it analogous to one. A suspect interrogated at a police station is not put under oath or punished by contempt if he refuses to answer. The Connecticut prosecutor should have been making these distinctions clear, not blurring them. Indeed this was something one would expect to find in the ACLU brief. The prosecutor's behavior raises questions, to say the very least, that *Malloy v. Hogan* was not a genuine "case" or "controversy" to which the judicial power of the Supreme Court extends, but a sham in which the lawyers on both sides of the case were working towards the same result.

On January 27, 1961, the Superior court issued a writ of habeas corpus ordering Hartford County Sheriff Patrick J. Hogan to produce William Malloy and show cause why he was being detained.[19] On the same day Justice Douglas wrote a letter of recommendation[20] on behalf of his former clerk, Steven Duke, to his friend Eugene Rostow, the Dean of Yale Law School. Before entering political life Justice Douglas, it should be pointed out, served as Sterling Professor of Law at that institution.[21]

I have your letter inquiring about Steven Duke for the Yale Law Faculty.

I can recommend him without any qualifications. Of the 25 or more law clerks I have had, he ranks among the first few in terms of a teacher's potential. In fact, I have seen but a few of all the law clerks to all the Justices who would compare with him in that regard.

---

[18] *Malloy*, 9, 10.

[19] Transcript, 2.

[20] The Papers of William Orville Douglas, container 278. Manuscript Division, Library of Congress. The letters are arranged chronologically.

[21] Urofsky at xiv.

He is quiet and unobtrusive as you know. But his fires burn brightly. He has a real dedication to the law as an instrument of justice, as an expression of the democratic ideal, as a reflection of the dignity and worth of the individual. I think he will be an outstanding teacher.

In the state courts Sheriff Hogan was represented by Hartford County Prosecutor John D. LaBelle and his assistants George D. Stoughton and Harry W. Hultgren, Jr.[22] The same was true in the Supreme Court of the United States. Were one simply to read *Malloy v. Hogan* in Volume 378 of the U.S. Reports, that person would have no reason to believe any other lawyer was involved in preparing the brief so useful to the other side.

But if you look at the brief itself, something very few would ever have occasion to do, you would ascertain that there was a fourth lawyer—Steven B. Duke. His name appears below that of Mr. LaBelle, but above that of Mr. Stoughton and Mr. Hultgren. This arrangement suggests it was Mr. Duke who wrote the brief, a fact that Mr. LaBelle has confirmed. In a telephone conversation on September 11, 1990, Mr. LaBelle told the author that Steven Duke wrote the brief and that he, Mr. LaBelle, edited it. According to LaBelle, he found Duke and not the other way around, leading us to wonder why a prosecutor and his two assistants would engage an outside lawyer to write a brief on a case involving a pool-seller.

From various directories we glean that Steven Barry Duke was born in Mesa, Arizona, on July 31, 1934, received a B.S. degree from Arizona State University in 1956, and a law degree from the University of Arizona in 1959. He then proceeded to Washington, where he clerked for Justice Douglas during the term ending in June 1960.

The following September found Mr. Duke in New Haven as a graduate fellow at Yale Law School. By January of 1961, when the

---

[22] *Malloy v. Hogan, Sheriff*, 150 Conn. 220, 187 A.2d 744 (1963).

case of *Malloy v. Hogan* began in Hartford, he had applied for and
was being considered for an opening on the faculty. The Douglas letter of recommendation and Malloy's writ of habeas corpus
are dated the same day. In June of 1961 Yale awarded Steven B.
Duke the degree of L.L.M., and soon thereafter Mr. Duke became
a member of the faculty of Yale Law School. This was his status
in 1964 when he wrote the Brief for Sheriff Hogan.

Apparently his defeat in *Malloy v. Hogan* was not held against
him, for in 1966 he became a tenured professor of law at Yale,
where he remained for many years. Professor Duke was something of a gadfly who spent a lot of his time fighting for meritorious
causes *pro bono publico*. Not long after *Malloy v. Hogan* was decided
in 1964, we find "Prof. Steven B. Duke, Yale Law School, New
Haven," working as a volunteer lawyer for the ACLU[23] reporting
on a case he hopes will be of interest to the members.[24] In *Who's
Who in American Law* he has listed himself for many years now
as a member of the American Civil Liberties Union as well as a
director of something called the "New Haven Legal Assistance
Assn. 1968-70."

A 1979 article in *Time*[25] magazine—entitled "Rescuer In Red
Velvet"—captured the professor in battle harness. There is even
a picture of "Duke in his Yale Office." His attire appears to be a
trifle medieval, as if he were about to argue a case at Camelot. My
colleagues, he told *Time*,

> do not consider me a good role model, says Duke, 39, who
> favors red velvet suits and wears his blond hair over the col-
> lar. "They say I do not know how to lose" . . . "Every so

---

[23] Civil Liberties Docket (XIV: 1968-1969). Ann Fagan Ginger, editor. (Berkeley,
California: Meiklejohn Civil Liberties Library, 1968-69). [JC 599. U5 C5811 Volume 14] page 106, subchapter 391.

[24] See also *New Haven Journal Courier* January 23, 1967, 1, "Yale Professor's Argument May Invalidate Two Laws."

[25] *Time*, January 14, 1979, 49.

often," says the tenured professor, "my dean and I have a little talk and since I have never done the outside writing that is expected, he wants to know what I am doing with my time."

The Dean of Yale Law School apparently had not been paying close enough attention to his crimson-clad knight errant with the flowing golden tresses. Perhaps this is because he was so quiet and unobtrusive and came so highly recommended. But the Rescuer In Red Velvet did "know how to lose," of that his colleagues could be sure.

"It was my life's greatest privilege," wrote Steven Duke of William O. Douglas in 1976, "to have served as the Justice's law clerk in the 1959 term, and to have counted him as a friend." But that "highly disciplined mind that when at work moves at electric speed, devouring facts and ideas like a giant threshing machine" must have stripped a gear when its proprietor saw the name of his former law clerk on the brief for the respondent Sheriff Hogan. This could blow their cover.

Someone apparently took this breach of security seriously enough to try to hide it. When the first report of *Malloy v. Hogan* came out in Volume 12 of the Lawyer's Edition of the Supreme Court Reporter, at page 1316, after the names of LaBelle, Stoughton and Hultgren, it is stated that "Steven B. Duke filed a brief for respondent." But by the time *Malloy v. Hogan* took its place in the United States Reports this statement had been deleted. The name of Steven B. Duke is never mentioned. But since the Lawyer's Edition is only an interim reference, few would ever have noticed. Once a case is published in the United States Reports the Lawyer's Edition becomes redundant. No one would ever have reason to refer to it.

Affirmative steps were required. Who took them? It is safe to assume that no clerk would have taken it upon himself to make this deletion. We may also dismiss modesty as a consideration.

Jokers who go to court in red velvet suits do not hide their light under a bushel. The order could only have come from on high. The behind the scenes roles of William O. Douglas and William J. Brennan, Jr. as the orchestrators of the incorporation process will not be fully documented until we find out.

CHAPTER 11

BY HOOK OR BY CROOK

WILLIAM J. BRENNAN, JR., sat on the Supreme Court for 34 years. His retirement in 1990 was followed by an outpouring of adulation unmatched since William O. Douglas had taken his leave 15 years before. No one was more fulsome than Harvard Law Professor Laurence H. Tribe, who crafted an ode entitled, "Justice William J. Brennan: Architect of the Bill of Rights" (never mind the founding fathers). "How can one pay adequate tribute," it began,

> to a judge who has already been called "the judicial scholar's scholar," "the most outstanding justice of our century," and "one of the greatest judicial scholars, public officials and human beings mankind has ever known?" I can only add to these well-earned accolades my own words of admiration for a man whose work will long occupy a prominent place in American constitutional law.[1]

To Professor Tribe, Justice Brennan's most significant contribution was the doctrine of "selective incorporation" which in the 1960's "fundamentally reshaped the law of this land . . . [O]f the key cases he authored only *Malloy v. Hogan* . . . which made applicable to the states the Fifth Amendment right against compelled self-incrimination . . . *Malloy* was the first decision to speak explicitly in 'incorporationist' terms and to make clear that the relevant provision of the Bill of Rights applied to the

---

[1] *Tribe,* 77 American Bar Association Journal, 48 (1991).

states exactly in the same way that it applied to the federal government."[2]

Professor Tribe was right about one thing. *Malloy v. Hogan* was the keystone of Brennan's theory of "selective incorporation." But his "behind the scenes role as one of the principal orchestrators of the incorporation process,"[3] contrary to Tribe's understanding, has not been documented as fully as it should be, nor have the other "behind the scenes" orchestrators been given proper credit.

In 1920, Roger Nash Baldwin founded the ACLU and went on to serve as its Executive Director for the next 30 years. After his retirement in 1950, Baldwin remained on the Board of Directors and was the guiding spirit of the Union until his death in 1981. In his obituary, the New York Times quoted the encomiums of Ira Glasser, the ACLU's director, and Norman Dorsen, its president, to the departed. Baldwin was "one of the titans of American history [and] in a way one of our country's founding fathers—they wrote the Constitution, and he invented a way to enforce it."[4]

The *Report of Activities* of the American Civil Liberties Union for 1986-87 provides a more forthright description of the Baldwin approach to constitutional law: "It is the job of the courts to enforce the Bill of Rights, but they cannot act on their own initiative. While Congress and the President can initiate action, the courts are powerless to fulfill their function unless an aggrieved person complains by filing a lawsuit."[5] The Report hastens to tell us who stepped into the constitutional void so thoughtlessly left by our Founding Fathers.

The ACLU was the missing ingredient that made our constitutional system finally work. Most of what we today recognize as constitutional rights were established within the past 35 years — barely more than the last 15 percent of the bicentennial period. In

---

[2] Id., 49.

[3] Id.

[4] "Roger Baldwin, 97, is Dead: Crusader for Civil Rights; founded the A.C.L.U." *New York Times*, August 29, 1981.

[5] *Report of Activities 1986-87*, American Civil Liberties Union, 8.

a very real sense, the ACLU and other organizations outside the government function, in effect, as a fourth and truly independent branch, part of the system that checks abuses of power. We are the ignition for the constitutional engine, the key that makes it run.[6]

The key which is inserted into the ignition for the constitutional engine is what the ACLU openly calls a "manipulated test case."[7] Constitutional law to the ACLU is, to paraphrase Clausewitz, simply a continuation of politics by other means. They care not whether Incorporation is an historical truth, or a valid interpretation of the Fourteenth Amendment. They see it only as a means to their ends.

The first eight amendments protect certain values by rule. All that can be defined to fall within the ambit of a rule is forbidden, whether or not this be fair or just under the circumstances of the case. This is a deductive judgment arrived at syllogistically. The judge must be a logical judge—an Aristotle. The major premise is the constitutional amendment in question, and the minor premise the facts in the case at bar. The task of the judge is to determine whether or not the latter comes within the meaning of the former. It is a process of classification or labeling in which the judge bears no moral responsibility for the outcome. He is an amanuenses. If the results be unfair or unjust in the case before him, that is the price the Framers were willing to pay to keep certain values inviolate.

In contradistinction, due process of law—like equity—required that justice be done in the case at hand. It cared not what something may be called or labeled, or whether or not it fell within the ambit of any rule. This was necessarily a judgment made a posteriori. The facts and circumstances of the case were weighed in the light of the judge's own knowledge and experience. He had to be a wise judge—a Solomon. In deciding a due process case a

---

[6] Id., 9.

[7] Peggy Lamson. *Roger Baldwin — Founder of the American Civil Liberties Union.* Boston: Houghton Mifflin, 1976. "In many instances the ACLU acted to achieve what they referred to as a 'manipulated test case,'" 157.

judge bore the full moral and political responsibility for the consequences of his decision. He was a plenipotentiary. If there was a miscarriage of justice, he had failed as a judge. The Constitution, and those who wrote it, were not to blame.

Cases in which due process of law required of the states that which a specific guarantee of the Bill of Rights required of the federal government, seldom reached the nation's highest court. One would suspect this was for the same reason the "learned" in Cicero's Case were rarely called upon to review prize claims for storm-battered ships brought to port by able-bodied seamen who stayed aboard through the tempest. They were always awarded to the claimants at dockside and there was no reason to appeal.

Due Process of Law and the specific guarantees of the Bill of Rights are not contradictories; the affirmation of one is not the denial of the other. Most often they should bring about the same result. If this were not generally true something would be terribly wrong with our constitutional scheme of things. This jurisprudence was known as fundamental fairness defined by the Court as "natural equity under universal law."[8]

In the 1890's, to widen a street, the City of Chicago took by eminent domain certain parcels of land including part of the right-of-way of the Chicago, Burlington & Quincy Railroad Company. The damages awarded the C.B. & Q. by the state court was the nominal sum of $1.00. The railroad appealed, claiming they had been "deprived of" their "property," without the "due process of law" required by the Fourteenth Amendment.

There was never any question but that the railroad was entitled to fair compensation for the real property taken by condemnation. However, the damages to the C.B. & Q. in this regard were somewhat more abstruse than those of the rest of the property owners on the block. The reduction in value to a person's house and lot, by having the front ten feet lopped off, and taken in fee simple absolute, will vary according to circumstance. It is something, how-

---

[8] *C.B.&Q. Railroad v. Chicago*, 166 U.S. 226 (1897)

ever, that someone familiar with real estate values in the area can appraise. What Chicago took from the C.B. & Q. was essentially an easement across its right-of-way, so that when the railroad was not actually exercising its franchise to run its trains east and west, we will say, city traffic could cross north and south.

The appraisal of the C.B. & Q.'s damages was found to be neither unfair nor unreasonable. The Court upheld the award and denied the appeal of the C.B. & Q. What the Fourteenth Amendment requires of the states with respect to the rights of property, held the Court, is natural equity under universal law. Not once in the Court's 30 page opinion is either the Fifth Amendment or its clause "nor shall private property be taken for public use without just compensation" so much as mentioned. Nonetheless, in *Malloy v. Hogan*, Justice Brennan took C.B. & Q. to be the birth of "Selective Incorporation."

> The extent to which the Fourteenth Amendment prevents state invasion of rights enumerated in the first eight Amendments has been considered in numerous cases in this Court since the Amendment's adoption in 1868. Although many Justices have deemed the Amendment to incorporate all eight of the Amendments, the view which has thus far prevailed dates from the decision in 1897 in Chicago B. & Q. R. Co. v. Chicago, 166 U.S. 226, which held that the Due Process Clause requires the States to pay just compensation for private property taken for public use.[9]

From history and their colonial experience, the Framers of the Constitution recognized certain areas as being fertile fields for abuse. This, in part, is why they enacted the Bill of Rights. The Bill of Rights consists of those guarantees of the specific articles of the first eight amendments plus the "due process of law" guarantee of the Fifth Amendment. That the first eight amendments spoke only to the federal government, and not to the states, is an

---

[9] *Malloy v. Hogan*, 378 U.S. 1, 4 (1964).

indisputable historical fact.[10] The Fourteenth Amendment, which does apply to the states, and only to the states, contains none of the specific guarantees of the first eight. However, a body of law had evolved under which the basic rights and freedoms of the people were protected from invasion by state governments under the aegis of Due Process of Law. *Gitlow v. New York*, Justice Brennan's next case,[11] spoke directly to that point.

Benjamin Gitlow was a member of the "Left Wing Section of the Socialist Party" who in 1919 published what he called "The Left Wing Manifesto," advocating the overthrow of government by force and violence.[12] He was thereafter tried and convicted of the crime of "criminal anarchy," a felony under New York law. When his conviction was upheld by the highest appellate court in New York, Gitlow appealed to the Supreme Court of the United States. The State of New York, claimed Gitlow, had deprived him of the liberty of expression guaranteed by the due process clause of the Fourteenth Amendment. The Court proceeded on the following assumption:

> For present purposes we may and do assume that freedom of speech and of the press—which are protected by the First Amendment from abridgment by CongressCare among the fundamental personal rights and "liberties" protected by the due process clause of the Fourteenth Amendment from impairment by the States.[13]

This is a clear and simple statement that the First Amendment and the Fourteenth Amendment both protect freedom of speech and of the press—the First Amendment from abridg-

---

[10] See *Barron vs. Baltimore*, 7 Peter 243 (1833).

[11] It was *Gitlow v. New York* which in 1925 "initiated a series of decisions which today hold immune from state invasion every First Amendment protection for the cherished rights of mind and spiritCthe freedoms of speech, press, religion, assembly, association and petition for redress of grievance." *Malloy v. Hogan*, 5.

[12] *Gitlow v. New York*, 268 U.S. 652, 655 (1925).

[13] *Gitlow*, 666.

ment by Congress and the Fourteenth from impairment by the states. These propositions do not admit of, much less support, a conclusion that the Fourteenth Amendment incorporated the First Amendment so as to make it applicable to the states. To the contrary, *Gitlow* dispels any such notion. Justice Holmes and Justice Brandeis, who voted to reverse Gitlow's conviction, were even more explicit. They also thought that the several states had more latitude in determining the scope of free speech under the Fourteenth Amendment than did the federal government under the First.

> The general principle of free speech . . . must be taken to be included in the Fourteenth Amendment, in view of the scope that has been given to the word "liberty" as there used, although perhaps it may be accepted with a somewhat larger latitude of interpretation than is allowed to Congress by the sweeping language that governs or ought to govern the laws of the United States.[14]

The Court held that "a State may punish utterances endangering the foundations of organized government and threatening its overthrow by unlawful means . . . Freedom of speech and press," said the Court, quoting Joseph Story, "does not protect publications or teachings [such as the Manifesto] which tend to subvert or imperil the government or impede or hinder it in the performance of its governmental duties."[15] Gitlow's conviction for "criminal anarchy" was upheld.

Except for a ban on bills of attainder and ex post facto laws there were no restraints in the original, unamended constitution on how the individual states should administer their criminal law. Three-quarters of a century and one civil war later, this was changed by the Fourteenth Amendment. The necessary result of any criminal conviction is that the defendant, at least to some

---

[14] *Gitlow*, 672-673.

[15] *Gitlow*, 667.

degree, is deprived of either life, liberty or property. The Four-teenth Amendment restrains the states in the execution of their criminal law to the extent that it ordains that such a deprivation may not be accomplished without that certain something called "due process of law." Due process is always ad hoc, as was *Gitlow*; it dealt with the case at hand and no other.

> The precise question presented, and the only question which we can consider under this writ of error, then is, whether the statute, as construed and applied in this case by the state courts, deprived the defendant of his liberty of expression in violation of the due process clause of the Four-teenth Amendment.[16]

In 1917, two years before Benjamin Gitlow published the "Left Wing Manifesto," Charles Schenck was convicted of distributing pamphlets intended to disrupt enlistment programs and cause insubordination in the armed forces of the United States during World War I, a felony under the Espionage Act. Even if the pur-pose of the pamphlets was to interfere with the war effort, con-tended Schenck, it was nonetheless "free speech" protected by the First Amendment from abridgement by Congress. *Schenck v. United States*, in which his conviction was upheld, is remembered for this famous passage:

> The most stringent protection of free speech would not pro-tect a man in falsely shouting fire in a theatre and causing a panic . . . The question in every case is whether the words used are used in such circumstances and are of such a nature as to create a clear and present danger that they will bring about the substantive evils that Congress has a right to pre-vent. It is a question of proximity and degree.[17]

---

16 *Gitlow*, 664 (emphasis added).

17 *Schenck v. United States*, 249 U.S. 47, 52 (1919).

It is hard to see, given the flexibility of the "clear and present danger" test, how the freedom of speech guaranteed Gitlow by the due process clause of the Fourteen Amendment from impairment by the states, is meaningfully different from that protected by the First Amendment from abridgement by Congress. But while that may be true in the case of *Gitlow*, it is not true across the board.

When a judge applies the First Amendment, he envisions a large circle inside of which are the cases of those whose voices have been repressed by overreaching officialdom. John Peter Zenger, a printer and publisher, whose conviction of criminal libel in pre-revolutionary America for exposing British corruption in New York City, tops the list. It was the Zenger case, more than any other, that was in the minds of the Founding Fathers when they drafted the First Amendment. When a case involving free speech is judged by the First Amendment, the answer is usually a simple "yes" or "no." If the complainant falls within the ambit of the circle he has cognizable First Amendment rights; otherwise he does not. But—and this is a most important "but"—all those within the hypothetical circle are equals; there are no degrees.

In 1989, for example, the Court, in an opinion written by Justice Brennan, struck down a Texas statute prohibiting the desecration of the flag.[18] Brennan cast the First Amendment net wide enough so as to include what he called "symbolic free speech." Had the Fourteenth Amendment and its standard of due process remained the test, the outcome might well have been different. The issue then would not have been whether a flag burner is entitled to due process of law, but rather what process of law he was due under the facts and circumstances of his case. And neither Gregory Lee Johnson nor the freedom of expression he laid claim to, were comparable to the case of John Peter Zenger. The exposure of political corruption is, while the desecration of the flag is not, a right "basic to our free society" and "of the very essence of

---

[18] *Texas v. Johnson*, 91 U.S. 97 (1989).

a scheme of ordered liberty." To label them both "free speech" does not make them equals.

Incorporation had always rested on the supposition that the 39th Congress, in framing the Fourteenth Amendment in 1866, had intended thereby to incorporate the first eight amendments so as to make them applicable to the states. This theory, whose great exponent was Justice Hugo Black, had been rejected in 1947 by the Supreme Court in *Adamson v. California* and thoroughly investigated and discredited in the 1949 *Stanford Law Review* article by Professors Fairman and Morrison.[19]

But to Justice Brennan incorporation was a strategic imperative without which his judicial revolution could not be accomplished. And neither ethical niceties nor intellectual honesty would be permitted to stand in the way. In the face of history and ninety years of constitutional precedent, Justice Brennan knew he had take a different approach. To distinguish it from Justice Black's theory—now dubbed "total incorporation"—it was called "selective incorporation" and was launched by Brennan in a Fourth Amendment case contrived by the ACLU[20] in which the Court split four-to-four. Brennan posited his brainchild on this passage from Cardozo's opinion in *Palko v. Connecticut*.

We reach a different plane of social and moral values when we pass to the privileges and immunities that have been taken over from earlier articles of the federal bill of rights and brought within the Fourteenth Amendment by a process of absorption. These in their origin were effective against the federal government alone. If the Fourteenth Amendment has absorbed them, the process of absorption has had its source in the belief that neither liberty nor jus-

---

[19] *Does the Fourteenth Amendment incorporate the Bill of Rights?*, 2 Stanford Law Review, 5-173.

[20] Scully, *Bombers, Bolsheviks, supra*, 311-315. The case was *Ohio ex rel Eaton v. Price*, 364 U.S. 263 (1960). As the same source shows, *Frank v. Maryland*, 359 U.S. 360 (1959) is of the same genre.

tice would exist if they were sacrificed. Twining v. New Jersey, supra, p. 99. This is true, for illustration, of freedom of thought, and speech. Of that freedom one might say that it is the matrix, the indispensable condition, of nearly every other form of freedom.[21]

This process of absorption, wrote Justice Brennan, "is not a license to the judiciary to administer a watered-down subjective version of the individual guarantees of the Bill of Rights when state cases come before us."[22] He repeated this dicta the following year, adding that he could not "follow the logic which applies a particular specific for some purposes and denies its application for others . . . surely only impermissible subjective judgments can explain stopping short of the incorporation of the full sweep of the specific absorbed."[23]

The answer to this, as Brennan well knew, is that in the cases he cited as being supportive of this proposition, the "judiciary" was not applying a "watered-down subjective version" of a specific guarantee of the Bill of Rights, they were not applying a specific guarantee of the Bill of Rights at all. And the opinions of the justices who decided these cases, particularly Benjamin Cardozo and Felix Frankfurter, did everything they could to make clear that the question decided by the Court did not turn upon a specific article of the Bill of Rights, but upon fundamental fairness.

Of course fundamental fairness was ad hoc—it dealt with the case at hand and no other. The "least a defendant must do," said Cardozo, "is to show that in the particular case in which the practice is exposed to challenge there is a possibility that injustice has been done."[24] The "logic" which determined what was fair and what was not definitely was subjective—a judge reasoned

---

21 *Palko*, 326.

22 *Eaton v. Price*, 364 U.S. at 275.

23 *Cohen v. Hurley, supra* 158.

24 *Snyder, supra*, 97.

a posteriori from the circumstances of the case; the scales of justice were his tools, conscience was his guide.

The most egregious example used by Brennan was *Palko v. Connecticut* itself in which Cardozo rejected Palko's argument "that whatever is forbidden by the Fifth Amendment is forbidden by the Fourteenth also. The Fifth Amendment . . . was not directed to states, only to the federal government."[25] Justice Cardozo then went on to explain that not all of the privileges and immunities protected by the Bill of Rights were of equal value. There was a hierarchy in which "the immunity from compulsory self-incrimination" was a constitutional creature of a lesser order.

> The right to trial by jury and immunity from prosecution except as the result of an indictment may have value and importance. Even so they are not of the very essence of a scheme of ordered liberty. To abolish them is not to violate a "principle of justice so rooted in the traditions and conscience of our people as to be ranked as fundamental."[26]
>
> What is true of jury trials and indictments is true also, as the cases show, of the immunity from compulsory self-incrimination. Twining v. New Jersey, supra. This too might be lost, and justice still be done . . . Justice . . . would not perish if the accused were subject to a duty to respond to orderly inquiry.[27]

Now one would think that this would have laid the question to rest. If the "immunity from compulsory self-incrimination" is not "a principle of justice so rooted in the traditions and conscience of our people to be ranked as fundamental," it clearly did not meet Cardozo's test. Unlike "freedom of thought, and speech," without which neither liberty or justice would exist, the "immunity from compulsory self-incrimination" therefore

---

[25] *Palko*, 322.

[26] *Palko*, 325.

[27] *Palko*, 326 (footnote omitted).

was not "absorbed" by the Fourteenth Amendment. Nevertheless, in *Malloy v. Hogan*, Brennan seized upon the metaphor of "absorption" to impute to Cardozo the antithesis of the views Cardozo had expressed in *Palko*.

Frank Palko, you will recall, had been tried for the first degree murder of a police officer. The defendant had burglarized a store one night and shot the policeman while making his escape. At his first trial Palko was convicted of murder in the second degree only. He was acquitted of murder in the first degree because the trial judge erroneously instructed the jury that in determining whether the homicide was premeditated, they could not consider the fact that Palko had armed himself beforehand.

Under Connecticut procedure the prosecution was permitted to appeal, and this they did successfully. The Connecticut Supreme Court reversed the conviction and ordered a new trial. At the second trial Palko was convicted of murder in the first degree and sentenced to death. He appealed to the Supreme Court of the United States on the ground that this constituted double jeopardy within the meaning of that clause of the Fifth Amendment.

Now there is no getting around the fact that Frank Palko, for the same offense, was twice put in jeopardy of life. In a federal case the question would have been whether what was done to Palko constituted double jeopardy. If it did, then his conviction for first-degree murder would have to be set aside. Palko could not be convicted or punished for first degree murder in a federal forum because the Fifth Amendment forbids it. The fact that he is guilty of that crime is beside the point.

But this is a state case to which the Fifth Amendment does not apply. The question here was whether Connecticut was attempting to deprive Frank Palko of his life without the due process of law required by the Fourteenth Amendment. This, said Cardozo, is not determined by reference to the Fifth Amendment or whether Palko's second trial constituted double jeopardy. Label it anything you wish, there was but one question to be answered here. Is it unfair, or is it unjust, under the facts and circumstances of this case, to execute Frank Palko? Does it violate those "fundamental principles of liberty and justice which lie at the base of all our civil and political institutions?"

> The answer surely must be "no." What the answer would have to be if the state were permitted after a trial free from error to try the accused over again or to bring another case against him, we have no occasion to consider. We deal with the statute before us and no other. The state is not attempting to wear the accused out by a multitude of cases with accumulated trials. It asks no more than this, that the case against him shall go on until there shall be a trial free from the corrosion of substantial legal error.[28]

Frank Palko, a/k/a Frank Palka, died April 12, 1938 in the electric chair at the Connecticut State Prison at Wethersfield. According to an article—"Palka Dies; Murderer Calm in Face of Death"—on the front page of the *Bridgeport Times-Star* of April 13, "Palka strode, almost swaggered, into the oaken electric chair where he met his death a few moments after 10 p.m." Had Benjamin Cardozo thought that any Fifth Amendment right of Palko had somehow been "absorbed" into the Fourteenth Amendment, Frank Palko's departure from this world would have been less abrupt.

⚡ ⚡ ⚡

Malloy v. Hogan was to the Fifth Amendment and the law of confessions what *Mapp v. Ohio* was to the Fourth Amendment and the law of search and seizure. Each was a "manipulated test case" in which the American Civil Liberties Union appeared as amicus curiae. In both *Mapp* and *Malloy* the office of the prosecutor was subborned into working under cover with the ACLU to bring about the desired result. In each case a ruse was used to discourage uninvited amici curiae or throw them off the scent.

---

28 Id., 328 (emphasis added).

Organizations involved in law enforcement had taken to monitoring cases on the docket of the Supreme Court. The way they did this, and the only way they could do this, was by reading the briefs filed in the Supreme Court prior to oral argument to see if a case involved issues which would have an impact on law enforcement, and if it did, whether their viewpoint had been adequately represented.

Under the rules of the Supreme Court in effect at the time,[29] the appellant—the party granted the right to appeal the lower court's decision to the Supreme Court of the United States—and had 45 days in which to file a brief on the merits and serve it on the adverse parties. His adversaries, now called the respondents, then had 30 days to file a reply brief. The rules required each party to file 40 copies of any brief so that it could be disseminated to law libraries throughout the country. Any amicus curiae could file a brief, as did the ACLU, with the written consent of all parties. Absent that consent, anyone who wished to appear amicus curiae had to file a motion, within the time allowed the respondents to file a reply brief, requesting the court's permission to do so. "Such a motion is not favored," say the rules.

Mapp v. Ohio was, beyond question, the most significant case regarding the exclusionary rule since it was written into the Fourth Amendment in 1914. Yet no mention of a search or seizure issue was made in either the brief filed on behalf of either Mapp or the brief filed on behalf of Ohio. The only allusion to the exclusionary rule is contained in the brief filed by the ACLU by which time it was too late for a real adversarial amicus curiae to make an appearance. Years later retired Justice Potter Stewart retold the story without ever realizing the implications of his words.

The substantial federal question that prompted the Supreme Court to hear the appeal was whether the Ohio statute was vague and overbroad in violation of the first and

---

[29] *Rules of the Supreme Court of the United States.*

fourteenth amendment's free press guarantee; the overwhelming portion of the briefs and virtually all of the oral
argument were devoted to this issue. In fact . . . the issue
that the Court ultimately was to decide had been mentioned
only by an amicus curiae, the ACLU. Its twenty-page brief
included only a three-sentence paragraph at the very end
asking the Court to overrule its 1949 decision in *Wolf v. Colorado*, which had held that state courts were not required to
exclude evidence seized in violation of the fourth and fourteenth amendments. That the ACLU's argument was not
regarded by the parties as even a remotely important issue
in the case was made clear at the oral argument.[30]

To organizations such as the National District Attorneys' Association, *Mapp v. Ohio* would have looked like a real yawner. They
would have no reason to suspect that a case involving freedom of
speech would overrule 75 years of precedent in search and seizure
cases. Naturally the Fourth Amendment had to make an appearance. And so it was, but just barely. The paragraph in the ACLU
brief, couched in precatory terms,[31] was just right: enough so that
no one could say the issue was never raised but not enough to alert
the opposition. The Association never filed a brief. After the decision was handed down, however, they filed a petition for a rehear-
ing which was denied without opinion.[32]

The District Attorneys' Association did appear as amicus curiae in *Malloy v. Hogan*. Since the brief filed on behalf of the Connecticut sheriff made no explanation of why Malloy had not been
granted immunity, the District Attorneys' brief focused on state
immunity statutes about which they made this erroneous assertion: "To honor these privileges without sacrificing vital investi-

---

[30] Potter Stewart, *The Road to Mapp v. Ohio and Beyond: The Origins, Development
and Future of the Exclusionary Rule in Search and Seizure Cases.* 83 Columbia Law
Review 1365-1367 (1983) (citation omitted).

[31] Scully, 341, 342.

[32] 368 U. S., 871.

gations of crime, all of the states have passed statutes that grant immunity from prosecution for any state crime revealed by a witness, in exchange for the witness' testimony."[33] Connecticut, as we have seen, was an exception to this rule, as the brief for the Respondent Sheriff Hogan should have pointed out.

There were four other briefs filed in *Malloy v. Hogan*, not one of which addressed, much less advocated, Justice Brennan's theory of "Selective Incorporation"—the ground on which the case was decided and the precedent for which it stands today. In a tactic which in another context is called "bait and switch," the ACLU filed a brief which argued for incorporation—the "total incorporation" argument advanced by Hugo Black in *Adamson v. California*. Connecticut's brief, as we have seen, had let the ACLU's revisionist history pass unchallenged. Dissatisfied with this "advocacy," the Attorney General of California filed a three page brief as amicus curiae.

> While we support the position of respondent, we do so upon grounds not stated in respondent's brief. The law was settled by this Court not sixty years ago. (*Twining v. New Jersey*, 211 U. S. 78.) Forty years later, Twining was reaffirmed. (Adamson v. California, 332 U. S. 46.) Just three years ago, both Twining and Adamson were reaffirmed. (*Cohen v. Hurley*, 366 U. S. 117.) We would regard it, therefore, as unthinkable were they to be hastened into oblivion by any concession of respondent that they are tainted by time, that they are inconsistent with other decisions of this Court, or that they should no longer be law. (See Resp. Br. Pp. 6-17.)
>
> In our view, the historical record does not require this Court to hold, and would not justify this Court in holding, that the Fifth Amendment privilege against self-incrimination was incorporated into the Fourteenth Amendment by virtue of the latter's adoption. We are aware, of course, of the

---

[33] Brief of National District Attorneys' Association, *Amicus Curiae*, 2.

case argued with such eloquence and vigor by Mr. Justice Black. (*Adamson v. California*, 332 U. S. at pp. 68-123.) But the weight of the evidence is to the contrary. (See Fairman, "Does the Fourteenth Amendment Incorporate the Bill of Rights? The Original Understanding," 2 *Stanford L. Rev.* 5-139.)[34]

It was Brennan's thesis that in any case where, because of its circumstances, it had been held that fundamental fairness required of a state something which in a federal case would also have been required of the federal government by a specific guarantee of the Bill of Rights, that it was the intention of the justices who decided these cases that this specific guarantee was thereby "absorbed" into the Fourteenth Amendment and made applicable to the states. In a law review article in 1961 Brennan made an inventory of "how many of the specifics of the Bill of Rights have been held to be absorbed by the Fourteenth Amendment?"[35] He found four.

Three of the cases he cited to support his position—*B&Q v. Chicago*, *Gitlow v. New York* and *Wolf v. Colorado*—have already been discussed. The fourth was *Powell v. Alabama*, supra, in which, according to Justice Brennan, it was held that "Due Process requires the states to appoint counsel for an accused charged with an offense punishable by death, in accordance with the Sixth Amendment's requirement that an accused shall have 'the assistance of counsel for his defense.'"[36] Cardozo had said just the opposite in Palko.

> The decision [*Powell v. Alabama, supra*] did not turn upon the fact that the benefit of counsel would have been guaranteed to the defendants by the provisions of the Sixth Amendment if they had been prosecuted in a federal court. The decision turned upon the fact that in the particular situ-

---

[34] Brief of the state of California as Amicus Curiae, 2.

[35] *The Bill of Rights and the State*, 36 N.Y.U. Law Review, 761, 769 (1961).

[36] Id.

ation laid out before us in the evidence the benefit of counsel was essential to the substance of a hearing.[37]

The same device was used in *Malloy v. Hogan*. A quote would be lifted from dicta which superficially lent support to his argument. The holding of a case, the precedent for which it stood, that which explains the quote and belies the import Brennan put upon it, would be conveniently omitted. This is how "the judicial scholar's scholar, the most outstanding justice of our century," restated the holding of *Twining v. New Jersey*.

It was on the authority of that decision that the Court said in 1908 in *Twining v. New Jersey, supra*, that "it is possible that some of the personal rights safeguarded by the first eight Amendments against National action may also be safeguarded against state action, because a denial of them would be a denial of due process of law."[38]

Putting the quote back into its context in *Twining* we see that:

This contention requires separate consideration, for it is possible that some of the personal rights safeguarded by the first eight Amendments against national action may also be safeguarded against state action, because a denial of them would be a denial of due process of law. If this is so, it is not because those rights are enumerated in the first eight Amendments, but because they are of such a nature that they are included in the conception of due process of law.[39]

Cardozo, Frankfurter, and the other justices who had written the prior decisions upon which Brennan relied, had done everything possible to dispel any intention of incorporation. It was imputed to them nonetheless. Denials and protestations notwithstanding, osmosis had taken place. The Fourteenth Amendment,

---

[37] *Palko* 327. (Emphasis added)

[38] *Malloy v. Hogan*, 378 U.S. 4,5.

[39] *Twining*, 211 U.S. 99 (emphasis added, citation omitted).

like it or not, is now and forever permeated with the commands of whatever specific guarantees a majority of the Court may label fundamental. Fairness will no longer matter; judgment henceforth will be by rule, regardless of the circumstances of the case.

Malloy v. Hogan had nothing to do with a gambler named Malloy, a sheriff named Hogan, or "pool selling" in Hartford, Connecticut. They were just props. The sole purpose of this charade was to procure a precedent saying that the third article of the Fifth Amendment applied to the states. That being the case, the admissibility of a confession in a state case will no longer determined by whether or not it was voluntary, but on whether or not the defendant was a person who was "compelled in any criminal case to be a witness against himself."

To the uncomplicated mind this would seem to be distinction without a difference. But "the most outstanding justice of our century," as his fawning apostle called him, had a mind which was anything but uncomplicated. His opinion in *Malloy v. Hogan* converted what always had been regarded as an issue of fact into a question of law. Brennan, as Professor Tribe observed, also had a "special ability to lay a foundation in his opinions for future cases to follow."[40] The "Architect of the Bill of Rights" looked into his crystal ball and what he saw on the horizon was *Miranda v. Arizona*.

---

[40] Tribe, 49.

CHAPTER 12

THE FRUIT OF THE
POISONED TREE

IT HAD BEEN THE LAW IN NEW YORK from the very beginning that a confession was admissible provided it was voluntary, and not induced by force, fear, or favor. The constitutional validity of this law had been challenged and upheld in many cases including *Stein v. New York*, the *Reader's Digest* murder case. A goodly portion of the Empire State's inmate population was in prison after a trial in which their confessions had been found by a jury to be both voluntary and true. Many, including Stein, had been executed.

On June 22, 1964, one week after their decision in *Malloy v. Hogan*, the Supreme Court of the United States, by a vote of five to four, held the New York rule unconstitutional in *Jackson v. Denno, Warden*. Warden Denno was represented by William I. Siegel, the sweet-talking King's County Assistant District Attorney who had represented Warden Fay against Charles Noia the year before.

On June 14, 1960, at about 1 a.m., petitioner, Jackson, and Nora Elliott entered a Brooklyn hotel where Miss Elliott registered for both of them. After telling Miss Elliott to leave, which she did, Jackson drew a gun and took money from the room clerk. He ordered the clerk and several other people into an upstairs room and left the hotel, only to encounter Miss Elliott and later a policeman on the street. A struggle with the latter followed, in the course of which both men drew guns. The policeman was fatally wounded and petitioner was shot twice in the body. He managed to hail a cab, however, which took him to the hospital.

A detective questioned Jackson at about 2 a.m., soon after his arrival at the hospital. Jackson, when asked for his name, said, "Nathan Jackson, I shot the colored cop. I got the drop on him." He also admitted the robbery at the hotel. According to the detective, Jackson was in "strong" condition despite his wounds.[1]

There are two points in this case we need not belabor. That the confession is true and the petitioner guilty of murder no one can dispute. The Court's recital of the facts makes it absolutely clear that Nathan Jackson shot and killed New York City police officer William J. Ramos, Jr. as surely as Harold Rogers shot and killed Dorothy Kennedy. The point is that all of this is irrelevant.

It is now axiomatic that a defendant in a criminal case is deprived of due process of law if his conviction is founded, in whole or in part, upon an involuntary confession, without regard for the truth or falsity of the confession, *Rogers v. Richmond*, 365 U.S. 534, and even though there is ample evidence aside from the confession to support the conviction . . .

Equally clear is the defendant's constitutional right at some stage in the proceedings to object to the use of the confession and to have a fair hearing and a reliable determination on the issue of voluntariness, a determination uninfluenced by the truth or falsity of the confession.[2]

The problem with the New York rule, said the Court, is that the "jury is at once given both the evidence going to voluntariness and all of the corroborating evidence showing the confession is true and that the defendant committed the crime. The jury may therefore believe the confession and believe that the defendant has committed the very act with which he is charged, a circum-

---

[1] *Jackson v. Denno*, 378 U.S. 368, 370-371 (1964).

[2] Id., 376-377.

stance which may seriously distort judgment of the credibility of the accused and assessment of the testimony concerning the critical facts surrounding his confession."[3]

No one would quarrel with that. Jurors are reluctant to believe, once they know it to be an established fact, that a man who would hold up a hotel and shoot a policeman, would draw the line at perjury. Also, felony-murderers tend to lie a lot, and juries find them less credible as a class than, say, detectives. They are more apt to accept the testimony of the detective concerning the critical facts surrounding the confession than that of the defendant.

> In Jackson's case, he confessed to having fired the first shot, a matter very relevant to the charge of first-degree murder. The jury also heard the evidence of eyewitnesses to the shooting. Jackson's testimony going to his physical and mental condition when he confessed and to the events which took place at that time, bearing upon the issue of voluntariness, was disputed by the prosecution. The obvious and serious danger is that the jury disregarded or disbelieved Jackson's testimony pertaining to the confession because it believed he had done precisely what he was charged with doing.[4]

> Under the New York procedure, the evidence given the jury inevitably injects irrelevant and impermissible considerations of truthfulness of the confession into the assessment of voluntariness. Indeed the jury is told to determine the truthfulness of the confession in assessing its probative value.[5]

> Will uncertainty about the sufficiency of the other evidence to prove guilt beyond a reasonable doubt actually result in acquittal when the jury knows the defendant has given a truthful confession?[6]

---

[3] Id., 381.

[4] Id., 383.

[5] Id., 386.

[6] Id., 388.

The impact of *Jackson v. Denno* was staggering. At least 14 other states and six federal circuit courts of appeal followed the same rule as New York. For confessed felons in these jurisdictions, *Malloy* and *Noia* are their passes through the prison gate. In fact before the Court's holding is even a day old, its precedent has been used to vacate convictions in 11 cases in four states.

> Certainly if having the voluntariness of their confessions passed on only by a jury is a violation of the Fourteenth Amendment, as the Court says it is, then not only Jackson but all other state and federal prisoners already convicted under this procedure are, under our holding in *Fay v. Noia*, 372 U.S. 391, entitled to release unless the States and Federal Government are still willing and able to prosecute and convict them.[7]

Any prisoner in these twenty jurisdictions whose confession was used in evidence against him may now proceed by way of habeas corpus in a federal district court to have his conviction reversed. They are entitled to what the Court awarded Jackson, a hearing or a new trial, failing which the prisoner is entitled to his release. The 11 cases vacated in one day by the Supreme Court is but a trickle which will become a torrent when the federal district courts begin acting on habeas corpus petitions brought by freedom-loving felons. You can bet that jailhouse lawyers like Willie Sutton were burning the midnight oil on June 22, 1964.

Malloy v. Hogan removed "voluntariness" as the test of confessions and *Jackson v. Denno* barred the admission of corroborating evidence showing the confession is true and that the defendant committed the crime. But it is one thing to lay down the law in the cloistered confines of the Supreme Court, and quite another to be a trial judge looking into the faces of a jury as they listen in stunned disbelief to your instructions that they may not consider the truthfulness of a confession in assessing its voluntariness.

---

[7] Id., Black, J. dissenting, 406.

One must consider also that most trial judges are elected. The grass roots of the American people are, like Justice Robert H. Jackson, against exclusionary rules which "discredit constitutional doctrines for protection of the innocent by making of them mere technical loopholes for the escape of the guilty."[8] Take, for example, the exclusionary rule which bars the use of evidence taken in a search and seizure said to be made in violation of the Fourth Amendment. It can, and often does, make impossible the conviction of vicious criminals who are guilty beyond any doubt. This does not sit well with the general public who are apt to remember this on election day, a fact which is not lost on liberal judges.

In 1955, in *People v. Cahan*,[9] the California Supreme Court adopted the exclusionary rule as a matter of state law. There was widespread criticism of this decision and trial judges were reluctant to apply it. Then in 1961, in *Mapp v. Ohio*,[10] the United States Supreme Court held that the exclusionary rule is required by the U.S. Constitution, a case, which, in effect, made *Cahan* redundant. In 1962 Justice William O. Douglas passed on to Justice Tom Clark, who had written the opinion in *Mapp*, some heartfelt thanks from embattled California liberals.

> This last weekend at a social occasion I saw Attorney General Stanley Mosk of California and his wife. He said out of the blue "Thank the good Lord for *Mapp v. Ohio*." I asked him what he meant and he went on to give an interesting account . . . which I thought I would pass on to you.
>
> He said that the California Supreme Court decision in the Cahan case was four to three and since it was decided, there had been two vacancies on the Court and two new appointments. He said that Phil Gibson and the others who were for the Cahan opinion held their breath until the nominees took office and until they could find out where

---

[8] *Stein v. New York*, supra.

[9] *People v. Cahan*, 44 Cal. 2d 434, 282 P.2d 905 (1955).

[10] *Mapp v. Ohio*, 367 U.S. 643 (1961).

these nominees stood on Cahan. It so happened that one of the two nominees was for the Cahan decision and one was against it. So far as the Supreme Court of California went, Mosk said that it was barely holding its own.

The newspaper campaign, however, against the Cahan decision, continued unabated. Mosk said that with the system of elective judges they have in California, pressure on the trial courts was very, very great not to apply the Cahan case or to find there were more exceptions to it, or in other words, try to get around it . . . He mentioned in addition to the newspaper pressure, the pressure of the head of the police in Los Angeles, a man named Parker who, I understand, is a lawyer and very vocal.

The result of *Mapp v. Ohio*, according to Mosk, is to take the pressure off the local judges to create exceptions and to follow the exclusionary rule and all its ramifications.[11]

The problem with cases like *Jackson v. Denno* is that it makes people think that liberals are soft on crime. A few more decisions like that might bring down the wrath of the electorate on their heads. There would also be pressure from police organizations which tend to become "very vocal" when admitted cop-killers like Nathan Jackson go unscathed. Political exigencies required that a fact-proof screen be interposed not only between the truth and the jury but the public as well. *Miranda v. Arizona* would provide that screen.

In 1963 an 18-year-old girl was kidnapped and raped near Phoenix, Arizona. Ten days later a suspect was arrested and taken into custody. In a Phoenix police station he was picked out of a lineup by the victim, and thereafter questioned by two police officers. Within two hours he gave a detailed confession and signed a statement admitting and describing the crime. His name was Ernesto Miranda.

---

[11] WOD to Tom C. Clark, January 25, 1962. Douglas Letters, 205 (footnotes omitted).

The victim had gotten off a bus on the night in question and was walking toward her home when the defendant "left his car, walked toward her, and grabbed her."[12] He forced her into the car at knife-point and drove out into the desert. He then raped her and drove her back within the city limits of Phoenix, where he released her. When she picked him out of the police lineup, Miranda said it was a case of mistaken identity; he and the girl had never met. His fall-back position was the preposterous claim that she had given her consent. Calculating that his situation was hopeless, he then gave a detailed oral confession. Afterwards he wrote out a brief statement admitting and describing the crime and signed it. This included the street intersections where the kidnapping began and ended. Those in Miranda's confession matched exactly those previously given the police by the victim, the girl Miranda denied ever meeting a few hours before.

Miranda v. Arizona had companion cases decided the same day. Before we examine them let us discard that which is not pertinent to our inquiry. It may be accepted as a certainty, albeit one which is irrelevant, that each of these defendants committed, and voluntarily confessed to having committed, the crime of which he was convicted.

In one case, Carl Calvin Westover was guilty of robbing two federally insured banks in Sacramento. Not only was he identified by a teller, but when he was arrested "he was still in possession of some of the currency which had been taken in the bank robbery, of which currency, by clever forethought, the serial numbers had been recorded by the bank, so that in the case of robbery it could be put in the robbers' loot as 'bait money.'"[13]

In a third case, Roy Allen Stewart was guilty of the robbery and first-degree murder of Miss Lucille Mitchell who, on January 19, 1963, "was beaten and robbed of a silver cufflink, a transistor earplug, a black leather case for such an earplug, a watch,

---

12 *Arizona v. Miranda*, 401 P. 2d 721, 722.

13 *Westover v. United States*, 342 F. 2d 684, 688

and a charge-a-plate."[14] On January 31 Stewart was arrested at his home after cashing some checks belonging to the husband of a Mrs. Wells, who had also been beaten and robbed.

> When the officer asked if he could search the house, the defendant replied, "Go ahead." During the search, the officer found Mrs. Wells' purse and wallet, Mrs. Miyauchi's coin purse attached to a key that operated the door to defendant's house, Miss Mitchell's watch, Mrs. Dixon's coin purse and initialed key, and Miss Ramirez' wallet. On February 3, during a further search of the house the police found Miss Ramirez' glasses and Miss Mitchell's cufflink, transistor earplug and case.

With respect to Miss Mitchell, the defendant expressed sorrow, saying "I didn't mean to kill her . . . He denied hitting Miss Mitchell on the head; he did say, however, that he could have kicked her in the head after she fell and while he was escaping." The police had already found Miss Mitchell's charge-a-plate before they searched Stewart's house, in case you are wondering what happened to it. They found it "on the ground about 18 inches from the place where Miss Ramirez had been lying."[15] This is the same Miss Ramirez whose wallet and glasses were found at Stewart's house.

But this, held the Court, is beside the point. None of the defendants had a lawyer present when he confessed, nor were any of them advised that he did not have to make a statement, that any statement he made could be used against him, and that he had a right to see a lawyer. The Court did not look to the circumstances of these cases to see whether or not the incriminating statements were voluntary. Instead, by another vote of five-to-four, they formulated a new exclusionary rule to apply to these cases and all cases tried thereafter. No matter what the circumstances:

---

[14] *People v. Stewart*, 400 P. 2d 97, 99.

[15] *People v. Stewart*, 400 P.2d 97, 98-99.

[T]he prosecution may not use statements, whether exculpatory or inculpatory, stemming from custodial interrogation of the defendant unless it demonstrates the use of procedural safeguards effective to secure the privilege against self-incrimination . . .

Prior to any questioning, the person must be warned that he has a right to remain silent, that any statement he does make may be used as evidence against him, and that he has a right to the presence of an attorney, either retained or appointed.[16] The defendant may waive effectuation of these rights, provided the waiver is made voluntarily, knowingly and intelligently. If, however, he indicates in any manner and at any stage of the process that he wishes to consult with an attorney before speaking there can be no questioning. Likewise, if the individual is alone and indicates in any manner that he does not wish to be interrogated, the police may not question him. The mere fact that he may have answered some questions or volunteered some statements on his own does not deprive him of the right to refrain from answering any further inquiries until he has consulted with an attorney and thereafter consents to be questioned.[17]

The Court concluded "that without proper safeguards the process of in-custody interrogation of persons suspected or accused of crime contains inherently compelling pressures which work to undermine the individual's will to resist and compel him to speak where he would not otherwise do so freely."[18] "Our aim is to assure that the individual's right to choose between silence and speech remains unfettered throughout the interrogation process."[19] *Miranda* was posited on the precedent established in another case

---

[16] The Morse Code neglected to mention the right to appointed counsel.

[17] *Miranda v. Arizona*, 384 U.S. 436, 444-445 (1966).

[18] Id., 467.

[19] Id., 469.

you might remember. If you were wondering what the fuss in *Malloy v. Hogan* was all about, *Miranda* will tell you why.

> Our decision in *Malloy v. Hogan*, 378 U.S. 1 (1964), necessitates an examination of the scope of the privilege in state cases as well. In *Malloy*, we squarely held the privilege applicable to the States, and held that the substantive standards underlying the privilege applied with full force to state court proceedings. There . . . we applied the existing Fifth Amendment standards to the case before us. Aside from the holding itself, the reasoning in *Malloy* made clear what had already become apparent that the substantive and procedural safeguards surrounding admissibility of confessions in state cases had become exceedingly exacting, reflecting all the policies embedded in the privilege, 378 U.S., at 7-8. The voluntariness doctrine in the state cases, as *Malloy* indicates, encompasses all interrogation practices which are likely to exert such pressure upon an individual as to disable him from making a free and rational choice.[20]

A large part of the opinion is devoted to a description of police interrogation techniques and stratagems. Nothing described in *Miranda* would undermine the individual's will to resist and compel him to confess falsely to a crime he did not commit. All are designed to implant in the mind of the suspect, if he is in fact the perpetrator, the idea that the police know more than they really do, so that he might as well tell them the rest and have done with it. All of these tactics recognize as a rule of human experience that innocent people accused of a crime generally respond differently in such a situation from those who are guilty. "The wicked flee when no man pursueth; but the righteous are as bold as a lion."

Until the latter part of the nineteenth century, the defendant in any criminal case was not eligible to be a witness. After this disqualification was abolished, he could if he wished, but not oth-

---

[20] Id., 463-465.

erwise, take the witness stand and testify on his own behalf. His right not to do so became known as the Exemption from Compulsory Self-Incrimination. If the defendant chose to take the witness stand, he was deemed to have waived it and could be cross-examined by the prosecution. As a unanimous Supreme Court held in 1936, the Exemption applied only to sworn, in-court testimony. "The compulsion to which the quoted statements refer is that of the processes of justice by which the accused may be called as a witness and required to testify."[21]

The guilty suspect who elects speech over silence, like my clients of the 1950's, invariably manifests it in the first instant by making exculpatory statements. When they do not stand up, he changes his story, as did Ernesto Miranda, making a bad situation worse. Professor John Henry Wigmore described this predicament long ago and nothing has changed since.

> The nervous pressure of guilt is enormous; the load of the deed done is heavy; the fear of detection fills the consciousness; and when detection comes, the pressure is relieved; and the deep sense of relief makes confession a satisfaction. At that moment, he will tell all, and tell it truly.[22]

These confessions were "involuntary" only in the definition of that word minted in *Malloy v. Hogan*. If you subtract from confessions made under such pressure as to fetter a suspect's "right to choose between silence and speech," those confessions brought about by pressures which might prevent an innocent man from standing by the truth, you are left with confessions that are voluntary in the real sense of that word. They are also true and the confessors guilty. It is a crime against a civilized people to let them get away with it.

But to a lawyer representing a suspect at the stationhouse his duty is clear. If his client tells him he is guilty, or he has any reason

---

21 *Brown v. Mississippi, supra*, 286.

22 Wigmore, *Evidence*, (3d Ed. 1940), 319.

to believe the client may be guilty, the lawyer must advise him to "say nothing, absolutely nothing." No admissions or confessions will occur except as part of a bargain. And what does *Miranda* do for the innocent suspect? Let Chief Justice Earl Warren tell you in his own words: "The person who has committed no offense, however, will be better able to clear himself after warnings with counsel present than without. It can be assumed that in such circumstances a lawyer would advise his client to talk freely to police in order to clear himself."[23]

With respect to a person who has committed an offense, to state the converse of the Chief Justice's proposition, it can be assumed that in such circumstances a lawyer will advise his client to say nothing whatever to the police. Let no one tell you the *Miranda* rule protects the innocent by preventing involuntary confessions and wrongful convictions. Its sole purpose and inevitable consequence is to prevent the guilty from making true confessions and suffering rightful conviction. *Miranda v. Arizona* covers 120 pages, of which the dissents account for 45 pages. Justice Byron White, joined by Harlan and Stewart, made this prediction:

> In some unknown number of cases the Court's rule will return a killer, a rapist or other criminal to the streets and to the environment which produced him, to repeat his crime whenever it pleases him. As a consequence, there will not be a gain, but a loss, in human dignity. The real concern is not the unfortunate consequences of this new decision on the criminal law as an abstract, disembodied series of authoritative proscriptions, but the impact on those who rely on the public authority for protection and who without it can only engage in violent self-help with guns, knives and the help of their neighbors similarly inclined. There is, of course, a saving factor: the next victims are uncertain, unnamed and unrepresented in this case.[24]

---

[23] *Miranda*, 482.

[24] White, J., joined by Harlan and Stewart at 542-43.

The following year, in *Griffin v. California*, by a vote of five-to-three, the Court struck down the California statute upheld in *Adamson*, which permitted comment by the trial judge or prosecutor on the defendant's failure to testify. Griffin, the defendant, was convicted of murder in the first degree after a jury trial. He "had been seen with the deceased the evening of her death, the evidence placing him with her in the alley where her body was found."[25] The prosecutor commented on the defendant's failure to deny or explain things which "if anybody would know, this defendant would know." Justices Stewart and White dissented.

> The California rule allowing comment by counsel and instruction by the judge on the defendant's failure to take the stand is hardly an idiosyncratic aberration, The Model Code of Evidence, and the Uniform Rules of Evidence both sanction the use of such procedures. The practice has been endorsed by resolution of the American Bar Association and the American Law Institute and has the support of the weight of scholarly opinion.[26]

Justice Harlan concurred "with great reluctance" because of "last Term's decision in *Malloy v. Hogan* . . . that the Fifth Amendment applies to the States in all of its refinements." He felt that this decision exemplifies the creeping paralysis with which the Court's recent adoption of the 'incorporation' doctrine is infecting the operation of the federal system." He concluded by expressing "the hope that the Court will eventually return to constitutional paths which, until recently, it has followed throughout its history."[27] Had Harlan taken his own advice, *Adamson* would have remained the law.

That all men are equal before the law is one of our fundamental precepts. In no case was this equality more clearly demonstrated

---

[25] *Griffin v. California*, 380 U.S. 609, 610-611 (1965).

[26] *Griffin*, 622.

[27] *Griffin*, 615-617.

than in the case of John W. Hinckley, Jr., who attempted to assassinate the President of the United States in Washington, D.C. on March 30, 1981. He succeeded in wounding President Ronald Reagan, the President's press secretary James Brady, as well as a Secret Service agent and a Metropolitan police officer. Hinckley was tried on a number of charges, the chief of which was the violation of the Presidential Assassination Statute.

Hinckley was given the warnings required by *Miranda* and indicated he wanted to talk to a lawyer. He was not thereafter asked any questions about the shooting. He was, however, asked the usual background questions customarily asked of an arrestee at the administrative procedure known as "booking"—address, marital status, family and employment. He was then photographed and fingerprinted.

Hinckley was later transferred to a federal institution to undergo psychiatric evaluation, where he was held in solitary confinement and kept under 'round-the-clock supervision. He took to writing letters with knowledge that his personal correspondence would be read. Some of it was seized. None of the information obtained from Hinckley as a result of the seizure of the papers or the booking was evidence in the usual sense. The prosecution did not try to use it to prove that it was Hinckley who did the shooting. As it turned out, Hinckley did not deny he shot the President; his defense was insanity.

The federal district court held that the *Miranda* rule required the suppression of all evidence surrounding the booking, and that under the rule of *Weeks v. United States*, the letters must be excluded as well. The government's position was that these exclusionary rules only forbid the use of such evidence in its case-in-chief. The prosecution does not bear the burden of proving sanity in the first instance. Should Hinckley come forward with an affirmative defense of insanity, the United States, it was urged, should be able to use Hinckley's oral and written statements to rebut it. Those agents present at the booking, if not permitted to testify as to Hinckley's statements, should be at least be allowed to testify as to Hinckley's demeanor.

While this might be true in the usual case it is not so here, held the D.C. Circuit Court of Appeals. The information ordinarily obtained through booking was clearly investigatory in the case of Hinckley. As a matter of fact, the FBI agent who conducted the booking interview testified that he wanted to find out if Hinckley had acted alone or as part of a conspiracy so that they could determine whether other officials were in danger.

The circuit court held that any information obtained during the booking must be suppressed. The agents would not be permitted to testify as to their observations of Hinckley or his demeanor during the interview. None of this could be used to rebut the defense of insanity. The seizure of the papers was "a serious invasion of Hinckley's right to privacy . . . was perpetrated by individual officers unguided by prison rules or even the instructions of their superiors."[28] They were suppressed for all purposes. None of these violations of Hinckley's rights should have ever happened; the federal agents involved should have known better.

> We are not confronted here with the typical police officer, but rather with the special concerns of highly trained agents whose job it is to prevent and investigate assassination attempts on major political figures. Such agents, we can assume, are fully aware of the critical importance of their demeanor testimony about a suspect arrested in the course of an attempted or actual assassination . . .
>
> Were we to curtail the exclusionary rule in the drastic manner the government urges, we would provide little or no deterrence of constitutional violations against defendants whose sanity is the principal issue in the case.[29]

---

[28] *United States v. Hinckley*, 672 F. 2d 115, 131 (1982).

[29] *Hinckley*, 133-134.

The failure of federal agents to observe Hinckley's rights, said the circuit court, cannot be justified by their concern to protect the nation's high officials from a possible ring of like-minded assassins. People are apt to get excited when the President of the United States is shot, particularly those charged with his protection. But they cannot have it both ways, according to Circuit Court Judges Robinson, Wright and Wald. They must choose between the safety of their "protectees"—their official duty—and being able to use the "illegally obtained" evidence to prosecute the man who shot the president. They opted for the former, and this is why John W. Hinckley, Jr. was never convicted of the attempted assassination of President Reagan nor punished for the dreadful harm he inflicted upon presidential press secretary James Brady.

⚥ ⚥ ⚥

The *Miranda* rule has accomplished its purpose. Not only is the truth kept from the jury, the truth is kept from the public as well. A motion to suppress evidence is usually argued in a hearing from which public and press are excluded. An order to suppress is accompanied by a "gag order" enjoining the disclosure of the incriminating evidence by those privy to that information. As a consequence, the truth only comes out if the motion to suppress is denied and the case tried. One such case came in 1984 when the Court created the "public safety exception" to the *Miranda* rule.

> On September 11, 1980, at approximately 12:30 a.m., Officer Frank Kraft and Officer Sal Scarring were on road patrol in Queens, N.Y., when a young woman approached their car. She told them that she had just been raped by a black male, approximately six feet tall, who was wearing a black jacket with the name "Big Ben" printed in yellow letters on the back. She told the officers that the man had just entered an A & P supermarket located nearby and that the man was carrying a gun.

The officers drove the woman to the supermarket, and Officer Kraft entered the store while Officer Scarring radioed for assistance. Officer Kraft quickly spotted respondent, who matched the description given by the woman, approaching a check-out counter. Apparently upon seeing the officer, respondent turned and ran toward the rear of the store, and Officer Kraft pursued him with a drawn gun. When the respondent turned the corner at the end of an aisle, Officer Kraft lost sight of him . . .[30]

One wonders what went through the mind of this policeman at this point. What lay around the corner, he must have realized, was a critical period of a criminal case to which the right of counsel attaches. An error in judgment on his part could result in a violation of Big Ben's constitutional rights and the exclusion of vital evidence, precipitating long and expensive appeals. Given the circumstances, however, Officer Kraft may be forgiven if his mind wandered to more personal considerations: Who will take care of my family if something happens to me? "Is it not better," as the saying goes, "to be tried by twelve, than to be carried by six?" Why did I not spend more time at the pistol range? Aim low, and always remember, "do not pull—squeeze." Big Ben Quarles must also have been uncertain of what legal presumptions attached under the circumstances, or at least of Officer Kraft's interpretation of them. We know that because when Kraft ordered him to stop and put his hands over his head, Quarles complied.

Although more than three other officers had arrived on the scene by that time, Officer Kraft was the first to reach respondent. He frisked him and discovered that he was wearing a shoulder holster which was then empty. After handcuffing him, officer Kraft asked him where the gun was. Respondent nodded in the direction of some empty cartons and

---

[30] *New York v. Quarles*, 467 U.S. 649, 651-652 (1984).

responded "[t]he gun is over there." Officer Kraft thereafter retrieved a loaded .38-caliber revolver from one of the
cartons, formally placed respondent under arrest, and read
him his *Miranda* rights from a printed card. Respondent indicated that he would be willing to answer questions without
an attorney present. Officer Kraft then asked respondent if
he owned the gun and where he had purchased it. Respondent answered that he did own it and that he had purchased
it in Miami, Fla.

In the subsequent prosecution of respondent for criminal
possession of a weapon, the judge excluded the statement,
'the gun is over there,' and the gun because the officer had
not given respondent the warnings required by our decision in *Miranda v. Arizona*, 384 U.S. 436 (1966), before asking him where the gun was located. The judge "excluded
the other statements about respondent's ownership of the
gun and the place of purchase, as evidence tainted by the
prior *Miranda* violation."[31]

In *Quarles*, by the narrowest of margins, the Court created an
exception to the *Miranda* rule. They agreed that Quarles was in
police custody when asked where the gun was, and that the facts
of this case come within the ambit of the *Miranda* decision as we
have subsequently interpreted it. "Thus the only issue before
us is whether Officer Kraft was justified in failing to make available to respondent the compulsory safeguards associated with the
privilege against compulsory self-incrimination since *Miranda*."

We conclude that the need for answers to questions in a
situation posing a threat to the public safety outweighs the
need for the prophylactic rule protecting the Fifth Amendment's privilege against self-incrimination. We decline to
place officers such as Officer Kraft in the untenable position
of having to consider, often in a matter of seconds, whether

---

[31] *Quarles*, 652-653.

it best serves society for them to ask the necessary questions without the *Miranda* warnings and render whatever probative evidence they uncover inadmissible, or for them to give the warnings in order to preserve the admissibility of evidence they might uncover but possibly damage or destroy their ability to obtain that evidence and neutralize the volatile situation confronting them.[32]

We hold that the [New York] Court of Appeals in this case erred in excluding the statement, "the gun is over there," and the gun because of the officer's failure to read respondent his *Miranda* rights before attempting to locate the weapon. Accordingly we hold that it also erred in excluding the subsequent statements as illegal fruits of a *Miranda* violation."[33]

Justice Thurgood Marshall, with whom Justice Brennan and Justice Stevens joined, dissented, castigating the majority for having abandoned the *Miranda* rule. "In a chimerical quest for public safety," wrote Marshall, "the majority has abandoned the rule that brought 18 years of doctrinal tranquility to the field of custodial interrogations. [This] public-safety exception destroys forever the clarity of *Miranda*."[34]

It would strain credulity to contend that Officer Kraft's questioning of respondent Quarles was not coercive. In the middle of the night and in the back of an empty supermarket, Quarles was surrounded by four armed police officers. His hands were handcuffed behind his back. The first words out of the arresting officer were: "Where is the gun?" In the majority's phrase, the situation was "kaleidoscopic." Police and suspect were acting on instinct. Officer Kraft's abrupt and pointed question pressured Quarles in precisely

---

[32] *Quarles*, 657-658.

[33] *Quarles*, 659-660.

[34] *Quarles*, 679.

the way that the *Miranda* Court feared the custodial interrogations would coerce self-incriminating testimony. Footnote omitted.[35]

According to Justice Marshall, there is no need for a so-called
"public safety" exception to the *Miranda* rule. He laid down some
useful guidelines so that ordinary citizens can tell when their
safety is "imminently imperiled" and do not panic and disgrace
themselves at the local supermarket. The timid tend to become
alarmed over the sight of a police officer, gun in hand, stalking a
fugitive down an aisle.

> The irony of the majority's decision is that the public's
> safety can be perfectly well protected without abridging
> the Fifth Amendment. If a bomb is about to explode or the
> public is otherwise imminently imperiled, the police are
> free to interrogate suspects without advising them of their
> constitutional rights . . .
>
> To a limited degree, the majority is correct that there is
> a cost associated with the Fifth Amendment's ban on intro-
> ducing coerced self-incriminating statements at trial. With-
> out a 'public-safety' exception, there would be occasions
> when a defendant incriminated himself by revealing a threat
> to the public, and the State was unable to prosecute because
> the defendant retracted his statement after consulting with
> counsel and the police cannot find independent proof of
> guilt. Such occasions would not, however, be common.[36]

The next case, decided by the Court in 1980, was a reprise
of the Pamela Powers murder case. The issue was "whether the
Respondent was 'interrogated' in violation of the standards pro-
mulgated in the *Miranda* opinion." Once again, Justice Potter
Stewart delivered the opinion of the Court.

---

[35] *Quarles*, 684-685 (footnote omitted).

[36] *Quarles*, 686-687.

On the night of January 12, 1975, John Mulvaney, a Providence, R.I., taxicab driver, disappeared after being dispatched to pick up a customer. His body was discovered four days later buried in a shallow grave in Coventry, R.I. He had died from a shotgun blast aimed at the back of his head.

On January 17, 1975, shortly after midnight, the Providence police received a telephone call from Gerald Aubin, also a taxicab driver, who reported that he had just been robbed by a man wielding a sawed-off shotgun. Aubin further reported that he had dropped off his assailant near Rhode Island College in a section of Providence known as Mount Pleasant. While at the Providence police station waiting to give a statement, Aubin noticed a picture of his assailant on a bulletin board. Aubin so informed one of the police officers present. The officer prepared a photo array, and again Aubin identified a picture of the same person. That person was the respondent. Shortly thereafter, the Providence police began a search of the Mount Pleasant area.[37]

At approximately 4:30 a.m. a patrol car spotted Thomas Innis, and he was arrested unarmed and without incident. Within minutes other officers arrived. The suspect had not thus far been questioned in any manner. "Captain Leyden advised the respondent of his *Miranda* rights. The respondent stated that he understood those rights and wanted to speak with a lawyer . . . While en route to the central station, Patrolman Gleckman initiated a conversation with Patrolman McKenna concerning the missing shotgun."[38] He noted that this was his patrol area and that there was a school for handicapped children nearby. "[T]here's a lot of handicapped children running around in this area," continued Gleckman, "and God forbid one of them might find a weapon with shells and they

---

37 *Rhode Island v. Innis*, 446 U.S. 291, 293 (1980).

38 *Innis*, 295.

might hurt themselves."[39] The defendant thereupon asked the police to return to the scene of his arrest.

> At the time the respondent indicated that the officers should turn back, they had traveled no more than a mile, a trip encompassing only a few minutes.
>
> The police vehicle then returned to the scene of the arrest where a search for the shotgun was in progress. There Captain Leyden again advised the respondent of his *Miranda* rights . . . The respondent then led the police to a nearby field, where he pointed out the shotgun under some rocks by the side of the road.[40]

Innis was convicted of the murder of the taxi driver after a trial in which the shotgun and the statements he had made to the police were admitted into evidence. But the murderer of John Mulvaney was not as lucky as the murderer of Pamela Powers. Unlike Robert Williams, held the U.S. Supreme Court, Thomas Innis had not been "interrogated."

> It cannot be said, in short, that Patrolman Gleckman and McKenna should have known that their conversation was reasonably likely to elicit an incriminating response from the respondent. There is nothing in the record to suggest that the officers were aware that the respondent was peculiarly susceptible to an appeal to his conscience concerning the safety of handicapped children . . .[41]

Justice Marshall, in an opinion in which Justice Brennan concurred, was outraged. Officers Gleckman and McKenna "knew respondent would hear and attend to their conversation, and they are chargeable with knowledge of and responsibility for the pressures to speak which they created. One can scarcely imagine a

---

[39] Id., 294.

[40] *Innis*, 295.

[41] *Innis*, 302-303.

stronger appeal to the conscience of a suspect—*any* suspect—than the assertion that if the weapon is not found an innocent person will be hurt or killed . . . As a matter of fact, the appeal to a suspect to confess for the sake of others, to 'display some evidence of decency and honor,' is a classic interrogation technique."[42]

---

[42] *Innis*, 306, 307.

CHAPTER 13

THE COUNTERFEIT CONSTITUTION

THE HIGHEST PRIORITY OF A NATION is the protection of its people from predators. This is the *raison d'etre* of governments; it is the reason why people get together and form them in the first place. The state protects its citizens from the enemy without by its armed forces; the enemy within the criminals care dealt with by the police and the courts. A civilization which fails in its duty to protect its people from crime must change or perish.

> Within the memory of most Americans, serious offenses were committed in the United States with only a fraction of their current frequency. For example, the statistics on reported crime for 1981 show a more than doubling of the murder rate, a quadrupling of the rate for rape, and a quintupling of the robbery rate as compared to those of 1961 . . .
>
> If government in the United States fails to correct this situation, it fails in discharging its most basic function—protecting the individual in the enjoyment of his life, liberty, and property, and maintaining the stability and order necessary for the pursuit of happiness and a meaningful existence. The freedom from criminal activity is the most basic of all civil rights.[1]

"According to one poll of Florida residents," continues the same source, "more than half of all respondents are afraid to walk

---

[1] *Truth in Criminal Justice, supra,* 426, 427 [Footnotes omitted].

outside their home in the evening. This rampant criminality seriously undermines the 'blessings of liberty' that the Constitution was meant to secure, and may sometimes make them wholly illusory."[2] Ironically this so-called price we pay for freedom is borne most heavily by black citizens, the very group the Fourteenth Amendment was passed to protect.

> [T]he impact of many serious crimes falls with particular severity on the poor and members of minority groups. For example, the black population is victimized by crimes of rape and robbery at close to double the rate of the white population, and includes nearly one-half of all murder victims.[3]

That we have come to this pass cannot be laid at the feet of the Framers. Those who wrote the Bill of Rights and the Fourteenth Amendment did not intend thereby that ordinary people in their everyday life should fear for their safety. The "domestic tranquility" the Constitution was intended to "insure" is but a hollow phrase to those in the inner city who cower each night behind double-locked doors. The statement that the "freedom from criminal activity is the most basic of all civil rights" is absolutely correct.

All of our travail comes down to the meaning given the four words "due process of law." In the field of criminal justice before 1961 due process of law was equated with fundamental fairness. In this sense fundamental fairness was the equity that Joseph Story said "must have a place in any rational jurisprudence, if not in name, at least in substance." Its ultimate goal was truth and justice. The jurisprudence of fundamental fairness was nothing but equity by another name, and as Story said, "Equity is synonymous with justice." *Minnick v. Mississippi* is an illustration of the irrationality of what *Miranda* has wrought.

Petitioner Robert Minnick and fellow prisoner James Dyess escaped from a county jail in Mississippi and, a day later,

---

2 Ibid., 427 [Footnotes omitted].

3 Ibid., 426.

broke into a mobile home in search of weapons. In the course of the burglary they were interrupted by the arrival of the trailer's owner, Ellis Thomas, accompanied by Lamar Lafferty and Lafferty's infant son. Dyess and Minnick used the stolen weapons to kill Thomas and the senior Lafferty. Minnick's story is that Dyess murdered one victim and forced Minnick to shoot the other.[4]

After his arrest in California as an interstate fugitive, Minnick was interviewed by FBI agents. "The FBI report indicates that the agents read petitioner his *Miranda* warnings, and that he acknowledged he understood his rights . . . After the FBI interview, an appointed attorney met with petitioner . . . [Two days later] Deputy Sheriff J.C. Denham of Clarke County, Mississippi, came to the San Diego jail to question Minnick . . . [After] Denham advised petitioner of his rights . . . [Minnick] told Denham about the escape and then proceeded to describe the events at the mobile home."[5] He told the deputy about his role in the double murder. The dissenting opinion of Justice Antonin Scalia tells us what happened after that.

> Minnick was later extradited and tried for murder in Mississippi. Before trial, he moved to suppress the statements he had given the FBI agents and Denham in the San Diego jail. The trial court granted the motion with respect to the statements made to the FBI agents, but ordered a hearing on the admissibility of the statements made to Denham. After receiving testimony from both Minnick and Denham, the court concluded that Minnick's confession had been "freely and voluntarily given from the evidence beyond a reasonable doubt," id., at 25, and allowed Denham to describe Minnick's confession to the jury.

---

4 *Minnick v. Mississippi*, 498 U.S. 146, 148 (1990).

5 Ibid., 148-149.

The Court today reverses the trial court's conclusion. It holds that, because Minnick had asked for counsel during the interview with the FBI agents, he could not—as a matter of law—validly waive the right to have counsel present during the conversation initiated by Denham. That Minnick's original request to see an attorney had been honored, that Minnick had consulted with his attorney on several occasions, and that the attorney had specifically warned Minnick not to speak to the authorities, are irrelevant.[6]

Today's decision, wrote Scalia, "is the latest stage of prophylaxis built upon prophylaxis, producing a veritable fairyland castle of imagined constitutional restriction upon law enforcement. This newest tower . . . was needed to protect *Miranda*'s prophylactic right to have counsel present, which was needed to protect the right against compelled self-incrimination found (at last!) in the Constitution":[7]

> Apart from the fact that this protective enterprise is beyond our authority under the Fifth Amendment or any other provision of the Constitution, it is unwise. The procedural protections of the Constitution protect the guilty as well as the innocent, but it is not their objective to set the guilty free. That some clever criminals may employ those protections to their advantage is poor reason to allow criminals who have not done so to escape justice.
>
> Thus, even if I were to concede that an honest confession is a foolish mistake, I would welcome rather than reject it; a rule that foolish mistakes do not count would leave most offenders not only unconvicted but undetected. More fundamentally, however, it is wrong, and subtly corrosive of our criminal justice system, to regard an honest confession as a "mistake." While every person is entitled to stand silent, it

---

6 Ibid., 158.

7 Ibid., 166.

is more virtuous for the wrongdoer to admit his offense and accept the punishment he deserves.[8]

An editorial in the *New York Times*—"Mainstreaming *Miranda*"—harkened the significance of *Minnick v. Mississippi*. "Just as impressive is the 6-to-2 margin and the strong majority opinion of Justice Anthony Kennedy, who rarely parts company with the dissenters, Antonin Scalia and Chief Justice William Rehnquist. *Miranda*, a 5-to-4 decision, is now endorsed—and enforced—by Justices who would never have voted for it in the first place."[9] According to two liberal academics, this marked a great victory:

> "Having this Supreme Court, which is widely viewed as unsympathetic to the rights of criminal defendants, acknowledge the importance of the Fifth Amendment right against self-incrimination is tremendously important," said Vivian Berger, a general counsel for the American Civil Liberties Union who is a dean at the Columbia University School of Law."
>
> "Its greatest significance may well be that it defeats the predictions in some quarters that a conservative majority would roll back the protections of the Warren and Burger Courts," said Laurence H. Tribe, a professor at Harvard University Law School.[10]

The liberals had every reason to crow. Here were two Justices—O'Connor and Kennedy—who would have voted against *Miranda* as an original proposition, voting 25 years later to uphold and extend its rule. They were joined by Justice Byron White, who did vote against *Miranda* as an original proposition. There is a certain irony that Ellis Thomas and Lamar Lafferty are two of the very people White had in mind in 1966 when he wrote in his

---

8 Ibid., 166-167.

9 "Mainstreaming *Miranda*," *New York Times*, Dec. 5, 1990.

10 *New York Times*, Dec. 7, 1990, B-7.

Miranda dissent: "There is, of course, a saving factor: the next victims are uncertain, unnamed and unrepresented in this case."[11]

One of the most urgent problems of our time is crime—violent crime—and the failure of the law to contain it. The primary obligation of protecting the individual in the enjoyment of his life, liberty and property lies with the individual states. Ninety-five percent of all the felonies committed in this country come under the jurisdiction of the states, and with respect to violent crime the figure is more like 99 percent. It is not that the states have abdicated their responsibility to protect their citizens from crime; the problem is that they have been deprived of the means with which to fulfill it. Here is a newspaper story appearing shortly after the Court's decision in *Minnick v. Mississippi*.

> Montgomery County prosecutors dropped charges yesterday against a man accused of ransacking an Orthodox Jewish school yesterday in Silver Spring, after a Circuit Court judge threw out the man's statement to police.
>
> Judge Paul A. McGuckian ruled yesterday that prosecutors could not use Jeffery Lee Eskew's statement to police that he was responsible for tens of thousands of dollars in damage at the Yeshiva of Greater Washington.[12]

The skin-headed Mr. Eskew was by no means a recalcitrant witness against himself. In fact he was quite pleased over the whole episode. In an interview with the *Washington Post*, Eskew said, "I did it basically to feel good about myself . . . I felt like I had to prove to Satan and to myself that I'm better and more powerful than any person who's into God or some other religion."[13]

When interviewed in a California jail, "Eskew did not specifically ask for one [a lawyer] when he talked with Montgomery

[11] *Miranda*, 542-543.

[12] "Judge's ruling throws out case against confessed vandal," *Washington Times*, Dec. 19, 1990.

[13] "'Hate' vandalism charges dropped in Montgomery" *Washington Post*, Dec. 14, 1990.

detectives, but he had indicated that he wanted legal counsel in the unrelated Los Angeles robbery" charge on which he was being held. The public defender had argued and Judge McGuckian agreed that "Supreme Court decisions state that attorneys should be present on such occasions and Eskew's statement was inadmissible at trial." "Rabbi Zev Katz, assistant principal of Yeshiva High School of Greater Washington, deplored yesterday's ruling" and wondered about the rights of the victims.

> "It seemed pretty cut and dried to me that the guy confessed to it. If he did this he should pay for this," Mr. Katz said.
> "You start wondering about all these technicalities and these protections of the rights of the criminal. You wonder what there is to protect us. There's more legal protection for him than there is for us."[14]

The Montgomery County judge and prosecutor cannot be faulted for their decisions. It would be a vainglorious waste of time and resources to try Eskew on the heels of the Supreme Court's decision two weeks before in *Minnick v. Mississippi*. Rabbi Katz "blamed neither police nor prosecutors for the dismissal . . . The system let us down."[15] What the American people don't know is how "the system" came about. To most people, like Rabbi Katz, it seems pretty cut and dried that if it can be proven, and proven beyond a reasonable doubt, that someone committed a crime, he should pay for it. If the law insulates the criminality of people like Minnick and Eskew, what does it do to protect us, the law abiding? Why, they ask, has the system let us down?

⚘ ⚘ ⚘

Fundamental fairness is gone and in its place stands an alien called "selective incorporation" in which the guilt or innocence

14 Id.

15 Id.

of the defendant is but a side show. The scales of justice which weighed in the balance the rights of the victim no longer exists. The lives of innocents like Ellis Thomas and Lamar Lafferty and the trauma to their families are given short shrift. The system certainly has failed them "in discharging its most basic function— protecting the individual in the enjoyment of his life, liberty and property, and maintaining the stability and order necessary for the pursuit of happiness and a meaningful existence." The people of this country don't need statistics to prove this; in many areas, the fear of crime pervades their daily lives.

No evidence of guilt was more trustworthy than the defendant's own words when corroborated by independent evidence. The two went hand in hand; rarely did the prosecution have one without the other. In one scenario, the accused, confronted with physical evidence found on his person or premises, realized that denial was useless and told it all and told it truly. In the other sequence he began by fabricating a story which did not stand up. Then, like Ernesto Miranda, he changed it to make a bad situation worse. Finally, trapped by his own inconsistencies, he confessed and led the police to evidence only the perpetrator would know of, a weapon, a stash of stolen goods or, like Williams, the body of the victim.

These were the investigating techniques the police had always used to separate truth from falsehood and guilt from innocence; many cases simply cannot be solved without them. Undoubtedly they cleared far more suspects than they incriminated. By outlawing them, "the system" stripped law enforcement agencies of the most probative and effective means of vindicating the innocent and convicting the guilty.

In 1968, insofar and only insofar as federal criminal cases were concerned, Congress abolished the *Miranda* rule in the Omnibus Crime Control and Safe Streets Act,[16] and restored the common

---

[16] Now 18 USC § 3501 et seq.

law test of "voluntariness." The Senate Judiciary Committee had this to say of *Miranda*:

> [The *Miranda*] decision was an abrupt departure from precedent extending back at least to the earliest days of the Republic. Up to the time of the rendition of this 5-to-4 opinion, the "totality of circumstances" had been the test in our State and Federal courts in determining the admissibility of incriminating statements . . . Mr. Justice White's dissent . . . demonstrates beyond question that . . . warnings as to constitutional rights were not required by the Constitution, and that the sole test of admissibility should be "totality of circumstances" as bearing on voluntariness . . .[17]

Attorney General Ramsey Clark forbade U.S. District Attorneys to offer in evidence any confession, voluntary or no, not obtained in conformity with the *Miranda* rule. That way the constitutionality of § 3501 could not be put in issue, and the will of Congress thwarted. This policy was reversed by Attorney General John Mitchell, and in 1975 the statute was upheld by the Tenth Circuit Court of Appeals as a legitimate exercise of legislative power.

But it was not until the year 2000, in *Dickerson v. United States*, that the issue made its way to the docket of the Supreme Court, and when it did it was opposed by Attorney General Janet Reno. Reno, the American Civil Liberties Union and "the House Democratic leadership" filed briefs amici curiae urging the Court to declare the statute unconstitutional and uphold the *Miranda* rule.[18] "Because no party to the underlying litigation argued in favor of § 3501's constitutionality in this Court, we [the Court] invited [Utah Law School] Professor Paul Cassell to assist our deliberations by arguing in support of the judgment below."[19]

---

17 S. Rep. No, 1097, 90th Congress, 2d Session, quoted in *Truth in Criminal Justice*, 513.

18 *Dickerson v. United States*, 530 U.S. 428, 430-431 (2000).

19 *Dickerson*, 441.

Charles Thomas Dickerson was tried and convicted of the robbery of a federally insured bank. Dickerson, before his trial began, tried to suppress statements he had made to the FBI. The district court granted his motion and the Government appealed. The circuit court of appeals reversed. "It agreed with the District Court's conclusion that the petitioner had not received *Miranda* warnings before making his statement. But it went on to hold that §3501, which in effect makes the admissibility of statements such as Dickerson's turn solely on whether they were made voluntarily, was satisfied in this case. It then concluded that . . . Congress could by statute have the final say on the question of admissibility."[20] The Supreme Court, in an opinion by Chief Justice William Rehnquist, said otherwise.

> We begin with a brief historical account of the law governing the admission of confessions. Prior to *Miranda*, we evaluated the admissibility of a suspect's confession under a voluntariness test. The roots of this test developed in the common law, as the courts of England and then the United States recognized that coerced confessions are inherently untrustworthy . . . Over time, our cases recognized two constitutional bases for the requirement that a confession be voluntary to be admitted into evidence: the Fifth Amendment right against self-incrimination and the Due Process Clause of the Fourteenth Amendment . . .
>
> We have never abandoned this due process jurisprudence, and thus continue to exclude confessions that were obtained involuntarily. But our decisions in *Malloy v. Hogan*, 378 U.S. 1 (1964), and *Miranda* changed the focus of much of the inquiry in determining the admissibility of suspects' incriminating statements. In *Malloy*, we held that the Fifth Amendment's Self-Incrimination Clause is incorporated in the Due Process Clause of the Fourteenth Amendment and

---

[20] *Dickerson*, 432.

thus applies to the States. 378 U.S. at 6-11. We decided *Miranda* on the heels of *Malloy*.[21]

The Court declined to overrule *Miranda*. Whether or not a majority of the Court would have agreed with *Miranda* when it was decided in the first instance, wrote the Chief Justice, "the principles of *stare decisis* weigh heavily against overruling it now . . . even in constitutional cases, the doctrine carries such persuasive force that we always required a departure from precedent to be supported by some 'special justification' . . . We do not think there is such justification for overruling *Miranda*. *Miranda* has become embedded in routine police practices to the point where the warnings have become part of our national culture . . . In sum, we conclude that *Miranda* announced a constitutional rule that Congress may not supersede legislatively. Following the rule of *stare decisis*, we decline to overrule *Miranda* ourselves."[22] Justice Scalia wrote a biting dissent, in which Justice Clarence Thomas joined.

> In imposing its Court-made code upon the States, the original opinion [in *Miranda*] at least asserted that it was demanded by the Constitution. Today's decision does not pretend that it is—and yet still asserts the right to impose it against the will of the people's representatives in Congress. Far from believing that *stare decisis* compels this result, I believe we cannot allow to remain on the books even a celebrated decision—especially a celebrated decision—that has come to stand for the proposition that the Supreme Court has power to impose extraconstitutional constraints upon Congress and the States. This is not the system that was established by the Framers, or that would be established by any sane supporter of government by the people.
>
> I dissent from today's decision, and, until §3501 is repealed, will continue to apply it in all cases where there

---

21 *Dickerson*, 432-434.

22 *Dickerson*, 443-444.

has been a sustainable finding that the defendant's confession was voluntary.[23]

Looking at the alignment of the justices, particularly that of the Chief Justice, one cannot help but suspect that Dickerson was as much a battle over "turf" as anything else. This thought also occurred to Linda Greenhouse, who for years has covered the Supreme Court for the *New York Times*. In an article appearing on the front page of that newspaper on June 28, 2000—"A Turf Battle's Victim: Opposition to *Miranda* Ruling Fell Prey to Justices' Desire to Win a Bigger War"—she explained:

> There might well have been a period, sometime in the last three decades, when the court would have overturned Miranda, a bitterly fought 5-to-4 decision that had appeared ever since to have an ever more fragile hold on the court's loyalties.
>
> But it was the bad fortune of opponents finally to get the justices' attention at the very moment when the court's interest in protecting its constitutional turf against Congressional incursions was at a peak unmatched in recent years.

Liberals take a more flexible approach to *stare decisis* than does Chief Justice Rehnquist. Hugo Black, for example, never deviated from his theory of incorporation; the Court's decisions in *Twining v. New Jersey* and *Adamson v. California* did not faze him one iota. And, after all, the judicial revolution of the 1960's was accomplished by overruling precedent that had prevailed for almost a century. In a 1985 address at Georgetown University, Justice William J. Brennan, Jr., gave the audience his views on the subject.

> Perhaps you see in it a refusal to abide by the judicial principle of *stare decisis*, obedience to precedent. In my judgment, however, the unique interpretive role of the Supreme Court with respect to the Constitution demands some flexi-

---

[23] *Dickerson*, 465.

bility with respect to the call of *stare decisis*. Because we are the last word on the meaning of the Constitution, our views must be subject to revision over time, or the Constitution falls captive, again, to the anachronistic views of long-gone generations . . . [W]hen a Justice perceives an interpretation of the text to have departed so far from its essential meaning, that Justice is bound, by a larger constitutional duty to the community, to expose the departure and point toward a different path.[24]

The doctrine of *stare decisis* is the underpinning of what is called "case law" in this country. Indeed, the subject of constitutional law concerns itself far more with the study of cases than with the text of the Constitution itself. *Stare decisis*, it is safe to say, rests on the implicit assumption that the axioms which make up our jurisprudence were created in genuine "cases" or "controversies" honestly arrived at.

The fact is, however, that American constitutional law has been subverted by bogus cases briefed and argued by liberal lawyers masquerading as adversaries when in truth they were allied in achieving the same end. The proposition that our case law be established honestly and not by trick and device seems too manifest a truth to require citation. However, since this approach calls into question the legitimacy of what has become part of our "national culture," a look at some cases where collusion was discovered in time—frauds that failed, so to speak—is in order.

About 150 years ago two characters named Lord and Veazie tried to pull a fast one on the City Bank of Boston. They contrived a case between themselves and brought it before the Federal Circuit Court in Maine for the purpose of settling legal questions upon which depended a large amount of property owned by themselves and the bank. Veazie being the designated winner in the

---

24 William J. Brennan, Jr., Address to Text and Teaching Symposium, October 12, 1985, Washington, DC. *The Great Debate: Interpreting our Written Constitution*. Published by: The Federalist Society, 24.

lower court, Lord had it brought up, by writ of error, for review by the Supreme Court of the United States.

The idea was to obtain an opinion of the Court in a test case manipulated by the two spurious litigants which later could be used as a precedent to control the outcome when they confronted their real adversary, the City Bank of Boston. The knowledge of this suit was kept from the Bank, for a while at any rate. But when the writ of error was entered in the Supreme Court, they got wind of it and exposed the fraud for what it was.

> The Court is satisfied . . . that there is no real dispute between the plaintiff and defendant. On the contrary, it is evident that their interest in the question brought here for decision is one and the same, and not adverse; and that in these proceedings the plaintiff and defendant are attempting to procure the opinion of this court upon a question of law, in the decision of which they have a common interest opposed to that of other persons, who are not parties to this suit, who had no knowledge of it while it was pending in the Circuit Court, and no opportunity of being heard there in defence of their rights.

"The objection in the case before us," continued the Court, "is that there is no real conflict of interest" between the parties, "that the plaintiff and defendant have the same interest, and that interest adverse and in conflict with the interest of third persons, whose rights would be seriously affected if the question of law was decided in the manner that both of the parties to this suit desire it to be." The Court set aside the judgment as a fraud and dismissed the writ of error. "A judgment in form, thus procured, in the eye of the law is no judgment of the court. It is a nullity."

> And any attempt, by a mere colorable dispute, to obtain the opinion of the court upon a question of law which a party desires to know for his own interest or his own purposes, when there is no real and substantial controversy

between those who appear as adverse parties to the suit, is an abuse which courts of justice have always reprehended, and treated as a punishable contempt of court.[25]

In 1889 the State of Michigan passed an act regulating the rates a railroad could charge for passenger traffic. "On the very day on which the law took effect, to wit, October 2, 1889, the defendant in error, plaintiff below, went to the defendant's office in Port Huron, and tendered $3.20 for a ticket from that place to Battle Creek, which was refused. Thereupon he brought this action in damages, to which the railroad company promptly answered."[26]

The Supreme Court of Michigan felt constrained to make the observation that the evidence suggested "that this was a friendly suit between the plaintiff and the defendant to test the constitutionality of this legislation." The counsel for the railroad did not deny this, but stated: "This may be conceded; but what of it? There is no ground for the claim that any fraud or trickery has been practiced in presenting the testimony."[27] The Court refused to rule on the constitutional question. Only when "the court must, in the exercise of its solemn duties, determine whether the act be constitutional or not" would it exercise that "ultimate and supreme" power[28]; and then only in a case when after "an honest and actual antagonistic assertion of rights by one individual against another, there is presented a [constitutional] question."[29] Beware of friendly lawsuits, a unanimous Court cautioned its posterity:

We do not mean to insinuate aught against the actual management of the affairs of this company. The silence of the record gives us no information, and we have no knowledge outside thereof, and no suspicion of wrong. Our suggestion is only to indicate how easily courts may be misled into

---

25 *Lord v. Veazie*, 49 U.S. (8 How.) 251, 254-256 (1850).

26 *Chicago & Grand Truck Railway v. Wellman*, *143 U.S.* 339, 340, (1892).

27 *Id.* 344.

28 *Id.* 345.

29 *Id.* 345.

doing grievous wrong to the public, and how careful they should be to not declare legislative acts unconstitutional upon agreed and general statements, and without the fullest disclosure of all material facts. Judgment affirmed.[30]

Half a century later, during World War II, much the same caper was tried in *Roach v. Johnson*.[31] In 1942 Congress had passed the War Emergency Price Control Act, which regulated, among other things, the rents a landlord could charge for residential properties in certain areas. Johnson, a landlord, contrived to have Roach, one of his tenants, institute a friendly suit for damages in the U.S. district court.

In his answer Johnson challenged the constitutional validity of the law and was successful in obtaining an order from the district court dismissing the tenant's complaint on the ground the rent control law was unconstitutional.[32] At this point the United States intervened and moved for dismissal on grounds of collusion. When this motion was denied the government appealed to the Supreme Court. It did not contend that "any false or fictitious state of facts was submitted to the court," only that "one of the parties has dominated the conduct of the suit" by controlling the attorneys on each side.[33] The Supreme Court dismissed the suit as collusive. "It is the Court's duty to do so where, as here, the public interest has been placed at hazard by the amenities of parties to a suit conducted under the domination of only one of them."[34]

Here an important public interest is at stake—the validity of an Act of Congress having far-reaching effects on the public welfare in one of the most critical periods in the history of the country. That interest has been adjudicated in a proceeding in which the plaintiff has had no active par-

---

[30] *Id.* 346. emphasis added.

[31] 48 F.Supp. 833 (1943).

[32] *Id.* at 835.

[33] *United States v. Johnson*, 319 U.S. 302, 304 (1943).

[34] *Id.* 305.

ticipation, over which he has exercised no control, and the expense of which he has not borne. He has been only nominally represented by counsel who was selected by appellee's counsel and whom he has never seen. Such a suit is collusive because it is not in any real sense adversary. It does not assume the "honest and actual antagonistic assertion of rights" to be adjudicated—a safeguard essential to the integrity of the judicial process, and one which we have held to be indispensable to adjudication of constitutional questions by this Court.[35]

United States v. Johnson, Lord v. Veazie, and *Grand Trunk Railway v. Wellman,* the three cases we have just seen, are decisions of the United States Supreme Court entitled under the doctrine of *stare decisis* to the same respect as *Malloy* or *Miranda.* Let us hope that the moral and ethical standards they enunciated, and which the American people have always taken for granted, will prevail. A nation which prides itself on the observance of the rule of law can do no less.

Malloy v. Hogan was a charade engineered by Associate Justice William O. Douglas; no one can contend that it was not. Douglas dispatched his clerk Steven B. Duke to Connecticut to choreograph a Star Chamber scenario which would be used to "selectively incorporate" the Fifth Amendment's prohibition against compelled self-incrimination. The quid pro quo was a professorship at Yale Law School. Duke was to cosset the case all the way to the Supreme Court of the United States, where he would do battle with the ACLU and fall on his sword. Somehow Duke was able to persuade Hartford County Prosecutor John LaBelle to let him use his office as a front. The facts speak for themselves.

Falsus in uno, falsus in omnibus—false in one thing, false in everything—is a legal maxim under which a trier of fact, once he knows that a party has tried to deceive him on one thing, may

---

[35] *Id.* 304, 305.

disbelieve him on all things. According to *Black's Law Dictionary*, "[t]his doctrine means that if testimony of a witness on a material issue is willfully false and given with an intention to deceive, the jury may disregard all the witness' testimony." This is a rule of human experience not confined to a courtroom. It is implicit in a relationship of every kind—marriage, friendship, business, everything. Once one party knows the other has tried to deceive him, the deceiver loses all credibility. All inferences may be resolved against him. Once you know how William O. Douglas "fixed" the case of *Malloy v. Hogan*, the presumption in favor of the legitimacy of *Fay v. Noia* begins to fade. Judge Jerome Frank was a doctrinaire liberal and a friend of long standing of Justice Douglas. Not only that, Frank owed his seat on the Circuit Court of Appeals to Justice Douglas, who lobbied President Roosevelt on his behalf. It would be hard to believe Frank wrote his "satanic" opinion without first consulting Justice Douglas.

It does not strain one's credulity to believe that Kings County Assistant District Attorney Charles Siegel was coopted into the cabal. It is a lot easier to believe that Siegel was playacting than that his behavior was genuine. Yes, Noia's confession was coerced, stipulated Mr. Siegel, and No, we don't have any other evidence besides the confession. So New York is holding Charles Noia in violation of the Constitution—so what? Under the exhaustion rule the federal courts can't do anything about it. But the law of habeas corpus has since been changed by statute so as to eliminate some of the more flagrant abuses brought about by *Fay v. Noia*. We shall revisit habeas corpus another time in another venue for another reason and discuss the inadequacies of these reforms, but for the present, any further discussion of that case would be moot.

What are not moot are other cases in which Douglas's vote provided the margin of victory, *Mapp v. Ohio* being the first to come to mind. A judge is not a legislator representing a particular constituency. His duty is to administer fair and impartial justice to all who appear before his bench, and *Malloy v. Hogan* shows that William O. Douglas was incapable of doing that on any issue that ran counter to his political predilections. All doubts should be resolved against him, and for the purpose of *stare decisis* his vote should be regarded as tainted.

And what does this say of the Architect of the Bill of Rights, as Lawrence Tribe described Justice Brennan, of "one of the greatest judicial scholars, public officials and human beings mankind has ever known"? Had it been tested in an adversarial proceeding honestly briefed and argued, Brennan's theory of "absorption" would have been exposed for the humbug it is. And it survives today only because the Court, in blind obedience to *stare decisis*, continues to apply the poisoned precedent of *Malloy v. Hogan* without the slightest idea of its illegitimacy.

But with regard to Justice Brennan, we need not rush to judgment. In his law review article, Professor Tribe was good enough to catalog a dozen or so cases—landmark cases—in which both Brennan and Douglas were in the majority, all decided by a closely divided Court. Before reaching any firm conclusions, we should see how many of these "cases" or "controversies" pass the smell test.

Malloy v. Hogan is fundamentally fraudulent by any standard. By the Court's own standard it is a nullity which must be expunged. A monstrous wrong has been done the American people. In the war against crime, we have been betrayed. And we must never forget that it was an "inside job" by liberal judges and lawyers sworn to uphold the Constitution and laws of the United States.

www.ingramcontent.com/pod-product-compliance
Lightning Source LLC
Chambersburg PA
CBHW021421170526
45164CB00001B/35